# DIVINE
# INTERVENTION

*The most controversial true story
of a spirit "walk in"
and spiritual enlightenment
you will ever read*

## HAZEL COURTENEY

CICO BOOKS
LONDON NEW YORK

## Dedication

*For Mum and Dad. I love you – and carry you both
in my heart forever.*

First published in this revised edition in 2011 by CICO Books
an imprint of Ryland Peters & Small Ltd

20–21 Jockey's Fields, London WC1R 4BW
519 Broadway, 5th Floor, New York, NY 10012

www.cicobooks.com

10 9 8 7 6 5 4 3 2 1

A CIP catalog record for this book is available from the Library of
Congress.

ISBN: 978-1-907563-50-8

**Other books by Hazel Courteney:**
*The Evidence For the Sixth Sense*
*Countdown to Coherence*
*500 of the Most Important Ways to Stay Younger Longer*
*500 of the Most Important Health Tips You'll Ever Need*
*Mind and Mood Foods*
*Body and Beauty Foods*

For more information on Hazel's work, log on to her website:
www.hazelcourteney.com

Cover design: Jerry Goldie Graphic Design

Printed in Great Britain by CPI Antony Rowe, Chippenham, Wiltshire

# Contents

| | | |
|---|---|---|
| Foreword by Professor Gary Schwartz | | 4 |
| Preface to the 2011 Edition | | 7 |
| 1. | The Beginning | 9 |
| 2. | The Madness | 12 |
| 3. | The Death | 26 |
| 4. | The Return | 48 |
| 5. | The Happenings | 57 |
| 6. | Another Death | 82 |
| 7. | The Birth of a Master | 105 |
| 8. | The Meetings | 128 |
| 9. | The Duchess | 139 |
| 10. | The Predictions | 144 |
| 11. | The Scientist | 156 |
| 12. | The Long Road Home | 167 |
| 13. | The Journey Back to Chaos | 181 |
| 14. | Return to America | 187 |
| 15. | The Move | 191 |
| 16. | Return to Mother | 206 |
| 17. | The Memories | 213 |
| 18. | The Higher Realms | 227 |
| 19. | The Journey | 234 |
| 20. | The Vision | 238 |
| | Epilogue | 242 |
| 21. | The Journey Continues Afterword 2004 | 250 |
| | Useful Books and Addresses | 270 |

**Author's Note:** This book is my own story written in my own words. During the past fifteen years I have read numerous books, features and articles and certain phrases remained in mind. Wherever possible I have acknowledged the source of these phrases and to those whose names I have forgotten, my apologies for any unintentional oversights.

**Acknowledgements:** Sometimes words are not sufficient to convey the emotion that accompanies them, and to all those who stood by me throughout my incredible experience, from the depths of my heart I love and thank you. For my husband Stuart for not giving up hope. Thanks to Dr John Briffa for being such a true friend and for coming to my rescue in my hour of need. A huge thank you to Bob Jacobs and Dr Richard Lawrence for their support and advice. For Norma and Lindsey for understanding and not judging. For Sheila and all we shared. Leila, Kelvin, Jacqueline, Meg, Bill and Celia – thank you for being who you are. To all the scientists and experts who helped me to understand what happened to me – thank you all. Special thanks to Dr Serena Roney-Dougal and Roger Coghill, for your patience. Also my dear friend Robin Morgan, thank you for all your encouragement during some of my darkest moments. I also owe huge debts of gratitude to Lord Feldman and Sue Brotherton for your valuable time and support. Thanks also to my publishers for having the courage to publish this book and to my editors Mary and Cindy who made the process of cutting 20,000 words from my original manuscript not as painful as I thought it would be. Finally to my daughter Victoria, my brother Bob and his wife Helen for all your support when I needed it most … Thank you all.

# Foreword By Professor Gary Schwartz, University of Arizona

Hazel Courteney says in the Afterword of this book, "Had I really heard from the spirit of Diana, Princess of Wales? Did I truly become some kind of enlightened spiritual master who could affect miracles? The answer is yes... and no."

My association with Hazel began during late August, 2003, when I received an unexpected and extraordinary phone call from a woman with a striking British accent. She explained that she lived in London, but she was calling from the West Indies where she and her husband were on holiday. I was in Tucson, where I am a professor and scientist at the University of Arizona. The woman said she had been given my phone number by the wife of the distinguished British psychical scientist Montague Keen (now deceased), a man I deeply admired. And so I listened. Hazel introduced herself and said that she really needed my advice and potentially my assistance. What she told me seemed unbelievable. Hazel explained that she was an award-winning health columnist, who had worked for the *Daily Mail* and *The Sunday Times* newspapers in London, that she has written several books on complementary and alternative medicine – but also that she had been through an incredible spiritual experience during 1998 in which she had almost died. In the process of her illness and ultimate recovery, this polite stranger claimed a host of remarkable experiences that included affecting electrical equipment, telepathy and communicating with the "dead". But Hazel's most outrageous claim was that she had been in contact with the late Princess Diana. Because of my research program on topics that include energy medicine and survival of consciousness after death, I tend to get strange phone calls from time to time. Many I dismiss, as over the years I have learned that people can claim many things – but it's verifying them under scientific controlled conditions that can in many cases elicit the truth!

Hazel wanted to know if there was some way that I could determine scientifically if any of her experiences were real. As Hazel brings to life in *Divine Intervention*, many of her experiences were witnessed by others. Most of the profound experiences reported by Hazel in this book I could not independently validate. However, one set of experiences demanded to be documented. As I describe in my books *The Afterlife Experiments* and *The Sacred Promise*, it is possible to document scientifically the existence of a specific deceased person under controlled laboratory conditions. To facilitate this, we use research "mediums" who are "blind" to the identity of both the sitter (the person wanting to hear from one or more deceased loved ones) and the deceased.

In our experiments with well-known mediums such as John Edward, whose gifts have been seen by millions of people on his television show *Crossing Over* plus equally gifted mediums such as Mary Occhino, the star of *Angels On Call* on Sirius XM radio, it is possible to conduct readings where the sitter is not allowed to speak – and at times they are not even in the same country. And if highly specific information is provided by the mediums under controlled conditions, conventional explanations such as fraud, cold reading, and other "tricks" can be firmly ruled out.

Therefore, I proposed to Hazel that if she really wanted to know if Princess Diana had indeed played a role in her dramatic spiritual experience, she should fly to Tucson and serve as a secret sitter, in a blind mediumship experiment. If positive results were obtained in such an experiment, this would help substantiate the reality of some of her claims. At the time Hazel called, two mediums who worked in my laboratory at the time, Laurie Campbell and Allison Dubois, were scheduled to come to Tucson for an unrelated mediumship experiment during October 2003 - and therefore I proposed to Hazel that we take advantage of this fortuitous opportunity and we scheduled a meeting. What you are about to read was described in my book *The Truth About Medium*.

Both mediums had separate 'blind' readings with Hazel. Before they were brought into the room with Hazel, I told them that the secret sitter was from overseas, that this was an unusual and important reading, and that they should not filter any experiences or information. I reminded them that no matter how strange or far-fetched the information might seem to them, they should report exactly what they were experiencing. Crucially, I did not tell the me/diums that the sitter was from England. Hazel had never heard of either of the mediums, and she was not allowed to speak at any time during the duration of each one-hour reading. When each medium in turn walked into that room to join Hazel and myself - they had no idea who Hazel was or where she was from. Neither party knew of the existence of the other until that moment.

What happened in those two readings was "jaw-dropping" to say the least. Both readings began with the mediums receiving information about Hazel's deceased family members. However, within ten minutes of the readings beginning, when both mediums independently and suddenly looked embarrassed and confused, stating that they recognized the presence of Princess Diana, I was stunned. In the seven years I had conducted research readings with Laurie, and the three years I had performed research readings with Allison, the Princess of Wales had never appeared. Nor had she shown up in any of our previous mediumship experiments involving hundreds of readings with other talented research mediums such as John Edward or Mary Ochinno.

What was especially important for me as a scientist, was my attempt to determine if the mediums could get any information, purportedly from the deceased, about the nature of Diana's unique relationship (if any) with Hazel, especially during 1998. The mediums did not mistakenly report that the deceased was family (Hazel is not related to Princess Diana), nor did they report specific outings or activities that Hazel had with the deceased. What the mediums actually reported felt "weird" and "unusual" to them. For example, one medium said that the deceased had an intimate but not sexual relationship with the sitter (Hazel), it was like their relationship had been, to paraphrase, mind-to-mind. The other said that Princess Diana helped the sitter in a crisis that had affected Hazel physically and spiritually.

As I listened to the mediums struggle with their thoughts and emotions as they recounted sometimes painful information from Princess Diana, I felt both humbled as did Hazel. In fact, many of the statements and sentiments communicated in these research readings were very similar in context and emotion to the messages from Diana as reported by Hazel. Did Hazel actually hear from the Spirit of Diana? The experiments strongly confirmed this part of Hazel's experience. During June of 2004 we conducted a further experiment with regard to Princess Diana with celebrity medium Sally Morgan and the results of that test were again amazing in their accuracy. All our tests regarding Hazel are documented in her sequel to this book, *The Evidence for the Sixth Sense* and my book *The Sacred Promise*.

Today (2011) after examining the totality of the evidence of survival of consciousness from a host of institutions around the globe, plus the results from more than a thousand research sessions from the past decade or so - I now firmly conclude that our consciousness survives physical death. We are receivers and transmitters of energy and our unique energy field which contains all information about us continues on after physical death. And this information can be retrieved by sensitive mediums. This is well explained in this and Hazel's other spiritual/science books. In fact I now firmly believe it's up to the sceptics to prove that consciousness does not survive physical death... Meanwhile, *Divine Intervention* has the potential to help us all to discover more about our true spiritual nature and as a scientist I believe that this book should be taken seriously. And even if you read it as a total sceptic - then it still remains a riveting read.

*Gary E. Schwartz*

Professor Gary Schwartz, University of Arizona

# Preface to the 2011 edition

Since this book was first published in December 1999 I have received hundreds of letters from men and women from all walks of life saying that my story has inspired and helped them on their spiritual journey. Also, this tale created considerable controversy and a few people judged me before knowing the whole story. Yet once they realised that I had far more to lose than gain in writing this book – and that my experiences went *way* beyond *only* hearing from the spirit of Princess Diana – attitudes have thankfully changed. Also, it's imperative to keep in mind when reading this book, that when I wrote it I was in an extremely heightened and at times confused spiritual state and today some of my statements make me cringe with embarrassment, whilst others make me laugh. But I wasn't laughing in 98/99.

I underwent an intense Spiritual Emergency, a term coined by renowned psychiatrist Professor Stanislav Grof who has spent over 50 years studying altered states, to describe when a spiritual transformation becomes a physical crisis. Even today I marvel that I survived and kept my sanity. During the past decade I have met hundreds of individuals who have gone through their own unique awakening, some of which mirrored my own experience.

Over the years, I have learned huge amounts from cutting-edge scientists, and in the sequel to this book called *The Evidence For the Sixth Sense*, I share good evidence on subjects ranging from Life After Death, Re-incarnation and The Science of Enlightenment - to Spiritual Emergency, Spontaneous Healing, Masters of the Self, How Miracles are made and more. And in my third spiritual/science book *Countdown to Coherence* published in 2011, being hailed as '*A serious attempt at offering good scientific ideas toward a Spiritual Theory of Everything*' I have found leading-edge scientists who are now coming to some staggering conclusions about who we are, where we come from and why miracles will shortly become more commonplace and much more.

Meanwhile, many of the statements that I remain convinced emanated from the spirit of Diana back in '98 have come to pass. She told me that Charles would marry Camilla, which he did in 2005; and that William would marry for love. She spoke of increasing global weather and other planetary changes and how we all needed to care more for each other and the planet. Indeed, the Green Movement is gathering pace yet we still have a long way to go. These days, I believe that her spirit has moved on to the higher realms and I long ago stopped attempting to contact her.

Yet this story is as relevant today as it was back in '99 – as the world remains in great need of the wisdom and universal truths it contains. Also, as spiritual crisis is a growing phenomena that desperately needs to be understood, I am keen to help people awaken in calmer circumstances and thus help them to safely understand who they and all of us *truly are*... Good luck on your journey, with love and light

Hazel Courteney, March 2011, www.hazelcourteney.com

In his TV series *Cosmos* in the 1980s, scientist Carl Sagan was pictured standing in the New York Library surrounded by millions of books. He pointed to a tiny section and said, 'It is only possible in one person's lifetime to read this many books.'

He then turned to the camera and said: 'The trick is to read the right books.'

When I was 14, a fortune teller predicted that one day I would write a book about my life.

How could she have known?

How can anyone know what the future holds?

No one – and everyone …

# 1 The Beginning

*The events I describe in this book actually happened.*
*I did not 'ask' for what happened to me over Easter 1998, it simply*
*happened. If you choose not to believe my story – that is your choice.*
*But it is true.*

**IN APRIL 1993, I WOKE** suddenly in the middle of the night and the word 'write' literally popped into my head. The next morning I told my husband Stuart that I was going to become a writer. 'Of course you are, my dear,' he said with a long-suffering smile. For some years I have believed that we all come to this Earth for a specific purpose, and when I heard that word 'write', I had no idea what I would write, or how to become a writer – but in that moment of inspiration I knew with absolute certainty that I had found my purpose. At the time, I was running a small villa rental company for my husband and had written nothing more than a few business letters since leaving school at 16. But the word 'write' struck a chord somewhere deep within me and I began writing about anything that came to mind. By late summer I had managed to persuade several local newspapers to print my features – and one thing had led to another. But after a lifetime of almost continual ill health, which had eventually been alleviated by alternative medicine and dietary changes, my real passion was to write about alternative health issues, nutrition and the power of the mind: subjects I had been researching in my spare time for several years. Somehow I wanted to make a difference.

In September 1993, I sat in the tropical garden of our home on the island of Barbados and scribbled a few pages of notes that simply flowed from my pen. On the cover of my note pad I wrote the word 'Imagine' and suddenly I knew with my whole heart that I had been born to write a very special book. I had no idea what it would be about, but I just knew that one day it would come about. My notes were left on a shelf to gather dust.

By March 1994 I had my own weekly alternative health column in the UK's most popular tabloid newspaper the *Daily Mail*. I was the UK's first national alternative health agony aunt and I loved every minute of it. During the next two years I answered thousands of readers' queries, recommending specific vitamins and minerals plus dietary changes and hints known to ease their ailments. I also wrote about nutritional medicine, alternative therapies, electrical pollution, pesticides and their relationship to cancer – anything to do with alternative health. When you are doing what you love and living it 24 hours a day, seven days a week, you learn very fast – or you get fired. I felt as though someone, somewhere must have been smiling on me as I made great strides in a very short time.

In January 1997 I moved to the UK's most prestigious broadsheet – the *Sunday Times*. It was incredible. I had received no formal training in alternative medicine or writing, and yet in June 1997 I was voted Health Journalist of The Year. Invitations to lecture all over the UK came in every week. I was on top of the world. But in April 1998, circumstances beyond my control forced me to resign from the *Sunday Times*. Now why would I do that?

*23rd April 1998 – London*

As I walked into the Savoy Hotel in London to interview Hollywood star Whoopi Goldberg for my weekly page, I was a little apprehensive. After all she is a big name and I have always been a huge fan. On the way to the hotel I stopped at a flower stall and bought her some purple tulips – highly appropriate I thought, remembering her wonderful film *The Colour Purple*.

To some this may seem like a corny gesture – but I gave them as a fan, not as a journalist. Whoopi was in London to promote her latest book and inscribed a message for me on the inside cover which read: 'There is nothing you cannot do if you keep calm and go forward…' What a magical lady. Whoopi could not have known how appropriate her message was, nor what had happened to me in the two weeks prior to that meeting.

I was lucky to be alive.

The interview duly appeared on 3rd May when I announced that meeting Whoopi had inspired me to leave my column to take time out to write my fourth book. In the moment that I wrote those words this was not strictly true. It was an excuse as to why I was really leaving my beloved column. The truth was that I was living in a nightmare. How would I ever be able to tell the whole truth?

Friends who knew me well were flabbergasted to read I was giving up my page. Why hadn't I told them? Was I mad? I had worked really hard for six years to reach the position of having my own page in Britain's best known Sunday paper and they were all aware that the column was, after my husband and daughter, my whole life. During the weeks that followed I received hundreds of letters from readers saying: 'Why are you leaving so suddenly? Your column and the information you give has changed our lives – please come back soon'.

I made so many excuses, but could not bring myself to tell anyone the truth. It was too incredible. I told them half-truths. Our friends knew about the dengue fever I had contracted from a mosquito bite in the Caribbean during mid-March. The illness had given me a high fever similar to malaria and left me feeling debilitated, and one particularly nasty symptom was a violent stabbing pain at the back of my eyes. So I told everybody that my eyes needed a rest, and that looking at my computer screen was agony, and it was.

But only I knew the truth.

# 2

## The Madness

*3rd April 1998 – Birmingham*

**OVER THE WEEKEND** I worked as normal on my next column, it was entitled 'A New Beginning'. But as I sat at my computer, I had no idea that within two weeks I would have left my job at the Sunday Times and almost lost my life.

It wasn't anything tangible, but on Friday 3rd April I began to feel different. Like most of my fellow evening commuters on the train from London to Birmingham, I was naturally tired after a fairly chaotic week but the feeling went beyond tiredness, it was more like a growing sense of unease deep within me.

Weekends offered a welcome respite from the constant telephone calls, and on Saturday I settled in front of my computer as usual to write my column. As the hours passed I began to work with a greater urgency than I had felt since my early days in journalism. I could not understand the intensity of my emotions as I wrote, but as the hours flashed by like minutes the weekend quickly disappeared.

Although I work hard I have always enjoyed a healthy appetite and make sure I stop for regular meals, but during that weekend I noticed that I did not feel hungry at all. Strange. I still ate my porridge with organic soya or rice milk for breakfast, but found myself craving bananas and developed an unbelievable thirst. Every day I drink at least six glasses of filtered water, but suddenly I was drinking a glass every 30 minutes or so. So maybe my body was telling me I needed to detox, but it had never prevented me from eating before, unless I was suffering from a tummy bug, which we all do from time to time.

By the time my cleaning lady Sheila arrived on Monday morning I had lost a couple of pounds. When you only weigh around 8 stone at the best of times, and are 5ft 9in tall, you don't need to lose weight. Why wasn't I hungry?

On Monday night I travelled to London as usual. The next day I went about my normal work, interviewing a naturopath about antibiotic overuse, which was going to make a great piece for my page, talking to Sky TV about a forthcoming programme appearance ... just life ...

Then the madness began.

*8th April – London*

My husband, Stuart, left at 6 am to drive to the site of our new home being built in Oxfordshire. I was due to meet him at midday for more meetings with the builders. Our driver, Paul, arrived at the house around 10 am and I decided to pop down to Harrods to pick up sandwiches for our lunch. In the car it was business as usual as I called my editor Lucas Hollweg to wish him 'bon voyage' before he went off on holiday that Friday.

As I shopped, I remembered that Stuart's mother Jean was coming to spend Easter with us, and the family were all gathering for Sunday lunch at our home in Birmingham, so off I went to pick up a few Easter eggs. Everything was so normal ...

When I entered the store I felt perfect, but as I began to shop, a strange feeling came over me. Nothing I could put my finger on, maybe I was a little tired as I had certainly been working long hours. I shrugged off my growing sense of unease and carried on. Paul has a passion for almond croissants and before leaving I thought I would pop along to the bread hall to buy his favourite treat. But as I walked into the turnstile in the bread hall, it stuck fast. I couldn't go forward or back. And during those few seconds, a searing pain shot down through my head into the centre of my chest, as if I had been struck with a long blunt hammer, which literally took my breath away. I gasped. Suddenly the turnstile moved. Feelings of panic began to overwhelm me, and as I quickly walked towards the exit, I caught sight of myself in a mirrored column. I looked grey.

Once outside I took a deep breath, I *had* to calm myself, but there was a loud voice in my head commanding me: 'Find a doctor – now'. Was I talking to myself? Where had that voice come from? On my mobile phone I dialled our doctor's surgery. Myra the receptionist answered.

'Is Brian still there?' I demanded.

'Yes,' she said, realizing from the tone of my voice that something was very wrong.

'I'm coming round now,' I shouted – and hung up. As Paul saw me walking towards the car he knew something had happened. He drove as quickly as traffic would allow to my doctor's surgery in Kensington. Fifteen minutes in a car believing that you might only have minutes to live is a very long time. I tried to be rational, but felt very frightened, my heart was pounding and my head throbbed.

As we drew up outside Brian's surgery, he was waiting on the steps. We have known each other for a long time and he knew I would not have made that call as a joke. I was breathing heavily, crying and felt very overwrought. Before I would allow him to examine me, I told Brian to tell Stuart and my daughter Victoria that I loved them very much.

Brian was more interested in taking an electrocardiogram, thinking that I might have suffered a heart attack. He quickly rang a cardiologist and played my heartbeat down the phone, then he came back to see me. My heart was fine. But somehow I already knew this and I suddenly became unbelievably calm, strangely calm. It was very weird. It was as if I was someone else, and in that moment I suddenly realized I was able to 'read' Brian's thoughts. He became even more concerned. He thought I was having a nervous breakdown, and it seemed pointless for me to argue. Perhaps this was stress. I have always known that prolonged stress can trigger practically every disease and health problem, but in my heart I knew that something special had happened during those few seconds in Harrods. I just couldn't work out what it was. Brian examined me thoroughly. Everything was fine, but he suggested I go straight home to bed. I called Stuart, said I was feeling rather tired and that I had seen Brian who had insisted I rest instead of going to the building site. Stuart sounded concerned, but I assured him I was all right and we agreed he would return home mid-afternoon.

Paul did not want to leave me as he was so worried and full of concern for me, but despite the shock of what had happened and the pain that I was still experiencing in my head and chest, I felt strangely calm. It was bizarre. Perhaps I should go to bed after all. I went into my bathroom to wash off my make-up, and when I looked in the mirror my eyes looked different. They were bigger, rounder and bluer than they had appeared in previous days. I felt different. Considering the fright I had just had, I looked really healthy. 'Oh well', I thought, 'maybe I should rest on the bed for an hour'. My chest still felt bruised and sore and I kept rubbing the area, but my heart was fine – Brian had told me so.

As I lay on the bed, I picked up the phone to call a friend, but my hand slowly and deliberately put the phone back in the cradle. I wanted to make the call, but my arm and hand seemed to be working of their own accord. With incredulity I realized that I was not 'being allowed' to use the phone. I began having strange thoughts. Suddenly, I seemed to know many new things and a little voice in my head kept saying: 'listen to the silence'. For years I had written not only about health issues but also about the power of the mind, telepathy, life after death and spiritual healing. And in that moment I seemed to 'know' all the answers to those profound questions that most people ponder. Why are we here? Where do we come from? Do we all have a destiny? Intuitively, I knew that what I 'felt' as the answer inside my head was an ultimate truth.

Suddenly, the room seemed to fill with a light white mist – was that my eyes – or was the mist real? The experience was almost beyond words. It was as if I was floating. My body felt as light as a feather – it was totally blissful. But then I heard my husband arrive home two floors below me, and I had to tell him something and quickly. Why had I not come to the site? Why had I gone to Brian's? After 18 years of marriage, we know each other's moods pretty well and as soon as he saw me Stuart knew that something had happened.

I tried to explain about feeling tired and having a pain in my chest in Harrods but that I was now feeling fine when something odd happened, and I started rambling.

I blurted out that I had become different. Stuart looked quizzical and asked: 'What do you mean by different?'

Well, I answered: 'I feel like a super being who can do many amazing things.'

'Like what?' said Stuart, looking very alarmed.

'Well in the same way that Uri Geller can bend spoons and use telepathy to communicate with others, I can do similar things'.

Stuart looked very worried and said that I needed a cup of tea. I tried to act normally. But I could not eat, I just felt so strange. Every night after supper we always go for a walk, but that night I did not feel like walking.

At 10 pm we went to bed. By midnight my brain felt as though it was cooking. I had developed a fever, the pain in my chest had returned and my head felt as if it was clamped in a vice. From my experience as a health writer, I knew that I wasn't having a panic attack, but something unusual was happening and I needed specialist help. Who could I call at midnight? Who would understand? Stuart was beginning to panic, and so was I. I ran downstairs and looked through my diary. At his surgery, Brian had told me that his father-in-law had just died and that he and his wife were going away to Scotland that afternoon, but to ring the emergency help number if I had any problems. My intuition told me not to call his practice: although I was suffering physical symptoms somehow I knew that the root cause of my problem was not inherently physical in nature.

I dialled my colleague Bob Jacobs, a scientist, naturopath and homeopath, and prayed he would be at home. Sleepily, he picked up the phone, thank God. I told him everything. Bob advised me to eat any food containing sugar as soon as possible. Sugar? Hazel, the health writer kicked in. Refined sugar isn't healthy as it lowers the functioning of the immune system. If it is not used up during exercise it converts into fat in the body and can make people, especially children, become hyperactive as well as trigger mood swings. My brain was already in overdrive: why on earth should I take sugar? Bob had been told by a spiritual master that when people have 'these types of experiences' they need sugar for the shock and it would help to quieten my brain. Hence the old adage give a shocked person sweet tea.

By this time Stuart was right behind me and the look in his eyes told me to get off the phone. I decided to eat a slice of Stuart's favourite ginger cake which was packed with sugar. I also took some paracetamol for my thudding head and to help bring down my temperature. I needed to appear normal for both our sakes. We went to bed.

Thursday dawned. I awoke feeling altogether better. I said all the normal things Stuart and I say to each other every day and then some. Perhaps I had been working too hard after all. Perhaps I needed a break. Perhaps I should call Brian after Easter in case my menopause was beginning. Stuart was thrilled that I seemed OK – he had his wife back. It had just been a strange day, but it was past.

I tried to act normally and went to our local organic supermarket to buy food for the coming weekend, but still felt decidedly odd.

As I shopped I realized I still wasn't hungry, but when I got home I forced myself to drink some fresh vegetable juice with added root ginger. At least this would give me some much needed vitamins and minerals in an easily absorbable form and the ginger would hopefully calm and warm my tummy. Perhaps it would also ease the queasy feeling that had returned to my stomach. Paul drove me back up to Birmingham. In the car, I wanted to make a few calls regarding the column I was due to write that weekend, but suddenly I found myself afraid of using my phone. This was ridiculous.

Lindsey, my PA, arrived for our usual Thursday afternoon session of letter answering and dictation. I told her all about the previous day and kept telling her to 'look into my eyes and you will know who I am'. The strange feelings were starting again. Lindsey is a very spiritual soul with the patience of a saint, but even she looked slightly alarmed. She knew something had happened to me, but like Stuart she suggested we have a cup of tea and get on with our work. People called me, but I still found it hard to speak on the phone – it just made me feel sick and strange, but I did the best I could to sound and act 'normal'.

Stuart arrived home and we had supper. I pushed the food around my plate but still had no appetite, which felt really odd. We had our usual walk and went to bed.

*10th April – Good Friday – Birmingham*

We were greeted on Good Friday morning by a blanket of snow that had fallen silently overnight. Not exactly what we were expecting for a spring bank holiday weekend. It was like a blizzard. I mentioned to Stuart that his mother might not make it all the way from Devon and suggested he should tell Jean to stay at home, but Paul had already set off from London to collect her. Stuart was adamant that his mother should still come as she had been looking forward to this trip for weeks. He was sure they would be all right and went off to work around 8 am.

I've never been a particularly religious person, so Good Friday seemed pretty much like any other day. Sheila, our cleaning lady, arrived at 10 am to help me for a couple of hours as she knew that Stuart's mum was arriving in the evening, and I wanted to begin writing my next column.

She was upset at how ill I looked. The fever was back but my skin felt like ice. I took Sheila into my office and told her to hold my hand to stop me shaking so much. Sheila suffers from a genetic eye condition known as retinitis pigmentosa, which causes tunnel vision and eventually almost total blindness. I had no idea what I was doing, but suddenly I grabbed her arm and stared deeply into Sheila's eyes and told her they would get better. She looked really frightened and yet I meant her no harm. As calmly as she could she suggested I go back to bed.

My mind was racing, what should I do? I called Bob Jacobs again and told him about the fever, my lack of appetite and the throbbing headache. He suggested I begin taking the homeopathic tincture Bach Rescue Remedy, which he said would really help reduce the shock.

'What shock?' I thought. I didn't feel shocked, just very weird. Bob said to take this remedy anyway. He believed that something very special was about to happen and told me it was important to 'stay grounded'. For years I had heard people say 'you need to keep your feet on the ground' and had never fully appreciated what being grounded really meant, until I had felt as though I might float away in our bedroom on Wednesday afternoon after the incident in Harrods. But Stuart's abrupt arrival home had literally brought me 'back down to earth' with a bang.

Bob said he would send me a tectonic aluminium plate to also help 'ground me' and I was to put it under my pillow to help calm my brain. I wasn't sure how the plate would work, but at that moment I would have slept on a bed of nails if I thought it would stop the confusing sensations that I was feeling. Before saying goodbye to me, Bob said not to forget to take the remedies, to rest and 'go with the flow' – easier said than done …

I called Lindsey and asked her to bring more Rescue Remedy, plus plenty of liquid vitamins and minerals which are more easily absorbed than tablets, especially when the body is under stress. Somehow I had to take care of my physical body until whatever was happening was over. Lindsey was shocked by my appearance, which had deteriorated considerably since the previous afternoon. In a week I had lost several pounds, my skin was grey, and my whole body was shaking. By this time Lindsey had also realized that whatever was happening might not be purely physical and, as I still refused to call a doctor, she rang my next door neighbour Norma, whom she knew had experience in spiritual matters.

Norma and I had become firm friends nine years earlier after the sudden death of her husband, Miall. After hearing about Miall's death, I decided to pop over and see if there was anything I could do for her. Much to my surprise she was not crying or distraught, but appeared very calm and controlled. We sat and had tea and as I sat listening to Norma I felt completely relaxed in the cosy atmosphere of her sitting room. It was as if we had known each other for years. She told me that since childhood she had always known that when people 'die' their spirits go on to another dimension, therefore she could communicate with her 'dead' loved ones almost at will. At the time I thought she needed valium and a psychiatrist. Norma sensed my unease and calmly explained that many people who lose a close relative can often sense their presence for weeks after they 'die'. According to her, as time passes this feeling fades and the loved ones simply remain in one's memory. But if a person is 'awake' to spirit, there is no reason why they should not be able to contact their loved ones whenever they wish.

I was fascinated. We talked for a couple of hours and she shared with me a tiny fraction of her knowledge. It's hard to put into words, but as the afternoon wore on, I just knew that what Norma was telling me was true.

Until that meeting, I was hardly what you would term a 'deep person'. Inherently, I was a loving, giving person, who was always willing to lend a hand when it was needed, but I was also at times dreadfully selfish and vacuous. Before my meeting with Norma all I could think about was buying clothes, looking good and being seen with the right people. I still know quite a few people who are like that today …

That meeting was to change my life. I had always been fascinated by health issues as I had suffered so much illness throughout my life, but

Norma helped to add a new dimension to my life – that of connecting with spirit. As a result of this meeting, I began researching every aspect of mind, body and spirit. I read dozens of alternative books and attended numerous courses. Norma became my teacher and had great patience, always reminding me that if I wanted to 'hear' spirit I would have to meditate regularly. She gave me a one-hour meditation lesson almost every week for three years. I listened and learned, but still I could not 'hear' spirit. Perhaps I never would. Then when I least expected something to happen, in April 1993, that word 'write' popped into my head.

By the time Norma arrived, I was in bed and felt too weak to get up. Lindsey and Norma sat and held my hands which were blue with cold. My feet felt like ice. The electric blanket was on full blast, as was the central heating. Everything was so bizarre. Outside snow fell silently. I told Norma to look into my eyes and she would 'know' who I was. Lindsey took charge again. She called my friend and fellow columnist Dr John Briffa at his home in London. I needed help and I needed it fast. But it was almost lunchtime and because of all the snow that had fallen that morning Euston station in London was closed, and all main roads out of London were now blocked.

John had made plans to go away for Easter with his girlfriend, but as Lindsey related the situation to him, he realized that something unusual was happening. John is a medically qualified doctor, but he is also an expert in nutritional medicine and, most importantly, he has some knowledge of spiritual experiences.

Thankfully, he agreed to come up as fast as he could. Ten minutes later the phone rang by the side of my bed and Lindsey took the call. Just the thought of holding a phone made me feel nauseous and I felt very afraid. It was Richard Lawrence, another friend from London, a doctor of theology with 25 years' experience in the field of psychic phenomena. John had called him and related what he knew about my situation in Birmingham. Richard told Lindsey that I might be possessed by an evil spirit. For goodness' sake.

Richard suggested that Norma should check if I was possessed by anything evil. She concentrated on me for a few moments, held my hands and looked into my eyes. I felt nothing, but soon realized that I was holding my breath. Norma smiled. Whatever was happening she said it was not evil. I sighed with relief. Yes, something was happening, but as Bob had said on the phone, Norma told me just to wait and see. Before leaving she suggested I should take a shower, as the water would wash away any 'negative energies' which I would have created around my body and in our bedroom by being so frightened. Norma said the water would also help to 'ground me'. Was this why I was becoming even thirstier and needing to drink a glass of water every 15 minutes …?

Stuart returned from his office at lunchtime and was appalled at how much I had changed. Perhaps I needed sugar again, my brain felt as though it was on fire, when I opened my eyes it felt like they were being stabbed by hot needles and my skin still felt ice-cold while the fever turned my face bright red. Everything was such a puzzle. Stuart was desperate to call our local doctor, but I knew that if he came I was likely to be sedated or even worse – committed to a psychiatric ward. I had to stay in control of my own mind, but why wouldn't my brain work and why couldn't I think clearly? I knew I could not ask for conventional medical help, and by now Stuart was sick with worry. John had rung back to say all the trains had been cancelled and that the roads out of London were closed but he would come as soon as he could.

I began to pray.

Lindsey went home and I dragged myself out of bed to take a shower. For Stuart's sake I had to try to appear as normal as possible. As I stood under the shower for a few minutes the warm, clear water helped to freshen me up. Then I cleaned my teeth again. Earlier in the day I had noticed a strange taste in my mouth, like rotting food. During recent months I had undergone implant surgery after my front tooth had been removed, along with seemingly endless other dental work, but I was careful with my teeth.

I flossed and cleaned them at least twice every day. Why was I getting this strange taste? As I began using my electric toothbrush my gums began to pour with blood – now what?

Perhaps I needed some minerals. I knew I wasn't anorexic, but I also know that when people go without food for some time, they go past wanting food and things can become serious. Zinc is often lacking in these cases, and perhaps a deficiency of this mineral was the root cause of the bad taste.

But I love my food and always take a multimineral supplement every day containing at least 25mg of zinc, so why couldn't I eat? Downstairs I heard Robert, a local freelance cook arrive. Because the family were gathering for the weekend, he had come to help out. I went down and swallowed some more liquid vitamins and minerals in a glass of freshly made organic vegetable juice. My body needed nourishment. Robert was visibly shaken by my unkempt appearance.

It was now around 4 pm. The skies overhead were grey and heavy with snow. I grabbed Rob's hands tightly, they were wonderfully warm, mine were blue. He tried to stay calm and said lightly, 'What do you think about this weather?'

I turned round to face him, looked deep into his eyes and in a strange voice said 'I – am the weather'. Dear God what was happening? The skies overhead darkened ominously, the winds grew in intensity, it all felt so surreal. I went back to bed.

Around 5 pm Stuart's mother Jean finally arrived from Devon. Luckily our driver Paul had left London early, before the snow had closed the roads, and after a very long day they had made it. Jean is 85 and partially blind, but even she could see sufficiently to be very shocked by my appearance. It seems I was 'shocking' all round. She brought me some beautiful yellow roses and Stuart put them in a vase on my bedside table. I did my best to reassure Jean that I was only tired, but she still looked terribly concerned.

Jean went downstairs so that I could rest. As I lay on the bed in silence watching the weather outside our window, the voice in my head that I had last heard in Harrods telling me to see a doctor returned.

Over the years I have met dozens of mediums, healers, astrologers and psychics, such as my friend Dr Richard Lawrence, and whenever someone 'gave' me a message from over there – wherever that is – I always asked 'Can you hear a voice in your head?' 'Can you see someone?' 'How do you do what you do?' Now as I lay looking at the ominous skies, firmly believing that in some way the storm was linked with what was happening to me, I suddenly 'felt' a thought in my brain, which I knew had not emanated from my mind.

It simply said: 'Wait until the death'.

The room began to fill again with a whitish, eerie mist. Was I going to die? I closed my eyes and screamed. The night of the long knives had begun – it was to last for more than ten days.

For supper I forced down a small bowl of vegetable soup. It cheered Stuart a little to see me eating, and he spent the evening dashing up and down stairs between seeing his mother and checking on me. By 10 pm we had all had enough, Stuart put our four cats to bed in their little conservatory, made our usual mug of camomile tea and came up to bed. Perhaps tomorrow this would all stop.

I took a sleeping pill and some paracetamol. We desperately needed some rest and I was trying to control my fever. In any event by this time I was past caring what was good or bad for my health. I felt that things couldn't get much worse – but they did.

At precisely 12.20 am I was suddenly woken up. It was as if I had been literally thrown awake by a tremendous shock and I found myself half in the bed and half out of it. I felt so cold I thought I might freeze to death. My mouth tasted repulsive, I smelled awful and I was unbelievably thirsty. My nightdress was soaked with sweat. How could I be so cold and yet hot at the same time? I crept into my bathroom, changed my nightdress, put bed socks on and went back to bed.

I always sleep on my side, but every time I tried to turn on my side some invisible force made me lay on my back. Suddenly I felt very afraid. My hands went 'into automatic' as they had done on Wednesday when I had wanted to use the phone. They crossed of their own accord over my tummy and it was cold and dark, as cold as the grave ...

In a flash, I knew where I was. I was laying in a lead-lined coffin on white satin, deep in the ground. But I, Hazel, was still lying in my bed.

I did not understand what was happening. The intense pain in my chest returned. My eyes were tightly closed, but as I lay there I could 'see' clearly. I was sitting in the back of a car, being driven at great speed. I felt a sickening thud, my chest and head hurt, I saw lights flashing all around me. Inside my head I was screaming 'help me, help me' but no words would come out of my mouth. Dear God in heaven, this could not be true. But in that moment I knew with every fibre of my being whose eyes I was seeing through – it was Diana, Princess of Wales.

I woke Stuart.

# 3 The Death

**BEFORE I RELATE THE** incredible events that took place over Easter, there are a few things I need to say. Since Diana's death I had seen the front page reports about her fund, her children, every minute detail the press managed to find out about her to continue selling newspapers. And I can almost hear all the cynics out there going 'Oh no, not someone else who wants to climb on the Diana bandwagon.'

Please remember, I did not ask for this to happen. It simply happened. I did not want to die … I had so much to live for. In under six years I had achieved so many of my dreams. I was a successful writer, broadcaster and author. I got paid, I had a secretary, I had a life.

Yes, I admired Diana. I thought she was a lovely lady and a great mum. But she was only human, we all are. Yes, she made mistakes, but then we all do. She tried to do the best she could to make a difference. And since Norma 'woke' me up nine years earlier I had tried to do the same in my own small way as have millions of others.

On that fateful day, 31st August 1997, the world was stunned to hear that Diana, Princess of Wales was dead. Gone forever from this physical world in a dreadful moment of madness. A few people could not understand what all the fuss was about. My neighbour Norma came for lunch on that awful Sunday and told me not to cry – surely I realized Diana was being looked after in the higher realms? But I was heartbroken. I cried all day. Diana was a very special soul, and like millions around the globe I felt as though a very special 'light' had been extinguished forever.

But I had to 'Think of England' as I used to joke – come rain or shine, life or death, high days and holidays – I still had to write my column for the *Sunday Times*. But first I composed two letters: one, which I wrote as a member of the public rather than as a member of the press, was to Mohammed Al Fayed who had lost his dear son Dodi. I had never met Mr Al Fayed, but my heart went out to him. Then I wrote to Her Majesty Queen Noor of Jordan to request an interview. For several days a press release had been laying on my desk, noting that Queen Noor would be in London during October to present The Woman of The Year Award. But I had done nothing about asking for an interview, as generally it's virtually impossible to obtain interviews with major royals, and most high-profile celebrities only grant an interview when they have a film or book to promote.

The theme of the lunch was 'Making a Difference'. If Diana had not died, I would never have written that heartfelt letter to Her Majesty Queen Noor. But on 31st August, I was angry that such a wonderful young woman had died in such a senseless way. Diana had done her best and I was damn well going to do mine. Queen Noor was so touched by my letter that we met in October '97 and her plea for peace and a reduction in the overuse of dangerous pesticides was read by millions in my Christmas column.

If Diana had not died I would not be sitting here today writing these words, I would be getting on with my column.

On the day she died I sensed that her death would affect the future of many people, and it has. Before I began typing I sat quietly and said a little prayer for Dodi and Diana. In a flash in my mind's eye I saw her on a cross, and heard the words, 'They have crucified me – I hope they are satisfied'. At the time I felt this was just my imagination working overtime.

There was such a huge emotional charge of energy that day and I felt sure that millions of people had similar experiences.

Over the years, whenever I had received messages during my meditations with Norma, I never really believed they were real. I wanted them to be real, to hear clearly like she did, but I was fairly hopeless at sitting quietly, and just figured I was talking to myself in my head. Perhaps I was, perhaps not.

Since writing the notes that I had entitled *Imagine* back in September 1993, I had planned that the book that I had been born to write would be based on John Lennon's magical song *Imagine*. As I sat writing those notes back in '93 I was amazed at how quickly and easily the words tumbled from my mind. I felt that they had come from some higher realm, as my pen just kept on flowing over the paper. I believed some of the messages might well have come from the spirit of John Lennon, but I was never able to corroborate whether or not the facts they contained were true. I tried to arrange meetings with George Harrison, Sir Paul McCartney, Julian Lennon and Yoko Ono – and I came very close on a few occasions, but they never happened. And I was about to find out why …

Back in February 1998 while chatting with my husband as we walked one evening, I discussed my concept for *Imagine* for the millionth time. Stuart said 'I'm so sick of hearing about this blasted book, why don't you just write it or forget it?' He was right.

I was writing my column every week, answering hundreds of letters, running two homes and a small travel business. Enough was enough. For the moment I would let 'Imagine' go. I thought to myself that maybe one day after we moved, or if the *Sunday Times* tired of my column, I would eventually find time to write it. Little did I know how that decision was about to change my life …

I had met Diana several times, and on two occasions we had managed to have a lengthy chat. The first was at a charity lunch at The Dorchester in the summer of 1993 where I had sat next to her. This was made possible by my dear friend Elizabeth Tompkins who had sponsored the lunch. At that time

I had just begun writing, but nothing had been published. As we sat down, I was so nervous, but Diana was so easy to chat to and she was extremely down to earth. We talked about having a purpose in life and Diana asked if I thought she would ever find lasting happiness and discover what her purpose was meant to be. In that moment I had no idea, which was just as well. She was such fun, so full of wicked wit and quickfire humour. As we ate, she joked about the press and how they used to bitch about her only having only achieved one 'O' level at school.

The last time we met was at a small lunch held in her private apartments at Kensington Palace in the late June of 1995. By that time I was writing for the *Daily Mail*, and I too was now a member of the press. Diana was kind but initially more guarded, as the press were then hounding her mercilessly. As I looked at her across the table, an enormous sadness came over me. I felt she was lonely and that her heart was sad.

As the lunch broke up, Diana showed me a little of her apartments and we joked about Prince William's pictures of Pamela Anderson. She knew that I would not repeat our conversation and as she walked with me to my waiting taxi we chatted about spiritual issues and life after death. I told her about 'hearing' the word 'write' in 1993 and how it led to my writing in a national paper. Diana looked wistful and said that she hoped that one day she might 'hear' too. We parted. I was never her 'friend' I was just another person she met along the way. There were so many ...

On Sunday 7th September, through my tears, I remembered her joke about only having one 'O' level – but two and a half billion people watched her funeral.

I watched it on TV in Birmingham. I had not intended to watch it all, but like millions of others I could not tear myself away. I wept for what might have been, for her sons, for her family, for Dodi and his family, and in my heart I wept for the world. What had brought us to this, where taking photographs of someone famous had taken precedence over saving a human life.

Love her or loathe her, Diana had done the best she could in her moment …

I know that many mediums all over the world have picked up different messages from Diana since her death. Richard Lawrence had called me early in 1998 and said we must meet as he had an urgent message for me that he was not willing to discuss on the phone. Richard told me that Diana was trying very hard to reach me and that in some way we would be working together … It was a lovely message, but I thought 'Yes sure, but why would she want to work with me?' Richard also said that many mediums would claim to have contact with Diana, but that not many were truly hearing her. I had no idea.

During February of the same year, while waiting to hear from the BBC in London as to whether the concept I had written for a TV show had been accepted, Lindsey told me about an unusual dream she had experienced the previous week. She had seen herself sitting in a theatre next to Diana. They were both watching me on the stage, it was a full house and Diana had turned to Lindsey with a huge grin on her face and said 'The show is about to begin'. Over a cup of tea, Lindsey and I had pondered the meaning of her dream. Perhaps the 'show' in her dream referred to my TV idea, and perhaps we would soon hear that it had been accepted. Then I forgot all about the meaning of the dream – until Easter.

## *1.30 am – Birmingham*

It was now around 1.30 am on Saturday. My husband was exhausted and almost at the end of his tether. He lay in bed patiently listening while I paced the floor for over an hour talking non stop. I could hear Diana's voice as clearly as if she was in the room with me – I was channelling her every thought. In that moment everything was so vivid it never occurred to me to write anything down. I was totally coherent and as I walked back and forth, I suddenly felt energized … but where was this energy coming from?

When I looked in my bathroom mirror, physically I looked half-dead, but my eyes shone – quite literally. As I stared at them in the mirror, I felt shooting pains stabbing at my eyes. Was I going mad, was I going blind? My physical body felt near to collapse and I was shaking with shock. I wondered whether I should call Norma again. I realized it was very late but she had said I could call any time. When Norma answered she told me to eat anything sweet such as white bread with a pile of jam on it. She said this would bring me ' back down to earth.'

Normally, we wouldn't have white bread in the house, but Stuart's mum only likes white bread. I forced down a piece of bread and jam, and for good measure took some more liquid vitamins and minerals plus some vitamin A to help my eyes, which were beginning to 'cloud over' again. I was frightened and yet I wasn't – everything was such a puzzle. I tried to work things out. Was I hardly eating because Diana had suffered eating disorders? Or was this a spiritual cleansing? I had vague recollections of reading about yoga masters fasting for long periods to enable them to become more 'enlightened'. Was I drinking so much water because I needed to cleanse my body? Was it because Diana was fanatical about cleansing? Was the water 'grounding' me? Or was I simply thirsty? Did she like bananas and porridge, or were they just the only foods I fancied at that moment?

Porridge is great for balancing blood sugar levels, which helps to prevent mood swings. It is also a rich source of B vitamins, which are great for calming the nerves. I took a vitamin B complex tablet along with the minerals magnesium and calcium – nature's tranquillizers. I needed all the help I could get.

I went back up to bed. 'Are you OK?' whispered Stuart.

I told him I had changed my nightdress as it was soaked again – which was true – and I had needed to get something to eat.

'Perhaps it's the menopause,' I suggested meekly. 'I hope that's all it is', he said. As I lay there in the dark I prayed with all my heart that in the morning I would wake and life would be back to normal, and I could get on with my next column.

But at 4 am, I was thrown awake again. And as I sat bolt upright in bed I could hear a woman's voice in my head saying over and over again, 'I have died and come back, I have died and come back.' This pattern of being woken suddenly at around 12.30 am each night and again at around 4 am was to continue for almost three weeks.

When I woke on Easter Saturday morning I could only remember a fraction of what I had said to my husband the night before and when I looked at my meagre notes, the writing was not in my usual handwriting. As I lay in bed wondering what might happen next, I tried to recall what 'the energy' had said through me, while I paced the bedroom floor for over an hour talking to my poor husband. It went something like: She wants me to write The Book, I have got to go to America, she wants people to know her truth, she has messages for the people of the world. Right … And of course everyone was going to believe me …

I felt confused, hungry, afraid and very cold. The shock of what had happened during the night was incredible, but somehow I had to keep control of my mind, and I needed to eat again. I went downstairs to call Dr John Briffa, Stuart and I both needed him now. As I picked up the phone, the voice I had heard during the night returned saying, 'Proof – you are going to need lots of proof'. My mind started racing, where was my small dictaphone recorder that I used for interviews? I called John to see what time he would arrive, but then the voice spoke again, saying authoritatively, 'Don't forget the proof'. So I grabbed my small tape recorder and started taping every word I and others said. In the midst of all this chaos I found my mother-in-law enjoying a quiet breakfast in the kitchen.

After a few minutes I felt incredibly weak and Stuart took me back to bed. I rewound the tape to listen to myself and as I came to the last words I had uttered before switching off the recorder, I let the tape play on. At the exact second I had finished recording I heard a familiar voice. It was Anita Roddick (now deceased) from The Body Shop saying 'I don't believe in life after death'. I realised I had taped over the recording of an interview done the previous September. To have picked up this particular tape seemed an incredible coincidence, since I had lots of blank tapes on my desk.

I rang Lindsey to ask her to pick up some more tapes for my recording as I only had a few left. She agreed to come to the house by 4 pm when John was due to arrive.

As I lay in silence, looking out at the depressing weather and trying to make sense of everything, I suddenly cried out: 'Why me, why are you doing this? No one will ever believe me.'

The voice returned to my head and said, 'Why not you? So many people say "Why me? Why me?" You are as good as anyone else and the world needs to know the truth, some people have turned me into a religion and this needs to be stopped. For months I have been trying to reach you. It is time for you to write your book. You are a respected columnist, you write in a language that anyone can understand. Like me, you had no formal training, but look at what you have achieved.'

As I lay there listening I had no idea at that moment whether I would survive long enough to write another word.

'Death is easy,' said the voice. 'We are trying to protect you, everything that has happened in your life until now has prepared you for this moment.' I knew this was true. After Norma, my neighbour had 'woken' me up, all those years ago, I soon began to realize that life is like a giant jigsaw and that every illness, operation, accident and event that had happened during my life had all served a purpose, they had all formed another piece of the puzzle.

At 16 I wanted to continue my education to fulfil my dream of becoming a doctor, but Dad had said we needed the money and that I would have to get a job. I prayed he would change his mind, and took a job in Stow-onthe- Wold in the Cotswolds as a children's nanny. It was to be the shortest job of my life, which began on 21st May 1966. At 6 am the following morning my brother Bob knocked on the door to tell me that our father had died of a heart attack during the night. I was numbed by shock – he was only 50 years old. I still could see no way of continuing my education and a couple of days after my father's death, I met my future husband in an employment agency. He even looked rather like the father I had worshipped. Within five months I became pregnant. My mother organized our wedding to take place on her day off from the store where she worked as a shop assistant – a Thursday in November 1966. I had wanted to get married on the Saturday, but fate took its course and as I walked up the aisle I began bleeding and lost my first child – a son – on my wedding night.

If only Mum had booked the wedding on the Saturday we might never have married … If only Diana and Dodi had stayed at The Ritz that fateful night.

My second child, Victoria, was born on 14th September 1968 and my husband left me soon afterwards. At the time I thought my world was falling apart, but it was the best thing he could have done for me. I revamped myself by having plastic surgery to rid myself of my huge nose. That alone changed my life completely. At 31 I married my second husband, Stuart, who had always made it plain he was not keen to have more children. This was just as well, because a few months later I underwent a hysterectomy. I was heartbroken that we would not have children, but life had provided me with my wonderful daughter. Everything turned out for the best – even when it did not seem so at the time.

It wasn't until I began writing that I fully grasped the jigsaw concept. That when you find a piece that fits easily into place, you really need to take notice, and eventually you start to see a bigger picture emerging. For instance, after hearing the word 'write' in my head back in April 1993, initially I worried about what I would write and who would want to read what I wrote. But once I had decided to become a writer, 'coincidences' began to fall into place.

Several years earlier I had met Christine Yorath, wife of Terry Yorath who then managed Leeds United football team … When she walked into the jewellery shop that I owned in London, we hit it off immediately and when she came to London we would occasionally meet for a coffee. In May 1992, her son Daniel collapsed and died suddenly of a rare heart condition while playing football with his father. Daniel's death was reported widely in the media.

Months later Christine rang me out of the blue, saying she had been to see a medium, who had told her things only she and her son could have known. Instantly I knew I had to write her story. Christine agreed to meet me for an interview. It took me three weeks to write what a professional journalist could have written in three hours. In October 1993 I managed to get it printed as a double-page spread in the *Daily Mail* without a single word being changed. Suddenly I had become a journalist. Doors were opening and in my heart I knew I had found my true purpose. It was not all easy, but when you know something is right, you keep going, and you don't give up …

So on Easter Saturday as I lay waiting for John to arrive I was determined once again not to give up. I also realized that if I had not read and learned so much about health and spiritual matters, the shock of what was happening might well have killed me. I knew from past experience that people in similar circumstances had been forcibly committed to psychiatric hospitals.

I recalled a young mother I had met on a healing course several years earlier. At the age of three she began seeing and hearing 'dead' relatives. Her parents thought she was telling stories and told her she was being naughty. In her teens her doctor diagnosed schizophrenia and had her committed to hospital. She was given electric-shock treatment against her will, and for ten years was administered drugs that kept her in a zombielike state. When at 25 she was allowed home she became so terrified of being sent back to hospital that she attempted suicide.

As a last resort, a relative suggested that she visit a spiritualist church. At first she was too frightened to go, thinking that spiritualists would be some kind of occult worshippers. But when she walked into the church and met helpful people of all races from many denominations, she was reassured that there was nothing to fear. And at long last she realized that she had never been mentally ill, but that she was simply a medium. Since then, I have heard dozens of similar stories. From my work, I know that many people thought to be suffering from schizophrenia are often only lacking in nutrients, especially B group vitamins and vitamin C, and I wondered if the 'voice' in my head was there simply because I had not eaten properly for many days. John would surely have the answers and I prayed for him to arrive soon. Meanwhile, I wanted to carry on asking the 'energy', as I had now began to call the voice in my head, various questions.

'Was I born to write "Imagine" and, if so, why could I never seem to get started?'

'Because I had not died yet.'

This statement blew my mind. I have never been particularly religious, but have always believed there is an ultimate higher energy called God, and, like most people, have pondered the meaning of life. I was in for some incredible shocks. I was so dumbfounded at the implications of what I had just heard I found it hard to breathe and the pain in my head was excruciating.

But I now knew the voice was truly Diana. I just knew. She continued speaking, 'In the coming weeks you will come to know that there are many realities and many truths. Everyone has to find their own truth. Certain events, such as my marriage and death have been "set in stone" for all time, but I did not realize these things until I reached this dimension. In the Bible it says "God's house has many mansions" – today you should call these dimensions or realities. There are hundreds of thousands of realities. I will explain more when you are ready.'

I was staggered.

Quickly I asked her: 'But what about your life, your marriage – the crash? Was the scene I had 'seen' the night before what really happened?'

Her voice continued: 'When I was young, like any child, I made up stories and adored fairy tales. Somewhere inside myself, call it my intuition, I always knew that one day I would have a special job to do. When I met Charles I felt sure we would marry and although I knew life in such a public role might not be easy – it was my own fairy tale. He was my Prince and I felt like Cinderella and I so wanted the shoe to fit, but I forced it on. I now know that destiny brought us together for a brief time, but we were never really on the same wavelength. Charles did his best under the circumstances and he tried, especially at the beginning, but I was too young to cope with so much change and pressure. Neither of us were saints and we both said and did some terrible things. There is no need to say more as every minutiae of our marriage has been dissected by the media. Everyone knows the story. Now I only wish Charles love, light and happiness. I feel that he has become a wiser soul since my death. But in our moment, we weaved magic together and made two beautiful sons.

'On that night as Dodi and I left the hotel for our date with destiny we were pursued by photographers, the leeches who had lived off every aspect of my life. Not all photographers are bad, but some have no idea when to stop. No scruples, no hearts. It's the same in any walk of life, in any business, there are good and bad. I was like a commodity to be bought and sold – they forgot I was only human.

'Many people believed that because I was famous, had money and position, that being constantly pursued and photographed went with the territory. But no one, no matter who they are, can ever understand and get used to such treatment and intrusion.

'In Paris I was truly happy with Dodi and the whole world knew it. Initially we were hesitant, but we had so much in common and there was a tremendous physical attraction. We were afraid of our feelings and their possible consequences – but we were like soul mates, and he had the ability to make me really relax – it was as though we had known each other all our lives. We took every day as it came, but during that fateful week Dodi had proposed and two rings were brought to our hotel suite and I chose the one

I loved. Before I could make any firm commitment or wear any ring, I wanted to discuss all the implications with my boys. And so, before going out for dinner, we left the ring at Dodi's apartment. We knew that if we married we would be breaking all the 'accepted' rules but we felt ready to fight for the right to be together. I desperately wanted more children and a loving family life, however in that moment I had no idea our physical time was running out.

'Since marrying Charles I had lived life in the fast lane, in a goldfish bowl with everyone looking in on our every move. Now I was in another fast lane, another car, another chase. I was frustrated but no more nervous than usual in such a situation and Dodi held my hand in the back of the car, saying it would all be fine. The world knows what happened next. The photographers were following us and as we tried to sink down further into our seats, there was a sudden jolt. Time stood still. And in those final moments I knew the end had come. Flashes of light exploded around us ...'

Was this my imagination going wild? How would I ever be able to prove what I was hearing?

As I had this thought, I suddenly felt a tidal wave of emotion sweep through my chest. Gone was the timid voice I had been hearing, now I screamed out loud as Diana's voice spoke through me: 'One second I had a new future and a new life before me, the next I was catapulted forward with incredible speed. There was a thud in my chest, my head swam. For a few seconds I was aware of all the flash bulbs. Yes, they took pictures of us all. No, they did not give us any assistance. I saw Dodi and knew he was dead. It was surreal, horrific, and then the shock really hit me. For a few seconds my mind was functioning but my body no longer seemed under my control. Shock is a terrible thing, as you Hazel, are now beginning to understand, but it also helps to deaden the pain. I paid the ultimate price for being who I was.'

As she said these words through me, I felt bile rise in my throat and the pain in my chest increase again. I wasn't sure if I could take much more emotion – it was tearing me apart. But she went on speaking in my head. Diana told me that she was only vaguely aware of being moved from the car and felt no pain at all. After that everything was 'darkness and shadow' until she fleetingly glimpsed bright lights above her – perhaps in the hospital … Once in the operating theatre she became aware that she was outside her physical body and 'watched with a morbid fascination' as the surgeon physically pumped her heart. From that moment she was aware of nothing until Prince Charles came to see her and the terrible reality finally hit her.

'As he kissed my forehead and cried, saying that he was so sorry, I realized I was 'dead' in the physical sense of the word. This was the first time that Charles had truly spoken to me from his heart and in that moment I cried out to him, "Why could you not have spoken to me like this during our darkest moments?" My anger knew no bounds. I saw my body looking as if it were asleep. I screamed, "Can't I go back? I want my life back."

'But "no" came the answer, "it is your time". I looked around and saw no one but Charles and yet felt no physical pain, only a seething anger and unbelievable shock. This could not be happening, I could not be dead – what about my sons?'

Waves of nausea and emotion swept over me. My hands and body were freezing cold, the pain in my heart and chest intensified, and I realized I was feeling every emotion as Diana had felt it during that August weekend. It was heart rending as she cried in my head, 'My sons, my sons'. It was too much to bear, I had to stop this.

It was now around 3 pm on Easter Saturday. I was emotionally and physically exhausted. Perhaps I was hallucinating. I remembered as my dear mum lay dying of cancer, she had seen my dad in the corner of her hospital bedroom. Perhaps Diana had come back to help me to die. Perhaps I was going mad. I just wanted to sleep forever and then hopefully it would all stop.

In the midst of all this, Stuart came upstairs with the local TV repair man, who had arrived to fix the video in our bedroom which had begun playing up earlier in the week. I must have frightened him half to death as he looked very keen to do his job and leave.

John and Lindsey arrived around 4.30 pm. Stuart came up with them. He needed answers – and soon. As they walked into the room, I felt as though I was half in this world and half in the next. As I stared out of the window I thought about my daughter in Australia; she would be devastated that I was leaving her and that she had not been with me at the end. But there was nothing I could do and as John came over to see me I thought how wonderful it was to have such good friends to share my last moments. I was very weak and, as best I could, I related my story. Much of what happened to me physically over the next two hours has become a vague memory.

But John could recall his reactions well, 'When I saw you in the bed, I could hardly believe how much you had changed. You had lost a lot of weight and when I held your hands they were exceedingly cold in a bizarre way beyond anything I have ever seen in my medical practice. You were very weak, extremely dehydrated and your tongue was dark green. On a physical level you looked well on your road to death. You stank of death. My initial reaction was to rush you to the nearest hospital. Yet at the back of my mind I felt almost certain you would end up on major tranquillizer medication and I shuddered to think how these might affect your experience, as they can have a permanent effect on mood and behaviour. After speaking to our friend, Dr Richard Lawrence, and hearing your story, I reasoned that while you were exhibiting no thoughts of harming yourself or others, the best place for you to be cared for was at home where you were surrounded by people who really care about you.' I distinctly remember staring into John's eyes and feeling a strange pulsing energy that passed through my eyes into his. I realized in that moment that I could read his thoughts and his fears. John seemed to sense this. I knew he was frightened and so was I. He knew my mind was okay because when I spoke I was totally coherent.

Towards the end of our first hour together I turned to Lindsey and asked her, 'Yesterday you said my eyes had gone cold and grey, are they still cold and grey?'

'Yes', she said quietly, as if answering truthfully might somehow be too much for me. Then I asked her to go into my bathroom and take out the cover photograph of Diana from the Diana Tribute Album I had bought after her death. 'What colour is that photograph?' I asked. 'Grey', Lindsey replied, looking very startled. 'Whose picture is it?' I demanded.

'It is Diana, Princess of Wales' whispered Lindsey. And in the exact second she spoke Diana's name the sky darkened and snow began falling outside the window.

Lindsey and John were stunned. John ran downstairs to fetch his medical bag and brought up an apple drink containing more liquid vitamins, minerals and herbs. I promptly threw up. He had put some Kava Kava root in the drink to help calm me down, but because I had a weak liver, my system could not take such a large single dose of herbs. Stuart went downstairs, but John and Lindsey remained.

My sight was fading and the room once again filled with a whitish mist. Dusk fell silently. I felt myself slipping away and asked John to hold my hand. I'm not sure what happened next, as time lost all meaning. I felt as free as a bird, there was no pain, no thirst, no stinking body, just total bliss.

The voice then returned, 'This is death. It is easy, but it is not your time. You must go back and continue your work, you have yet to fulfil your destiny.' When I eventually opened my eyes again, Lindsey and John were still there. John seemed to know something special had happened as his eyes were full of tears and he squeezed my hand. My senses eventually returned. The sweet, sickly stench of death pervaded the room, it was appalling. My mouth tasted repulsive, beyond anything I had ever imagined. I felt as though I was beginning to decompose, the stench was so strong.

John stroked my forehead lovingly. He said he was going to talk to Stuart, but that he would pop up every few minutes. John continues the story, 'My rational mind was in chaos, I had never witnessed anything like this before. In every sense of the word, Hazel appeared to be dead and yet her physical body was still alive, but only just – it was a mind-blowing experience. There is no way she could have acted her symptoms. Stuart was desperately worried. He did not know what we had just witnessed and I wasn't going to tell him. It was already hard enough for him to comprehend. He thought Hazel had suffered a complete nervous breakdown. But I told him her symptoms were not consistent with such a scenario, and reassured him she was not going mad.'

John also realized that Stuart and I badly needed some sleep. I was becoming terrified of the dark, and yet any type of artificial light caused my eyes terrible pain. John went off with Stuart to find a late-night chemist and get some sleeping pills. Lindsey sat with me and held my hand. Suddenly the energy returned and my temperature soared. Although my skin was like ice, the heat and intense spinning inside my solar plexus were tremendous. I looked deep into Lindsey's eyes and could 'see' her thoughts and her possible futures and in that moment I realized that her future was not set and that she could change it.

I was puzzled because earlier the voice of Diana had said that her death was set in stone. As I had this thought, her voice returned, 'Certain major events are set in stone, my death was one of them. Other events for you and Lindsey and for the world are at this moment just probabilities. The problem right now is that the Earth and all its inhabitants are in for a few surprises, some of which are already set in stone – some are good and some are terrible – you will come to know these in time. There are many possible futures for you all on Earth and it is time for you to understand that you can all help to alter some of these futures, but you must act quickly.

'You all come with a blueprint for a specific purpose, but how many roads you travel and the choices you make along the way before reaching your destination, goal or purpose, are your own. From what I have learned in this dimension I now know that we all come to Earth to learn various lessons through experience, and to help each other. But life on Earth for many is chaos: the delicate balance needed for good health and the health of the planet is disappearing.'

She wasn't joking, my mind was in total chaos.

Her voice continued, 'Some people are starving, others are rich beyond their wildest dreams. Accidents happen and things go wrong. You live on a physical planet, and sometimes you are simply in the wrong place at the wrong time.'

I was getting confused and needed some further clarification, so I asked, 'So what you are saying is that all accidents are just that, accidents, or are they pre-planned for a reason?'

She continued, 'You remain on a physical planet and accidents and other events do happen. Sometimes accidents or illnesses serve a greater purpose but, for the most part, people involved in accidents are simply in the wrong place at the wrong time.'

'So were you in the wrong place at the wrong time? Was your death an accident or were you murdered?' I asked.

'My death was set in stone', she replied. 'Again there are many realities. Yes, there was a plot being set in motion at the highest levels and there was a future probability that I might have been killed if I had decided to marry Dodi and bear his children, but by having the accident I beat them to it.'

This was all becoming totally surreal …

'And who are these people?' I interjected.

'They are above governments', came the reply. 'One day you will come to know who they are and understand what they are capable of, and it will terrify you. But right now it makes no difference, as I am physically dead. I now know much more than I did on Earth, I have seen more of what you term "the bigger picture" and I know that it is time for every living person to begin making a difference. No one can afford to sit on the fence any longer.'

I knew exactly what she meant.

After Diana's death I had written in my *Sunday Times* column on 5th October 1997: *I was privileged to have met Diana on several occasions. She desperately wanted people to rise above all the trivia written about her personal life. Like me, she believed that we all have a purpose to fulfil in our lifetime, and felt that her purpose was to raise global awareness of the huge number of people who need help. Diana was convinced that if we could see the 'bigger picture', we would realize that we can all make a difference, no matter how small. She had an inner knowing of the job she had come to do and had the integrity and strength to carry it through. I believe her death was somehow pre-destined, and was meant to trigger a positive response, a raising of consciousness within us all.*

*Since her tragic death there has been an incredible demonstration of people power. In everyday life many people have said to me, 'I had no idea Diana achieved so much, I'm going to do my best from now on to somehow help others in need. This is exactly what she would have wanted.*

The voice in my head continued, saying, 'I had no concept of how important I was to the bigger picture until I was "dead". You, Hazel, were born to write a special book, but if you die now because of the shock we gave you in Harrods, we will find another to take your place.'

One minute I felt like some all-knowing being but as she said this, what was left of my ego was completely shattered. Her voice softened, 'Hazel, you are special, you always have been, but you have never known it. You have very little self-esteem and suffer from moments of black despair just as I did. Before I died I too was on a journey of 'awakening' and had learned to love myself a little more. During my last years I had found a new inner strength, as I let go of a lot of my anger and frustration. I realized that holding onto negative emotions just holds you back. For years I had fought for recognition and to overcome feelings of inadequacy and frustration which almost destroyed me. But from all my trials and experiences came a new strength, an inner knowing. I wanted to be like the fairy godmother from my childhood fantasies, I wanted to put so many wrongs right. It wasn't easy, but I had found my true path in life. But I needed to be loved for myself and Dodi filled that void. When I finally accepted myself, warts and all, I found happiness.'

Was it real? Could I really be hearing Diana? It certainly felt real. As I swallowed John's concoction by my bedside I made a pact with God. If He would allow me to survive, I would make time to write this story. But at that time I still had a long way to go.

Lindsey went down to help Jean prepare a supper for everyone as John was also staying overnight. As I lay there I could feel a fantastic energy pulsing through my eyes, but my body felt as though it was burning out. The voice in my head continued: 'Hazel, you already know about auras, the electric field that surrounds every human, animal, fish, plant and living being, but every one of you also emits your own unique frequency. You are an electrical being with billions of circuits encased in a physical body. We in the higher realms can tune to your specific frequency so that we can communicate with you, in just the same way that you use a telephone on Earth. In the spirit world, we are energy or frequency, and just as you cannot see the signals coming into your radio and TV, the majority of you cannot see us but that does not mean that we do not exist. Just as we can tune to your specific frequency – you can also tune into ours. At first you will find it is hit-and-miss as many over here want to send messages to loved ones. But as you practise, you will easily be able to distinguish who you are hearing. We are merely in another dimension. In Harrods we turned up our frequency to full volume, which is what gave you such a tremendous physical shock.'

'But why, why did you do that?' I asked.

'Because you had let go of the book, which is your soul's purpose in being here for this lifetime and we had to try and get you back on track. We had tried to reach you before and failed. And so a great deal of discussion ensued and we decided to take drastic action. We trusted that you would be able to cope with everything that you would hear and everything you'd see.'

'And what do you call this drastic action?' I enquired ...

'It is known as Divine Intervention', came the reply. 'We are not allowed to interfere as such, we just wanted to force you to listen ... Then allow you to choose. On Earth, most of you have the freedom to choose what you do, and you have known for several years that you must write a book. You chose this lifetime before you were born, as I did, as Charles did, as all of us do. Every soul that is on the Earth chose to be here. No one is forced to return. But many never remember what they came to do and simply stumble through life, not realizing that we all came for a purpose. Again there are many realities, and we will explain further when you are feeling stronger. Meanwhile you are still in a physical body and the shock has made you very ill and you must fight to survive.'

It was incredible, I wanted to listen for ever, but my mind and body were totally drained. Stuart and John returned and gave me a sleeping pill and I went straight to sleep.

But at 12.30 am I was shaken awake and felt as cold as ice again. Stuart slept on peacefully beside me. Diana began talking again. She told me that after her earthly death, she was in such a dreadful state of shock that she 'hung around' her physical body for days. She did not want to die and fought hard to remain here, but ultimately realized that it was 'her time' to go. I lay in the dark weeping quietly as she told me of her moving reunion with her father who came 'to hold her hand' and give her support until after her funeral, after which she was taken into the next dimension for another reunion − with Dodi ...

She had felt incredulous at the outpouring of grief after her earthly death. She said, 'With all the death I had seen around the world, I was amazed that so many people cried for me. But as time has passed over here, I realized that I carried a special energy inside me. (She said I would understand what this meant in a few weeks). I was born to be the Princess of Wales, to do my job and to move on. My death was meant to trigger a worldwide raising of feelings, to bring emotions to the surface and to encourage people to think about their lives. To consider how short a time we have on Earth, just how precious life is, and above all to encourage every one of you to begin making a difference whenever and wherever you can. When I first came over, my grief and anger over the circumstances of our accident and leaving my sons behind was beyond words. We grieve over here just as you do. But every day I watch over my boys. We were joined at the hip and they know if they need me I am always listening for their call. I am in their hearts, now and forever, and one day we shall all meet again.'

As she spoke, I wept and wept with the intensity of her emotions as they swept through me. In life she had been proud of her body and had gone to great lengths to keep herself in shape as it gave her more confidence. She hated the fact that her 'shell' was lying in a coffin, but realized that it was necessary. Her funeral was 'stupendous' and she loved the fact that Sir Elton John gave the proceeds of his song, *Candle in The Wind* to charity – she thanked him for that. She was transfixed by her brother's speech as he said everything that she would have wanted to say. As we cried at the funeral, she also cried. She wept for her sons as they walked behind her coffin, for her brother and for her family and for what they were feeling on that day. She wept for Dodi and his family, for her friends and for the life that she had left behind.

Her voice returned. 'Another death is coming.' I tried to scribble odd notes using only my bedside torch for light, but I was too exhausted.

'Please – please whoever you are,' I cried. 'Just let me sleep, please let me sleep.' I took another of John's pills. So much for being a health writer.

# 4 The Return

*12th April – Easter Sunday – Birmingham*

**WHEN I WOKE IN THE** morning I looked at the pieces of paper by my bedside, and could hardly decipher my scrawl. But one name stood out – Paul McCartney. Perhaps, as the title for my book was to have been 'Imagine', and it was originally to have been based on John Lennon's song, maybe I was supposed to be interviewing Sir Paul and Linda McCartney.

As I lay in bed looking out at the sunshine, I recalled that the voice had also said to me, 'another death is coming'. My mother-in-law was getting on in years and she wasn't looking too well when she arrived on Good Friday, perhaps she was going to die. I began to panic. What was happening was more than enough. I stayed in bed, still feeling too weak to get up. John returned at 10 am.

Looking back on that day John remembered, 'You were still very poorly, but as we sat and talked I noticed how you changed from moment to moment both mentally and physically. One moment you were icy cold, looking like death and physically very weak, then as the 'energy' arrived, you became very flushed as your temperature shot up and you spoke with complete lucidity, but sounded like someone else. You appeared to have multiple personalities, one that I recognized as Hazel, albeit a very sick Hazel, and another one which I hadn't experienced before. You knew how ludicrous what you were saying sounded to us all, and yet I knew you were totally rational. It was incredibly dramatic, you seemed very wise and all-knowing and then in other moments you would look as though you were going to die.'

I asked John what he had thought was happening. 'On the face of it you seemed to be exhibiting what could be described as psychotic symptoms. Yet what could have been taken to be mad thoughts and ideas, were embedded in complete rationality. You were totally aware of who you were, where you were and the date and time. More importantly, you had a complete insight into the things that you were experiencing and the effect this was having on the people around you. You were well aware that a lot of what you were saying must have sounded utterly ludicrous to any rational person. But you expressed real concern for Stuart, and stressed, it was important that I did what I could to explain to him that you were not going mad. You remained consistent in what you said was happening to you. For these reasons I resolved to support you in any way that I could. It was as if the "energy" that we called Diana was giving you a taste of what it was like to have experienced what she went through. 'When you said certain things about her not being able to say goodbye to her family, there was a tremendous surge of emotion. It was incredibly profound.'

John suggested that I try and take a shower before all the relatives arrived for lunch since they were bound to want to visit me. He was right – I smelled awful and our bed sheets had the same smell of death as my mother's hospital room on the night she had died back in May 1991.

When I looked into the bathroom mirror to my amazement my eyes were a pure cornflower blue. They are normally dark blue. As I stared into the mirror they turned dark grey. Perhaps I was just seeing things, as my eyes hurt like hell. Back in the bedroom the voice instructed me to: 'turn on the TV'. Like a robot I did as I was told. I found myself watching *Fluke*, a film about a young man who is killed in a car crash and whose spirit returns to try and help his family. A coincidence? Maybe. I changed channels, to see Harrison Ford in *Sabrina*, a film about a young woman who finds happiness in Paris. I turned the TV off. It was as if she was giving me messages through the media.

'But why not,' the voice said. 'Almost everything I did appeared in the papers or on TV. There are many subliminal messages in the media that you are not aware of. All we are doing is making you more sensitive, so that you are aware of these messages.'

I went back to bed. At lunchtime, Stuart's sister Cheryl, her daughter Irena and granddaughter Daisy all arrived for lunch downstairs. One by one they came up to visit. Cheryl thought I was having a nervous breakdown. What could I say? I told her that I seemed to have become more psychic and believed that her mother may have come for the weekend to say goodbye. Cheryl was not amused.

During the afternoon as I lay gazing out at the sunshine, Irena came up with six-year-old Daisy. This was only the third occasion I had seen little Daisy. As she ran in the room, she climbed up on the bed and said, 'Auntie Hazel, you are very sick, can I give you some of my magic?' I was astounded. Here was a small child full of love and fun, offering to give me some healing. She went on, 'I can do magic and my daddy can do magic too.'

'What kind of magic?' I asked.

'Well, he can switch the washing machine on and off just by standing next to it, and he can change the TV,' she said. Her mother and grandmother laughed and told her not to tell stories, but I knew better. Scientists have known for years that the electromagnetic field is so strong around some people that they can set off electrical instruments and shatter light bulbs just by walking past them. Daisy placed her tiny hand on the exact spot on my head that had been thudding incessantly since Friday, and then without any prompting she moved her hand to my chest which was still extremely sore. As she lay there on the bed I felt full of love for this little child but also thought, 'I don't normally get on with children.'

Then the voice inside my head said: 'Children are full of magic and wonder until we take it from them. They have no fear until we plant our seeds in their heads. At this time, many special children are being born, and because they have a knowing which their parents do not have, some of these children are either bullied or thought to be telling lies. It is imperative that parents learn to distinguish children that are truly special from those who are simply being naughty so that their "talents" can be nurtured. Loving discipline is needed.'

Daisy smiled up at me and proclaimed very grandly, 'I can change the weather too.' Her mother laughed, but I was stunned, because as she said these words, snow flakes began falling through the sunshine. It was incredible. Suddenly exhaustion overwhelmed me and they left me to sleep.

But my brain went into overtime. The weather, she had mentioned the weather and then the snow came. Another coincidence? The voice was back, 'Yes, you are the weather. Almost everything you do on Earth affects the weather. Many of you think it's up to governments to stop the global emissions of chemicals and gasses that are destroying your ozone layer and triggering changes in weather patterns, but every single one of you is the weather. You can all do your bit to help look after the air and the Earth, then slowly but surely your cumulative efforts will kick in. The extreme weather conditions would ease and many sicknesses would no longer plague you. Everything could be perfect. It may take several generations, but it can happen, it must happen. You may think that what you do in your own home and at work makes no difference, but it's like a chain reaction. And you are all links in a huge chain. Many people have woken up to this fact, but billions more need to be educated as to how they can help – and very soon.'

She was right. For years I have watched the environmental lobby grow and have done my best to help protect the environment.

John broke into my thoughts as he crept back into the room. He told me that he would stay one more day, he wanted to be sure I was going to pull through.

That evening, Stuart suggested that we should watch a video to lighten our mood and he put on the film *Overboard*, starring Goldie Hawn and Kurt

Russell. Goldie plays an heiress who falls off a yacht in the middle of the night when trying to retrieve her diamond engagement ring from the deck. As Goldie's character plunged into the ocean, my thoughts turned to Diana and Dodi in the south of France and how happy they had seemed. Stuart could see I was becoming extremely agitated but I did not want to alarm him unnecessarily: I had to act normally. My eyes hurt again and I thought I would switch the TV off, but as I walked towards the set, the screen began to fuzz over with static lines. Stuart was annoyed, as the video player had been repaired only the day before, and told me to leave it on for a few more minutes. As I backed away, the picture came back on again, surely it couldn't be me doing that — could it?

I went for a walk around the landing. The stench around the house was becoming overpowering, why couldn't John, Stuart or his mother smell it too? Surely this was not just me? I began opening all the windows. As I walked into Jean's bedroom I noticed that the flowers that had been placed in her room by Sheila on Friday were dying, but the roses she had brought for my bedside were fine and blooming.

Was this a sign that Jean might be dying? I was certainly having some weird thoughts. I crept downstairs to check on her, and found her watching TV. As I looked deeply into her eyes it was as if I could read her thoughts of sadness. She told me that on Easter Monday it would be exactly seven years to the day since her husband had died and that she longed to follow him …

As I worried about her dying, I became very agitated and went back upstairs to have a relaxing bath in the hope of calming my anxious mind. As I put on the bathroom lights it was like being stabbed in the eyes. Was that because Diana had been in the darkness of a grave for so many months? No, that was silly — she had already told me that at the moment of earthly death, or soon after, the spirit energy or essence of an individual leaves the physical shell behind. Then what was causing the terrible pain in my eyes? Everything was such a puzzle.

Norma had said that water would ground me and I certainly needed a bath because I stank. I put some lavender in the water in the hope that the wonderful fragrance might help to calm me down. As I lay in the bath, I let go, closed my eyes and took a deep breath. I felt my body begin to rise up through the water and as I breathed out I sank back into the bath. But not for long. Suddenly my body began to rise again, and to my total horror I realized that I was floating just above the bath water.

I grasped the handles on either side of the bath and pulled myself back into the water. What on earth was happening? I needed this to stop. As I looked up again at the lights and the pain stabbed through my eyes it triggered memories of a visit to an Indian astrologer two years earlier who had said something about my eyes. Of course, he had given me a tape, so I got out of the bath, walked into my dressing room and began searching through my collection of tapes.

I couldn't believe my luck when I found it, dated 10th April 1996, a reading with Chakrapani Ullal – a Vedic astrologer. I put it on the tape player in my bathroom. It was all pretty boring, about how I should be in the media, but then he predicted, 'that around the time of the millennium, you will earn a lot of money and do great humanitarian work, but you must be careful with your eyes. You are going to have problems with your eyes.' I wasn't sure about the money part, but he was spot on about my eyes. How could he have known?

The voice returned in my head, 'Don't you remember? Certain events are set in stone and you came into this lifetime with a blueprint that you would write this book at this time. Remember what the fortune-teller told you when you were only 14.'

Yes, this statement evoked the long-forgotten memory of a local fair when I had paid sixpence to have my fortune told. The only statement I remembered was that one day I would write a book about my life. That prediction sounded like an impossible dream all those years ago, and yet at the age of 43 I had become a writer and with luck I would now fulfil my destiny. I thought about all the times I had visited fortune-tellers, psychics and mediums. Long ago I had learned not to take these readings too seriously. Yes, they gave me guidance and occasionally comfort during black times, but at the end of the day, it's your life and you have to make your own decisions.

We cannot keep handing absolute responsibility for everything that happens in our lives over to others. Often I realized that these people were just telling me what I wanted to hear. They would literally mirror my hopes and dreams back to me. So if a fortune-teller says to someone, 'there is going to be a death in the family or you are going to have problems with your marriage, or whatever else they might say. If we really believe what they tell us and think about it enough, we can sometimes bring these prophecies into reality. I remember years ago someone saying to me, 'whatever is expected tends to be realized', meaning that when we think and believe certain events are going to happen, we can literally bring them into being. What you think about the most is what you will have in your life. If you think about losing your job, not having enough money, not being happy enough, then this is what will expand and become your reality.

At the end of the day we should all remain as much as possible in charge of our own futures – after all, most of us can still choose what we want to do. It is true that some things might be set in stone, but the rest of life is a moveable feast. So should I believe what I was hearing now? Was Diana some kind of all-knowing spirit guide whom I should allow to tell me what to think, what to believe, and what to do with my life?

Her voice was back again, 'You are right to a degree. Just because I am now in spirit I have not become an all-knowing soul – I am still only Diana. That's why when someone on Earth receives a message from a relative over here, they should treat it in the same way as if that person were still alive. Yet I have also met great beings and masters of light from the higher realms who are helping me to understand more realities – and there are thousands of them. As I have said before, people still have to make up their own minds,

I can only share with you what I have learned until now, but there will be more to come in the future. As one learns one evolves and grows. In the higher realms everything can be perfect – God is perfect – and believe it or not I now know that if all people could change overnight into truly positive and caring individuals, all your futures could be changed in a flash to much happier ones. But we are realistic and this transition is not going to happen overnight and so, yes, certain events are still set in stone.'

'Is it possible that we could all hear spirit?' I asked.

'At this moment only one person in every million is truly psychic,' Diana replied. 'But you all have the ability to hear us. You are also capable of doing many amazing things which we are going to show you …'

I winced. 'You mean like the TV, like trying to heal Sheila, like my sensitivity to smell and light? …' I said. I dreaded to think what else lay in store for me. It felt as though she was roaring with laughter as she continued: 'You are so frightened, but there is no need. You are capable of much more than you know and one day you will all be able to do many fantastic things. It will all become second nature to you.'

'So there's more to come?' I asked, incredulously.

'Much more,' came the reply. 'There are great and exciting changes coming to you all and as more people go through their own unique awakening process they will need help. Then they will not have to suffer as you have done. They will know what is happening to them and they will know what to do.'

I could hardly believe that such a responsibility was being placed on my shoulders. But it reminded me of an incident that had taken place almost eight years earlier. Stuart and I had driven to Broadway in the Cotswolds for a Saturday lunch. Our car had broken down. And guess who got to wait for the rescue services, while Stuart returned home in a taxi? Right …

As I walked into the Lygon Arms hotel I saw a friend I had not seen for several years. I had plenty of time to kill, so we had tea together. She asked me what I was doing and I told her all about Norma and how I was researching alternative subjects. Her eyes started to glaze over. Angela ran a large perfume business and she wasn't remotely interested in hearing about spirits or saving whales and dolphins. She began to yawn, so I changed the subject. I did not imagine that Angela and I would be getting together again for some time.

Three days later I was extremely surprised to receive a telephone call from Angela, sounding incredibly agitated. What on earth was wrong? She told me she was hearing voices, notably a man's voice in her head. Her husband had told her to see their doctor, who had prescribed valium. What should she do? After asking her about the voice and what the man was saying, it was obvious that Angela had 'woken up' and could hear spirit and somehow our meeting had acted as the trigger, just as Norma had acted as mine. I was sick with jealousy that, overnight, Angela was able to hear so clearly when I had been receiving lessons for years. I told Angela she had been given an amazing gift, but she didn't quite see it that way. I told her to come straight over and see Norma, who helped Angela to integrate her newly discovered psychic abilities into her everyday life.

I realized that I too was being given a gift, but on that Easter Sunday evening I wasn't very appreciative either. I had been aware for many years that humans have not yet realized the true potential of their minds and thought about how Uri Geller and many others like him can perform seemingly impossible tasks. I was already fairly telepathic, in that when I concentrated I could feel what people were thinking. I had become sensitive to electricity and artificial lighting, also to smell and sound. And as I prepared for bed I wondered what Diana meant by 'much more'.

Physically I felt totally exhausted after my foray downstairs to see Jean and the episode in the bathroom, and yet there was an awesome energy inside my solar plexus area spinning around and around. As I turned off the light in my bathroom I caught sight of the black circles under my eyes, which were now a bright emerald green. Stuart and I went to bed.

# 5 The Happenings

*13th April − Easter Monday − Birmingham*

**I BEGAN TO DREAD THE** nights with a passion. They dragged on for what seemed an eternity. The voice in my head would come and go, and I would drift in and out of sleep. Since my mid-twenties I had suffered from chronic insomnia, and now I knew why. Because I had worried too much about whether I would get enough sleep. Now I no longer cared, I was alive and that was sufficient. As I crept into my bathroom and began scribbling notes at 2 am in the morning I realized the writing was not mine. Was this how Diana wrote? After we had met she had written me a lovely letter but I had mislaid it. I made a note for Lindsey to try and find it and then I would compare the styles.

I went downstairs and made myself some porridge. My weight had dropped dramatically and if God had heard my prayers and was going to keep his side of the bargain, I needed to start eating again − even though I still didn't feel hungry.

As I thought about all that had happened, it suddenly struck me that the incident in Harrods had only happened six days earlier, but it felt as though I had lived a whole lifetime since then. I thought about just how much

Diana fitted into her brief life and how much she had achieved.

I thought about everything Norma had taught me about guides and helpers from the higher realms. I remembered hearing John Lennon back in 1993, and I thought about my meeting with Barry Manilow in January 1998. Barry had told me how a painful time in his life had led to his 'awakening' a few years ago, and each day when he meditated he could hear his own guides. I wondered who his guides were. Barry had also advised me to trust – simply trust that life, the universe, one's guides, the higher realms – would help us through.

Was Diana guiding me now? Would I be able to hear other voices too? After my mum died of cancer in 1991, I was heartbroken and whenever I thought of her I would often cry myself to sleep. I used to imagine what she might say to me in various situations and this brought me great comfort, but I longed to hear her voice and cuddle her again. After her death I was given many messages that could have only come from my mother, and so I already had a firm belief in life after death. Since beginning work as a writer I had also interviewed dozens of people who had heard from loved ones in the higher realms.

Then at a TV studio in 1994, I met a wonderful lady from Exeter called Jacki Humphries who had lost her son Philip in a tragic car accident. As the night wore on, I went and searched in my study and read through that interview again. Not only did Jacki hear from her son, she also saw him again, as she told me: 'After Philip was killed, I went with my husband to identify his body. I was frightened, but I had to say goodbye to our son. It was my Phil, and yet what had made him special, his essence – whatever you want to call it – was gone. So if he was not in that room – I wondered where had he gone?' Jacki then went to a spiritualist church to see the medium Stephen O'Brien and recalled, 'I always thought that spiritualism had something to do with the devil, but I was desperate and would have done anything to know that my son had gone on. So many people had said to me that dabbling with death was evil, but for 2,000 years we have prayed to Jesus and he has been dead for a very long time, so I felt it could not be that bad.'

Jacki was surprised that there were over 300 people in the hall from all walks of life and many religions and she felt only an overwhelming sense of love. She had never met Stephen and yet he gave her a very specific message that she knew had come from her son. From that day, Jacki attended meditation courses and learned how to hear spirit for herself. At first when she began to hear voices she thought she was going mad but as the months passed she learned to cope. Then a miracle happened.

'After many months of meditating, early one morning as I sat quietly I became aware that Phil was in the room with me. I opened my eyes and there before me stood my son. At first I cried so much with shock and joy I could hardly see him, but as the months passed I could see and speak with him as clearly as I sit and speak with you now …'

When Jacki's story appeared in the *Today* newspaper on 9th November 1994, many people dismissed this as a mother's grief-stricken tale but as I sat in the cold and dark of the wee small hours I, like Jacki, realized that we all have the capability to hear spirit and wondered if one day I too might also be able to see spirit clearly. Now I know that there are hundreds of thousands of people out there having similar experiences, but they are too afraid to speak out for fear of being ridiculed. It was as I pondered Jacki's experiences and my own fears that I heard Diana again: 'When I was at my most vulnerable and feeling totally bereft I too had visions, but no one would believe me, they just thought I was mad.'

Just the thought of anyone appearing before me sent shivers down my spine, I desperately wanted to stop this, I needed some sleep. But the voice interrupted, 'For years you have read and written about life after death, the power of the mind, guides etc., but you never really understood the concepts of letting go and trusting, and neither did I. When you let go of your physical body on Saturday, you truly let everything go, caring about yourself, money, life – nothing had any meaning for you in that moment other than the total bliss that you felt. Now to get through everything we are going to tell you and show you, you must simply go with the flow and trust that everything will work out – and it will.'

I wearily agreed, and as I climbed back into bed I kept saying to myself, 'Let go Hazel, let go and go with the flow' and mercifully I slept until dawn.

Sheila arrived at 9 am on Easter Monday. She had known from my behaviour on Good Friday that something was going on and had agreed to come in and help me out on that Bank Holiday morning. She was appalled at how much weight I had lost, and she also saw that I was different. Sheila recalls: 'You looked dreadful, but I could sense there was something different about you. I saw a deepness in your eyes that I have never seen before, it's hard to put into words but they looked very knowing. In your bedroom the atmosphere felt very calm and strange, I don't know how to explain it, but the house seemed full of love. As I made your bed a little bird kept flying at the glass, trying to get in through the window – in the nine years I have been working at your house I had never seen that before.'

I noticed that Sheila was limping and she complained that her left knee was causing her considerable pain. I asked her to sit by me on the bed, and I pulsed the energy through my eyes into hers and placed my hand on her knee. 'What could she feel?' I asked. 'Ice,' she said. She explained that she felt an icy, cold sensation pulsing through her jeans into her knee. When I had first sat on the bed with her my hands had been warm. As I touched her knee my hands turned blue with cold. Maybe Diana wanted to heal through me and when my hands turned to ice, I would know the 'energy' was there helping me. As I sat hoping to heal Sheila's knees, after about four minutes my hands began to warm through and I knew that whatever energy had been there was gone. Sheila went back to work, without limping, and within an hour her pain had disappeared. But whatever I had done had drained my energy and I had to go back to bed. I just couldn't figure it all out.

John stopped by for lunch before returning to London. He had been my rock and Stuart's too, and one day I would repay his kindness. John came and sat by me and we held hands. I stared deeply into his eyes and I could feel the energy pulsing from my eyes to his. It felt as though I was giving him a gift, but I had no idea what it might be. Tears flowed down his face. 'What was he feeling?' I asked. 'An incredible "knowing", incredible emotions', was all he could say. What did I know? Nothing.

I told him that my next *Sunday Times* column was due in that day, and thank God it was a bank holiday and my editor was away. Perhaps on Tuesday I would be able to start writing. John hugged me goodbye and told me to 'hang on in there'.

In the early evening I went down to see Jean. What a terrible weekend she had endured. I felt very guilty. As I walked into the living room where she had spent much of her time, I noticed that the plants were dying, just like the flowers in her bedroom. But they had all been delivered fresh on the previous Thursday, as I had wanted the house to look good for Easter weekend. I thought that perhaps they needed some water, but the soil was damp. Was it possible that her energies were killing the plants?

I have long known that we all emit energies – our thoughts are energies – and if you walk into a room full of people who are thinking angry, negative thoughts, you can feel the heavy atmosphere. Also if you were to walk into a room full of happy people, you can feel the good vibrations, the positive thoughts, which then create a happy atmosphere. Thought creates … Think about it. Nothing comes into being until it is thought of first. At that time I believed that my mother-in-law was dying like the plants because of the message 'another death is coming' that I had heard on Saturday night. Now I know it was her negative thoughts and fears about what was happening to me that was killing the plants.

The negative energies had become trapped in the room where she had been sitting. I flung open the door to help release them. I now understood why – when you visit certain sites or places where highly emotional events have taken place, you can literally 'feel' or 'sense' the energies – good or bad, hot or cold.

On Tuesday, Jean went home, I got dressed for the first time in four days and Lindsey came back to work. Stuart was delighted to see me out of bed, but I looked and felt very drained. He was busy photographing furniture so that he could do the furniture layouts for our new home, and as he passed my study he snapped a picture of me and Lindsey – I looked awful.

Lindsey went off to collect some shopping for me and I switched on my computer in the hope of beginning my column, I knew my editor would be ringing shortly to ask for my copy. As I looked at the screen, it was like being stabbed in the eyes – the same pain I had experienced during the previous days when I had switched on the lights in my bathroom. But this was worse, and when I forced myself to look at the screen all I could see was blackness and my vision began to blur. Perhaps I was going blind? I had heard the phrase 'they made me blind so I could see' – maybe spirits were making me blind so that I could see them. I began to panic.

As I got up from my desk I knocked a cup over, and called for Sheila. She was hoovering upstairs and could not hear me. I fumbled my way to the kitchen, and began talking to myself, 'calm down, calm down, take a deep breath, you will be OK.' And I was. As I became calmer, my eyes began to clear. Once all this was over I would consult an eye specialist, meanwhile I would keep taking all the vitamins and minerals I knew of to help nourish my eyes. Perhaps whatever had happened over the past week had made me sensitive to the radiation from my computer as well as light? I had become sensitive to my mobile phone during the past year and had written regularly about the dangers of its longterm use. But what could I tell my editor when he called? That I had died and come back; that I had been, or still was, possessed by the spirit of Diana? Right …

When he did call, I waffled and said my mother-in-law was not well (remember I had thought she was about to die) and that I was having trouble with my eyes. How long would he give me to file my copy? He said he could give me until Friday. Great, I felt sure in a day or so everything would be back to normal.

Lindsey returned and suggested we should go out and get some fresh air. As we stepped out onto the patio the sun broke through the clouds. It was strange but sunlight did not trigger tremendous pain in my eyes as artificial lights had, and as I closed them and looked up towards the sun I instantly 'saw' a huge ball of yellow which then turned to a fantastic red. It was fabulous. I could literally feel my body soaking up the red and yellow colours, it was amazing. When we see different colours in a rainbow we are simply looking at light moving at different frequencies. For years I had written about the effect of colour on health and how if the body does not absorb and receive a full spectrum of all the colours found in sunlight: red, orange, yellow, green, blue, indigo and violet, then we become ill. I obviously needed the frequencies of yellow and red. I knew that the frequency of yellow would help to calm my solar plexus, digestion and nervous system, while the frequency of red would help to give my physical body more energy.

As I sat in the sunshine the voice returned: 'The sun was never meant to harm us, it gives us life. Without sunlight, humans, animals, plants and the planet will die.' It is now well-known that sunlight helps to raise serotonin and other hormone levels which elevate mood and boost the production of vitamin D which protects our bones and teeth. Ultraviolet light helps to lower blood pressure and cholesterol, assists with weight loss and is an effective treatment for psoriasis. There is hardly a person on the planet who does not feel better and healthier after spending some time in the sun.

Today, because of the thinning ozone layer, too many harmful rays are getting through, triggering an increase in skin cancer and cataracts. But our accumulative actions are causing this to happen – we are all responsible. Standing in the sunshine for a few minutes certainly helped to lift my spirits, but I still felt incredibly weak, so Lindsey helped me back up to bed. I smiled as I looked again at my mother-in-law's yellow roses. Over the weekend I had found myself staring at the flowers and I had wondered if yellow had been one of Diana's favourite colours. Now I realized that my body had simply craved yellow. I would eat another banana.

As the week wore on I began to crave other colours. On Tuesday it was orange, the colour associated with the gut. When I wrapped an orange scarf around my waist and my stomach, which was so sore it felt as though it had been kicked, it really helped. I also ate papaya, an orange-coloured fruit which soothes the gut. Then I was drawn to red. Red is for energy and goodness knows my physical body needed more of that. I picked red tulips and put them by my bedside. So now I was sensitive to colour as well as electricity, artificial light and smell. I wondered what it might be next.

I didn't have long to wait. Stuart came home on Wednesday evening and sat down to eat a piece of cold chicken for his supper. But for me, even being in the same room as that chicken made me feel extremely nauseous. This was strange because previously I had eaten organic chicken and fish quite happily. I was still surviving mainly on fruit and porridge and was able to face the odd bowl of vegetable soup. It was as though to 'hear' spirit my body had to be as pure as possible.

Diana was back: 'Yes for the moment it is preferable for you to remain as pure as possible, but again there are many realities. And because you are now so sensitive you are becoming aware of how the dead animal in your presence met its death – you are ultra-sensitive, but this will pass. From here, we see not only huge amounts of untold suffering that millions of humans are experiencing, which in most cases is totally unnecessary and preventable, but also the millions of animals who are treated with appalling cruelty.'

I have long advocated organic farming methods and in this area Prince Charles has certainly led the field. Demand for organic meats and foods and non-genetically engineered food is now so great that producers cannot keep up with demand … We need more organic producers – right now.

Diana spoke again: 'When an animal is killed in an inhumane way, the fear the animal experiences resonates throughout its entire body and releases negative energies. And when people ingest too much invisible, negative energy they can become sick. Animal species will remain on the Earth longer if you love them and treat them with more respect, but those that are mistreated will become extinct. But be assured that they are cared for in our realms and pet lovers should know that their animals go on as we do.'

In the meantime, as I sat with Stuart, the noise from the kitchen TV was beginning to get on my nerves. In fact as the week progressed, it became increasingly difficult for me to watch any TV, especially violence of any kind, which I realized emits huge amounts of negative energy that can physically affect us. I was able to read large print on the front of newspapers, but if I picked up a paper, I could feel the negative energies emanating so strongly from the 'bad news' stories that I would have to drop it on the floor.

The voice continued, 'For years you have written about the huge number of people who are becoming sensitive to man-made chemicals and pesticides, highly refined and processed foods, plus certain food additives and preservatives. You have often written about food allergies and food sensitivities, which are often triggered by an accumulation of these toxins within the body. But as you have purified your body and mind during the past few weeks, you are more able to sense other dimensions and realities. You are becoming sensitive to subtle frequencies and energy, and also to us in the spirit world.'

My whole being craved silence and I desperately needed to get away from the sight of Stuart's food. But I didn't want to alarm him either. As the feelings of nausea swept over me, I casually opened the kitchen door and said I was going out for some fresh air. Stuart looked concerned and I gave him a reassuring smile. Once outside I gulped in the air and began to calm down. I sat overlooking our fountain, drinking in the peace – the rhododendrons, azaleas, daffodils and tulips reminded me of the miracle of nature. My eyes closed and after a few moments I felt a swirl of energy around me. As I opened my eyes the air was peaceful, but I could see faint 'blobs' of light in the trees and around our garden. They danced before me like ballerinas on a stage and, as I concentrated, my eyes grew wide with child-like astonishment. I realized that the blobs of light manifesting in front of me were in fact nature spirits. It was incredible, I could see tiny beings from other realms and I now know that fairies and angels really do exist. Sir Arthur Conan Doyle was not so eccentric after all. Stuart shattered the moment when he called from the kitchen – he wanted to know that I was all right.

The next day, after Sheila and Lindsey had gone and Stuart was at work, I thought that if I began doing a few everyday, down-to-earth chores such as emptying the dishwasher, all the weird happenings might stop and I would be able to write my column as the deadline was fast approaching. But it was not to be. As I stood polishing the wet cutlery, suddenly it evoked memories of my saying to Stuart that I was going to be like Uri Geller, so I held the spoon and willed it to bend. Nothing happened. Then I started rubbing it with my fingers just as Uri had taught me to do when we had met a few months earlier on a TV show. It did not bend – but the silver turned a dirty black-grey colour.

I decided I would do some ironing, which would surely take my mind off things. I went into our small laundry room, switched on the iron and began singing to the radio. This was great, it felt normal. Then the radio started playing up. Perhaps Sheila had not tuned it in properly. I fiddled with the tuner and got a clear sound. As I turned to hang a shirt on the door the radio went strange again, it was full of static. Was I affecting it? I backed away from the radio and all I could hear was static, then I walked towards it and it came back on. This was the opposite to what was happening with the TV. My heart was thumping wildly and I could feel myself getting upset again. Couldn't this all stop, just for a minute? Then it hit me, when I had watched the Goldie Hawn film I had been upset about the boys being without their mother. The more upset I became, the more my solar plexus area had hurt and the TV had gone crazy. My husband had witnessed this incident. If I could stay calm, I thought, these weird things would stop.

The voice was back. 'You can create with your thoughts, just learn to play with the energies.' At this moment I had had enough. I would call her bluff. If I could create with my thoughts I would go completely over the top. I had heard that the spiritual master Sai Baba in India can easily manifest pieces of jewellery, and so I made a sketch of an emerald cut diamond ring that I had admired in a jeweller's window. Then I sat quietly in my office and concentrated on the sketch in my hand which had begun to burn and tingle. My solar plexus area above my navel starting spinning wildly, totally out of control, but I wasn't going to stop. The more I concentrated the more my body seemed to spin, at any moment I thought I would simply burst into flames or explode into millions of pieces and disappear. Then something amazing happened. As I stared at my hand I could see the shank of a gold ring begin to appear. I totally freaked out. And in that moment of blind panic the partial ring disappeared.

Enough was enough. But still it went on. And just as I thought, 'I feel sick', bile rose in my throat and I ran back into the kitchen and threw up. I knew that I could control what was happening, so I sat down and started saying out loud, 'everything is perfect, everything is perfect, everything is perfect.' But I was alone and felt petrified. Then I thought of Norma, perhaps she could help me. And just as I was thinking 'I am really scared' as I walked through the hall towards the back door, the smoke alarm began ringing. I ran across the lawn, praying that Norma would be at home.

Thank goodness, Norma was in. She instantly took control. She sat me down and forced me to take a few deep breaths as I was so distressed. The top of my head felt as though it had a gaping hole in it and she said that all my energy centres – chakras – were wide open and spinning out of control. Each chakra controls a different part of the body, and as my solar plexus felt like it was on fire, Norma placed her hands just above my navel to calm it down. 'OK I can control this,' I kept repeating to myself, and as the moments passed the warmth from her hands soothed my solar plexus. We had a cup of tea ... the apparent panacea to all the world's problems!

Norma said that whatever was happening, I must learn to take control by telling spirit when I would be willing to work with them and then commanding them authoritatively to leave me alone when I needed to rest. I felt this might be easier said than done when I was continually shaken awake at night and the information seemed to flow in through the 'hole' in the top of my head. Norma said that most communication from spirit comes in through the crown chakra and into the pineal gland (situated in the centre of the brain) or the 'third eye'. She told me to practise 'shutting down' at night by visualizing that I had an iron sliding door situated in the top of my head. When I wanted to shut spirit off, I should simply imagine pressing a button to close the gates which would close off my crown chakra.

After an hour or so, thanks to Norma, I felt more in control and as I walked back across the lawn I felt much calmer. Diana was back … 'You are such a drama queen, all we were trying to do was to help you to realize how your thoughts create your reality in the moment. But because you are so sensitive right now, you are not utilizing this knowledge to its true potential. Stay calm – we are helping you. Over the coming weeks you will integrate much of this knowledge into your life and one day, you will desperately want these abilities back …'

At that moment I thought she was very sick indeed … All I wanted was my life back to normal and soon.

It was now Wednesday and my editor expected a column. In my heart I knew I would have to leave my job. I couldn't cope with everything that was happening to me and carry on as normal. Nothing was normal any more. I took a deep breath and, with a shaking hand, dialled my editor's number. After five years of being a columnist it was so hard to make that call, and I could not lie to him. So I told part truths. I said that my eyes were causing me great pain, that I was having difficulty focusing and that I could not read or see the screen properly.

I realized that my editor knew there was more going on than I was willing to share but he was fantastic, he said if I could just manage this one last column, they would find someone else to carry it on. As I put the phone down, I wept and wept. Everything I had worked for was gone. That evening Stuart desperately tried to cheer me up. He said I had proved I could do it, that with no formal qualifications I had been voted health journalist of the year in June 1997, and that I had dozens of published features and columns to my name.

Diana's voice returned, 'Hazel, you are still alive, you can still fulfil your purpose. You can still see your daughter, but I have lost my physical life and can no longer hold my sons. Now it is truly time for you to really get the bigger picture. We know you are sad, but please trust us. You were going in the wrong direction and we had to do this. Trust us. Everything will work out for you.' I could hardly retort, 'That's all very well for you to say,' could I?

She continued, 'You can now choose whether to write your book. You have a husband who has stood by you and can afford to support you. You have been given your life circumstances for a reason, just as I was, and everything has been for a reason. Believe it or not, we have quite a lot in common in the sense that what people see on the surface is not really who you are – I was the same.'

I knew she was right. When I was young, my mum and dad had struggled so hard to give my brother and me a good home. It wasn't elaborate, but Mum made it great. Our toilet was a shed at the bottom of the garden and our weekly treat had been to share a tin tub of bath water in front of the kitchen stove. Mum nursed me through so many problems, while Dad went down the pub with his friends …

I used to suffer from constant ear infections that made me scream with pain. Today I realize these were triggered by our diet, which contained too much saturated fat and dairy produce. I was always prescribed antibiotics, which would work for a while and then the infections would return. And I always seemed to be sick. Measles, scarlet fever, German measles, chickenpox and the like.

My dear mum was always there to pick up the pieces. One week I would twist my ankle, then my wrists, then I broke my arm and jaw. In my teens I suffered terrible acne, thrush, glandular fever and chronic fatigue. Today I know that my diet left a lot to be desired. I also realize the continuous antibiotics I was prescribed for almost 15 years laid the foundations for many of my health problems in later life.

In those days we had no concept that many antibiotics kill not only the bad bacteria within the gut but the healthy ones too. In those days, doctors knew nothing about nutritional medicine and even today they are lucky if they receive six hours' training in nutrition during their five years at medical school. And so we continued to eat plenty of dripping sandwiches, fried foods with chips, white bread and jam, and took plenty of sugar in our tea. Our weekly treat consisted of roast lamb or beef on Sunday and we were expected to eat all the fat on our plate. No wonder my dad died of a heart attack. He was always stressed and the more stress he was under the more cigarettes he smoked. He drank moderately but not to excess and he didn't take enough exercise … If only I had known then what I know now, if only … They were just caring for the family as best they could. Millions continue in the same vein today.

Then thanks to the bullying at school, being called Pinnochio because of my huge nose and having to wear callipers to try and straighten my spindly legs, I learned to laugh at myself. At an early age I found that bullies mostly leave you alone if you can make them laugh and show that their scare tactics don't work.

But if Dad had not died on 22nd May 1966, I would never have married or divorced, never had my daughter, never met and married Stuart and I would not have gone to Harrods on 8th April …

I have vague memories of my mum working as a cleaning lady for a homeopathic doctor, but in those days our neighbours believed homeopathy was akin to witchcraft. Thankfully attitudes have changed, but it has taken an awfully long time.

After losing my first child on our wedding night back in 1966, my first husband and I went to run a small beach-side restaurant in Jersey in the

Channel Islands. We were young and it was fun. We worked seven days a week, twelve hours a day during the summer of 1967 and loved every minute of it. In the autumn we travelled to the Canary Islands and I managed to get a job as a children's nanny and cleaning lady.

Even the Princess of Wales had worked for her sister as a cleaning lady and the whole world knew her as the children's nanny who captured Prince Charles' heart … I was lucky that my parents never divorced but my father's death had a huge emotional impact on me. All my friends had a mum and a dad and suddenly they began treating me differently. Diana must have felt a similar stigma when her mother left home. We all carry so much emotional baggage, even when it's not of our own making. Today, one in five children suffer from a mental health problem before they are old enough to leave home. Divorce, arguments, violence, abuse, alcoholism, inconsistent or unclear discipline and a lack of basic parenting skills are usually the problem. Life has definitely changed …

After giving birth to Vicki in September 1968, I began training as an auxiliary nurse at our local maternity hospital and the fascination with health stayed with me. I loved caring for people. But after my husband left I could not live on my wage of £6.10 shillings a week. It was time to move on. After working for the civil service for a couple of years compiling telephone directories, I soon realized that if I did not break free I would end up regretting it. And I wanted to do something with my life. So at 20, I applied to British Airways to become an air stewardess. I did not tell them about my daughter or my divorce. In those days being a single mother (even one who had once been married) was not readily accepted. They thought I had the right personality in the interview but one of the panel took me to one side and said, 'If only you could do something about your nose …'

I had hated my nose all my life and I didn't need a better excuse. Diana also confessed that she did not like her nose and had considered plastic surgery at one stage. An aunt lent me the money for my 21st birthday and I underwent plastic surgery. When the plaster came off I felt re-born.

Suddenly, good-looking men began chatting to me. I felt like an ugly duckling who had become a swan. I gained more confidence and at 22 finally got a job with British Airways. At 23, I met Stuart and we married eight years later. I too had found my prince, he just took a bit longer to make up his mind.

All through my flying years my chronic thrush, cystitis and fatigue continued. And as time passed I added vastly to my medical history: amoebic dysentery in Calcutta, ulcerated colitis in Singapore, salmonella poisoning in Perth, I collected illnesses the way others collect souvenirs – and in doing so I became a first-class hypochondriac. Eventually, I suffered so many haemorrhages, which I am now convinced were triggered by taking the Pill for ten years, that I underwent an emergency hysterectomy.

After marrying Stuart in July 1980 my illnesses continued. Then one day my husband asked, 'Well, what is your disease of the day?' I felt really shocked. How could I have let myself slip down such a slope of ill health? The answer came easily – it was because I had placed complete responsibility for my health in the hands of my doctor. The poor man … he was not responsible for my stress levels, for my long working hours, for my dreadful diet. But he knew very little about how diet affects our health – he only knew about drugs. And in the long term they had caused more problems than they had cured.

Then my brother Bob told me about a newly qualified nutritionist named Kathryn Marsden who, for the princely sum of £20, would come to my home and help me to change my life. Just as my meeting with my neighbour Norma changed my life, so did my meeting with Katy – who is still a dear friend today. She explained that I was suffering from vitamin and mineral deficiencies because I had not been eating enough of the right foods (such as brown rice, lentils, brown bread, fruits, vegetables, oily fish etc.). This was why I continued to suffer from chronic bouts of thrush and fatigue. She also said that the dozens of courses of antibiotics I had taken throughout my life had undoubtedly destroyed the healthy bacteria in my gut, lowering my resistance, and that I was suffering from severe candida – a nasty yeast fungal overgrowth that causes symptoms ranging from bloating, irritable bowel, chronic headaches, exhaustion, to thrush and food cravings, particularly for yeast-based foods and sugar.

Kathryn suggested a course of healthy bacteria, acidophilus bifidus, in capsule form, and for a few weeks I cut out all yeast and sugar from my diet to starve the candida from my system. Kathryn also explained that millions of people who have taken too many antibiotics also often suffer digestive problems as they are not absorbing sufficient nutrients from their diet. Not only are we made of what we eat, but also what our guts are able to absorb. Until that moment it had never occurred to me that my diet could in any way be connected with any of my conditions. Nor had it occurred to my mother or father, their parents or their parents before them. No wonder they had all died early deaths from cancer, strokes and heart attacks.

From that moment, I was hooked on the concept of taking more responsibility for my wellbeing and I began researching how diet affects our health. I read every health magazine I could find and tried numerous alternative remedies. My diet changed and so did Stuart's. Out went the sugar in our tea and coffee. Stuart's cigar smoking days ended abruptly. Fizzy drinks packed with sugar and sugar substitutes such as aspartame were replaced by healthier juices and water. Wholemeal bread replaced gooey white bread and slowly but surely I began to feel better.

As the years passed I widened my interests to include the power of the mind and developed a fascination with the possibility of life after death. And so when I visited Norma on that fateful day nine years ago, I was ready for the next stage in my apprenticeship. Every illness, every meeting and every 'coincidence' had played some part in my jigsaw and I now truly understand how incredible life is. There is a master plan in existence, a much bigger picture than most people realize. Without doubt, we all come to Earth for a purpose. It's merely a question of discovering what that purpose is and for many people this is easier said than done.

Diana was back. 'If people want to know what their purpose is, all they have to do is to ask the higher realms for help. Once people offer to work for the light, they are never refused. Remember after Norma 'woke you up' it was four years before you heard the word 'write'. But because you had the intention to help others and your motives were honourable, the higher realms helped you. It takes time to set things in motion and you had to help yourself. This you did by reading so many books and going on courses. You did not sit and wait for things to happen – you went out and made things happen of your own free will. You created your own reality.' We also live on a planet that allows most people free will and those of us who have it are free to choose what and who we want in our lives. We moan a lot if things go wrong, but if we look at virtually any situation objectively, we still have choices.

Diana retorted, 'Yes, you can choose, but remember there are many whose only choice this day is whether to live or die. Now that I am in another dimension I realize just how out of balance many lives have become. We see your possible futures. Some incidents are already set in stone and you, Hazel, will come to know these during the coming weeks and months. It is not too late to change, but time is of the essence. We come now from the higher realms to offer you healing, light and hope.'

Her words made me cry with guilt and shame. When I had called my editor I was only thinking about myself and what I had given up. I had to pull myself together. OK, so I made my choices. I had left the column, I would write the book, trust that what was happening was real and if it sold well I would give a percentage to whomever Diana requested.

But I was longing to know who she was referring to as 'we' whenever she spoke. Instantly I heard her reply, 'There are many here who want to help with your work and anyone on Earth who works for the good of others without thinking about what's in it for themselves, will always receive help and guidance if they ask for it. No one is ever truly alone. Souls such as Queen Victoria, Martin Luther King, Mother Teresa, Gandhi and even your old friend John Lennon, are all here working for peace and 'getting through' to people like yourself when they can. For now I am simply their spokesperson. As there have been attempts by some people to turn me into a quasi-religious figure it was decided that it would be appropriate for me to make a dramatic entrance over Easter.'

She wasn't kidding.

This lady must have had a wicked sense of humour. I suddenly thought of the spoon turning black. Was that her? I always thought black was associated with evil. I felt her laughing again as she said: 'There is good and evil in every single one of you. Some people thought I was some kind of saint, others thought me to be a terrible sinner. I was everything, we all are. This will be explained to you later.' I could hardly wait.

Meanwhile, I somehow had to write my last column. I was able to type by looking down at my keyboard but I could not look at the screen. My hands were shaking as I began typing and everything felt weird. My solar plexus area began spinning again and I felt as though I might faint. I clung onto my desk, took a few deep breaths and closed my eyes. And when I opened them and moved my hands the area underneath was covered in a fine, dark grey powder. Where on earth could that have come from? I wiped it away with a tissue and carried on working.

It took me two days to write my last column, which I e-mailed on Friday 17th April. It was only nine days since what I had begun to term 'the madness' had come upon me in Harrods, but it felt like 20 years. Finishing that column had completely drained my energies. I had lost almost a stone and looked appalling, but I had survived. Lindsey suggested I should ask our friend

Shonagh to pop in and give me a healing treatment. She had introduced me to Shonagh months earlier when I had needed healing after some particularly painful dental surgery and I had really enjoyed her warmth and friendliness. Shonagh has worked as a spiritual healer for almost 15 years and when she walked into the bedroom I could see the shock in her eyes – I knew I looked awful. She recalls the moment, 'When I saw you I was appalled at how drained you looked, both physically and mentally. You did not tell me what was happening and I didn't need to know. All I could do was channel some healing energy into you. But I knew something highly unusual was going on as there were three distinct energies around you. One was your own physical energy, the other was a pure and very powerful spiritual energy within the room, and there was a third energy I could not identify.'

She was right. And as I sat in the armchair soaking up the warm energy emanating from Shonagh's hands I remembered what Diana had said about our thoughts creating our reality. I had been so sad about ending my column, hundreds of negative thoughts had come into my head which added to my lethargy and exhaustion. Shonagh reminded me of something that I had known for years – that every time I had a negative thought I should instantly replace it with a positive one. And as I sat with Shonagh my attention was drawn to the small collection of crystals that sat in a small glass bowl on a table next to the bedroom chair. I picked up a piece of amethyst, and as I held it in my hand it slowly began to cool, and after ten minutes or so it felt like a piece of ice. When Stuart came up to show Shonagh out I asked him to hold the crystal.

'How does it feel?' I asked.

'Like ice,' he said looking concerned. I smiled to allay his fears. I had begun to call Diana the 'Ice Queen' and it was as if she was trying to let me know through the crystal that everything would be all right. I have long known that crystals act as transmitters and receivers, hence their use in radios, TVs and computers. Diana was somehow transmitting her healing energy to me and it felt wonderful.

Over the weekend I rested and continued taking the vitamins and minerals and eating porridge and bananas. I had realized that it wasn't Diana who craved these foods, it was simply my body's way of telling me which foods would help to sustain me the most – and they had. Stuart insisted that when I returned to London I must see Brian MacGreevy, our London doctor, who had not seen me since the incident in Harrods. I agreed in order to appease him. What would I tell Brian, how could I possibly even begin to explain what was going on?

As I sat in my study trying to make sense of everything, I spotted a book on mental health by a friend of mine, nutritionist and psychologist Patrick Holford. Flicking through the pages, the heading 'Addicted to Stress' caught my eye. It stated: 'As a consequence of prolonged stress your energy level drops, you lose concentration, get confused, suffer from bouts of brain fog, fall asleep after meals, get irritable, freak out, can't sleep, can't wake up, sweat too much, get headaches' … Was this the answer? My fever, my headaches, the confusion in my head, had everything that was happening just been caused by stress? I know that stress thickens the blood, which can drive up blood pressure and that prolonged negative stress and its numerous side effects is the main trigger for most major killer diseases, but hearing voices?

I recalled a fascinating lecture in London presented by Dr Abram Hoffer, a Canadian psychiatrist and scientist who has pioneered research on the use of nutritional supplements and diet to conquer schizophrenia, numerous types of depression and other mental conditions. After 40 years in this field he had found that most of his patients responded positively to specific doses of vitamins B, C and minerals such as magnesium and zinc. In medical trials, food allergies were shown to trigger severe depression, nervousness, anger, loss of motivation and mental blankness. And the foods and chemicals that his research found produced the most severe mental reactions were wheat, cow's milk, cane sugar, tobacco smoke and eggs. In other tests 80 per cent of a control group suffering from schizophrenia were found to be allergic to cow's milk and eggs. Orthodox medicine is only just beginning to understand the enormous implications of this type of work.

I decided to call Patrick and ask his opinion on what was happening to me. Patrick listened while I told my story to date, although I could not bring myself to mention Diana's name. Patrick responded by saying there were so many realities and for him to explain them all would take a very long time. Where had I heard that before? Initially, I asked Patrick about people who have hallucinations – after all, I had 'seen' through Diana's eyes on Easter Friday and I wondered if I had been hallucinating.

Patrick told me that pioneering researchers such as Dr Hoffer and Dr Carl Pfeiffer in America have found that when the body becomes deficient in certain nutrients it can produce substances which act very much like hallucinogenic drugs. But these people's visions or voices tend to be of a very fearful nature and in the majority of cases when treated with specific amounts of vitamins most especially B3, B12 and folic acid, their hallucinations usually stop.

My initial experience had certainly been fearful, but for years I had taken plenty of B group vitamins ... Patrick agreed, saying 'In my classes over the years when I ask my pupils if they have heard voices or had visions which have in some way uplifted them and given them a new perspective on life, about one-third answer 'yes'. For thousands of years, mystics and psychics have had these types of experiences which have been well documented, but these experiences are in a different category to hallucinations. Then there is a third type of experience called psychosis where the patient loses all sense of reality, has a classic nervous breakdown and goes off into their own world. But from what you have said you were not psychotic and you have not lost your sense of reality.'

Thank goodness for that.

Patrick felt my experience was some kind of spiritual breakthrough rather than a physical breakdown. He said if a spiritually orientated monk living in a monastery had had my type of experience, in a very stable, calm environment with people around who could explain what was happening, then he would find it somewhat easier to cope. But to have had such an overwhelming experience while out shopping, with no conception of what was happening – well – it was no wonder it had been such a shock. In certain communities in India, when a person has mystical experiences, Patrick had heard that they were placed in a room with lots of bananas and water, and let out when it's all over. I roared with laughter, no wonder they talk about people 'going bananas' …

For anyone out there suffering in silence who would like to know more about the link between nutrition and mental health problems, I recommend you read Patrick's book (see page 271).

Meanwhile, since the nights were my worst times I had begun to ask Stuart to lay his hands on my solar plexus area just as Norma had done earlier in the week. Somehow it helped ease the spinning feeling that made me feel so nauseous. Here was my dear businessman husband, who has little concept of spiritual healing, doing his best to help his wife. It was touching beyond words.

I had discussed healing with Stuart over the years and told him that Norma could hear spirit, but he thought it all rather weird, so I kept quiet. Like millions of people, Stuart adheres to the idea that unless something has been proven in scientific terms, it cannot be true.

Whenever I had interviewed or received healing from a practitioner and felt the heat emanating from their hands I would often ask them, 'Where does the energy come from?' Each healer would have his or her own answer. Some would say it came from a universal source and that the energy entered through the top of their heads, down into their hands and into the patient. Others, who were more religious, would say the healing came from God. As I lay on the bed feeling the heat emanating from my husband's hands, it suddenly hit me where his healing was coming from. It was coming from a frequency situated within and around his heart.

Diana was back. 'There are millions of frequencies. Every living thing emits its own frequency, as do TVs, mobile phones and other electrical equipment. But there is one frequency of light and knowledge that pervades everything – it is the frequency of pure, unconditional love, which lives as a tiny spark in your body. Some people carry more of this spark than others, but every person on the planet carries a spark and has the potential to carry more of this specific frequency. You are now carrying a huge amount of this frequency – it is also known as divine energy and it is everywhere. All you need to do is to have the intention of helping others and the light will expand and grow with you.'

So, I asked, 'because my husband had the intention to help me, he literally transmitted pure love and that's why his hands felt so warm?' Did that also mean that he could now give healing?'

She replied, 'You all carry the potential to heal, yourselves and each other, you just don't understand frequencies fully, but you will in time. In simplified terms the amount of healing energy a healer is able to expend depends on how much of the pure frequency his or her body can hold and channel. This pure healing frequency usually channels out through the hands of the healer into the energy field of the person they are healing, which encourages the body to heal itself. How much of this pure frequency each person can retain depends on the individual. In Harrods we filled you to capacity with this special frequency, and you are receiving more light every day – we just had to take the chance that you would survive.'

'So what happens to most people if they receive this "light" and they don't have the help I have?' I asked.

'If you were all to be zapped with such a large dose of this very pure frequency some of you would die, while others would go mad,' Diana answered.

Incredible.

I had also noticed that when I had been ill in the past, some healers had been able to help me more than others. Of course … our frequencies were more compatible. If you try and put a 13-amp plug into a 110-volt socket, they would not be compatible. Stuart and I had always said that we were on the same wavelength, and we are. Diana had told me that she and Charles were rarely on the same wavelength. So, if you are with a person whose frequency does not 'fit' your own, you will never really get on. But was it really that simple? I thought of all the times I had met someone and thought, 'I don't like this person very much'. Often they are charming and you cannot put your finger on it, they are great people who mean you no harm, you may even have a lot in common, but you just know they are not for you.

Conversely, nearly all my true friends are people that I instantly gelled with, even when I hardly knew them. We had compatible frequencies.

So many realities had gone through my head during the past 12 days, I had begun to wonder what was truly real. My brain and head felt as though they were on fire, Stuart and I both needed to sleep and as I switched out my bedside light I noticed a get-well card that Stuart had given me at some point during the past week – the message was in French. Paris … Diana … It made me smile, another small coincidence.

# 6

# Another Death

**ON MONDAY 20TH APRIL** we woke to the news that Linda McCartney had died over the weekend. 'Another death is coming,' Diana had said. And she was right.

The previous October I had gone along to the Royal Albert Hall in London to attend a press conference for the UK premier of Sir Paul's symphony, 'Standing Stone'. There were around 700 press and photographers in the hall and I sat in the front row well ahead of time. We waited. Paul appeared and waved a friendly 'Hi' to everyone.

His PA asked for anyone who wanted to ask the first question to raise their hands. No one moved. Up went my arm. Before Paul came in the hall I had written two questions on my note pad. His PA pointed to me and my legs turned to jelly. I rambled on about how I believe that ancient stones carry knowledge and asked Paul if he believed this to be true. Paul was incredibly kind, even though I could see his eyes looking slightly alarmed at the length of my diatribe.

He answered that he wasn't sure whether the stones contained knowledge, but he felt they held a fascination and magic, and whenever he was in Scotland and Ireland he loved touching them. My second question was to have been 'How's Linda?', but I was not allowed to ask a second question.

As I sat listening to the news of Linda's death I realized that when an opportunity presents itself you must grasp it, and on that October day when I had the chance to ask Paul just one question I should have spoken from my heart rather than trying to please his PR people by asking about the symphony.

The voice of Diana returned. 'No matter how rich or famous anyone is – they are only human. They get sick, have accidents and die just like anyone else. On Earth many of you worship people because they are famous, wealthy or have great standing. Linda made a tremendous difference and she is a very special soul who is being well cared for in our dimension. But every single one of you is special, most of you don't realize just how special, and what a huge difference you can all make.'

During the remainder of that week as more details were released about Linda's death, for the first time I truly appreciated what a huge difference she had made, especially in her work for animal rights and the environment. Yet again I was reminded how one person can change the way millions think. When I heard that Linda had been cremated, I 'felt' that Diana would have preferred cremation too. It was as though she wanted to be free in the wind; she was proud of her physical body and hated the thought of it rotting in the ground. She also does not want the island where she is buried to become a shrine, saying over and over again, 'I was no angel, I was no saint'.

She was a high-profile, caring, warm and wonderful young woman, but she does not want to be worshipped or thought of as a martyr. She simply wants people to start doing what they can, when they can, to help each other, and not to keep thinking, 'what's in this for me'. Diana's voice carried on saying, 'I now truly see that what goes around really does come around. Everything comes full circle. If you send out negative and angry thoughts they come back to you. If you hurt someone – one day you too will be hurt

– something negative will happen to you. What you give out you get back. Cause and effect. It really is that simple. This is a universal law.'

I have read these sentiments many times and realize that there is some kind of universal regulator out there. I remember all the times I hurt my mum either through telling lies or through my actions, and how my misdeeds had always came back to haunt me. On one occasion during my years as a stewardess I lied to my chief steward about the numbers of headsets I had sold on a flight from America. Needless to say, I got a well deserved ticking off and made a conscious decision never to be so stupid again. When I got home I found my boyfriend had been sleeping with a close friend. Coincidence? Sure – life's like that. But it's also pay back.

A few months later I met a chap in a pub who regaled us with stories of his life as a car thief. He was openly bragging about what he did, while I was ashamed about the headset episode. And yet which one of us was worse? We had both taken something that did not belong to us. Who was I to judge? A few weeks later I heard that his new flat had been stripped by burglars. Pay back. What you give out is what you get back. Conversely, when you help someone, you also help yourself. During the early 1980s when I had a jewellery shop in London, one day I received a call from a man who wanted to order a ring to cheer himself up. It was obvious from his voice that he was not well and we got chatting. Bill lived near Cheltenham and had cancer. He had undergone almost continual chemotherapy for 15 years. We became telephone friends and I took to calling him once a week.

As the months passed I sent him the occasional fruit basket and flowers. One Sunday he called me at home in Birmingham and said he was lying on the floor unable to contact his neighbours. So I packed up some soup and filled a basket with food and drove to Bill's. He was in dire straits and I managed to reach his doctor who admitted him to hospital. I could hardly believe it when Bill told me that his sister lived just down the road and he had not seen her for almost five years. How can people be like this to each other? And yet on numerous occasions I had treated my own mother badly.

Bill died in hospital a few weeks later and his doctor called to thank me for the little help I had given. A week later I received a small tax refund out of the blue, the strangest 'coincidence' was that the tax refund was the exact amount I had spent on food for Bill during his last few weeks – payback? Who knows. After his death I always felt that Bill became my guardian angel to thank me for what I had done. His sister apparently cleared his house, even though Bill had wanted all his possessions to be sold for charity. I wonder who might help his sister if she ever becomes ill …

Diana interrupted my thoughts. 'What you are saying might sound to some people like "an eye for an eye" – this is not what the higher realms intend. If you hurt someone intentionally, the great universal laws come into effect and you pay one day, either in this lifetime or in the next, but this is something you bring on yourself. Everything that you give out, you get back. The phrase "an eye for an eye" was wrongly interpreted so many years ago: it was intended that people should realize there are universal laws and if they are broken the person will have to repay a debt. In some philosophies this is called karmic debt or cause and effect. If you hurt someone, you also hurt yourself. I sometimes used to think during my worst moments, 'Don't get mad – get even' and occasionally I did, but it was often a hollow victory, which usually made situations worse.

'From experience you know that if an irate individual or group bombs an embassy or whatever, it serves no purpose and often kills innocent bystanders. Then the "other side" retaliates and more innocent people are killed. For what? Most arguments usually stem from one's own ego, and all war is a waste of life, time, money and energy. If all the money spent on war and weapons (and the money needed to re-build communities after any war) could be spent on helping people, no one would need to be hungry and you could make Heaven a place on Earth. As you write there are millions in need, and yet what remains on the front pages of most papers and magazines? Who's sleeping with who. Who has the biggest boobs.

Really mind-blowing stuff. You all need to wake up.'

I think it's fair to say that on many occasions the media reduced Diana to total and utter despair.

Diana's voice interjected in my head: 'I received huge amounts of negative press which became increasingly abusive and intrusive over the years. I was only one person, I did not have the wisdom of Solomon. I ask every one of you to try and imagine what it is like to see minute details of your personal life in the papers virtually every day. To be followed. To be shouted at. To be thought of as public property. It became a nightmare. It would not have been so bad if they could just have reported the facts, but it was the judgmental comments that hurt so deeply, especially when they were made by people you have never even met.'

This made me think of how often we pass judgement on someone in a particular situation, only to find ourselves in a similar predicament a few weeks, months or years later. When we see that the situation is not as easy as we thought, we often wish that we had not judged that person so harshly.

Remember everything comes full circle. If you judge someone and consciously hurt them, one day you will find yourself on the receiving end yourself, and it's not very pleasant.

Diana added, 'I had lots of good press too, and most of the people I met were incredible; their love and affection, their letters, and the children and families I met, sustained me through some of my worst moments. At only 19 I chose to marry Charles and in those heady, early days it seemed all my childhood fairy tales were coming true. Then the intrusions grew and grew until the pressure became unbearable. How many young brides are reduced to tears of frustration before their wedding and during the months that follow as they adjust to their new relatives and new life. I ask everyone to imagine what it is like to try and adjust with practically the whole world watching your every move. 'Charles and I were rarely alone. There were always others around: secretaries, staff … It may sound wonderful, but in time you realize your life is no longer your own. My sense of loss of identity was enormous. All my life I had felt rejection in one form or another and childhood memories leave their scars. I longed for Charles' full attention, but just as you have tested your husband to the limits of his patience since this situation began, I sometimes tested Charles' patience to the limits too.

'I did not receive sufficient understanding during my early married life to help me through the emotional onslaught and I became ill in mind and body. I had very little self esteem, I did not love myself and I could not understand or cope with the huge interest in my every move, which took an incredible emotional toll. But as the years pass you learn from experience. Towards the end of my life I had at last found my purpose – it was to be a fairy godmother to those in real need. I knew that when I visited sick people and held their hands, I somehow gave them healing. But I could hardly say to anyone: "I have healing hands" as I knew the press would have a field day with any such statement.'

Without doubt I felt that during her last few years, Diana was truly awakening to spiritual issues. Her voice returned: 'By visiting countries where children were (and still are) being blown to pieces or dying of Aids and malnutrition, I knew the world would be watching. If they wanted to watch me so badly, let it do some good. Now we watch with delight that you are signing treaties to ban the use and production of land mines in many countries. There is victory in death.'

It all seemed so sad. I kept thinking of how much more she could have achieved had she not died.

'Like Kevin Costner in his film *No Way Out*, there was never going to be a way out for me, her voice added. I was stuck between a rock and a hard place. I wanted out long before I was allowed out. And they wanted a quiet exit, and I vowed never to go quietly – and I certainly kept that promise.' She sure did …

Meanwhile the time had come for me to try and get back into my life, so on the evening of Monday 20th April I travelled down to London. The mist over my eyes was clearing and I could read larger print when my eyes were not tired. As the fields lining the motorway sped by, I began to feel nauseous again – strange, as I had never suffered from car sickness. I thought perhaps the 'energy' inside me disliked the speed and I asked Paul to slow down. Stuart had insisted I should see Brian, our doctor, as soon as I reached London.

When Brian arrived at the house I told him that I had a special energy inside me. I would not tell him who or what this was but said I now had an incredible sixth sense. He looked alarmed. Brian recalled, 'You were speaking very quickly and had lost an awful lot of weight. I understood you had undergone a profound spiritual experience but because there is a fine line between a spiritual experience and a psychotic one, I thought it might be sensible for you to see a psychiatrist.'

I remember 'reading' his thoughts, which were full of care and concern, but I thought 'no thanks' – I did not want to end up living on tranquillizers nor to be branded mentally ill. Brian wanted to do some blood tests as he could see that when I became excited, what I called 'in energy', I would flush bright red and become very hot. He thought it might be the onset of my menopause. I agreed to have the tests and reassured him that I was eating again. He was not altogether happy, but said he would wait and see how I progressed. Thank God for that. Brian stayed for well over an hour and he and Stuart fired non-stop questions at me. By the time Brian left, I was totally exhausted. I needed some spiritual help and soon.

As I prepared for bed, the face staring back at me from the mirror looked ancient and worn. I was becoming far too thin. My sparse diet had kept me going for a month, but somehow I had to eat more. After all how many times had I written and lectured that the body is made 100 per cent of what we eat, drink and breathe. To survive, the human body needs 50 factors including 13 vitamins, 21 minerals, nine amino acids, two essential fatty acids, plus carbohydrate, fibre, air, water and light. And as our bodies cannot manufacture these factors, we must take them from external sources from our diet and through supplements.

Diana had told me that when the physical body dies, we still look the same as we have a spirit or etheric body, but it appears like a body made of light rather than a dense physical one. And for almost two weeks I had felt as though I was more 'up there' than 'down here' and this feeling was getting worse.

The next morning was my worst since that Easter weekend. I decided to travel over to Islington and see my friends Bill and Celia Whitehead, who are very specialized spiritual healers. Originally, Bill trained as an osteopath, but over 20 years ago he broke away from conventional medicine to practise his own unique healing methods. Intuitively, I knew they would understand what had happened and would help me.

At the time, Bill and Celia didn't answer their telephone as they were too busy giving healing, so you could not call and make an appointment. If you wanted to see Bill you had to be willing to go and knock on his door. I made my way across London, praying that they would be home. As I walked up their garden path, total exhaustion overwhelmed me. To say I felt like a zombie, like the walking dead, is truly no exaggeration and how I reached their door I have no idea. I felt as though I was being 'carried', I was at my lowest ebb. When Bill opened the door, he looked shocked by my appearance. I almost fell into a seat and simply stared straight ahead. Bill said, 'C'mon girl you have to talk to us, what's going on?' I kept repeating like some kind of robot: 'I have died and come back, I have died and come back' and then I began to cry. Bill seemed to understand immediately saying, 'My goodness they (I knew he meant the spirit realms) have given you the full monty'. He and Celia helped me into Bill's treatment room and I lay down on his couch. Celia rushed into the kitchen to get some magnesium-rich sea salt for me to swallow with water, to help ground me.

Meanwhile, I began to levitate, my body floating a few inches above Bill's couch. It felt wonderful. Bill acted swiftly and placed two tectonic aluminium plates underneath my back, which brought me down to earth with a bang. These were the same plates that Bob Jacobs had sent me over

Easter to put under my pillow. Bob had explained that they were made from a crystallized type of aluminium which creates an energy field within and around the body that helps to calm it down. Celia made me sit up and take another large pinch of salt with water and gradually I began to feel more normal.

Bill used kinesiology, a system of muscle testing, to check for my most serious nutrient deficiencies. He recalls, 'Your serotonin (a hormone-like compound secreted by the pineal gland in the brain that regulates mood) levels were on the floor. Your brain bio-chemistry was out of balance because it had been totally overworked.'

I was not surprised. Bill also found that I was deficient in the minerals magnesium and potassium phosphate which he said I desperately needed to normalize my brain function. I had already been taking these supplements but it showed just how quickly my brain was using them … During the two hours that Bill worked on me, it was as if I was half in this world and half in another. I literally felt as though I might disappear. The voice inside me said, 'This is what would happen if you were to move from the third dimension into the fourth and fifth dimensions, you would no longer be visible in the third dimension.'

I had heard of great spiritual masters who can disappear and re-appear at will but I prayed this was not going to happen to me, after all, I said to myself, 'I'm only Hazel, not some spiritual guru.' And I was having enough trouble being who and where I was.

Bill kept talking to me to bring me back into the moment and every 30 minutes he gave me another pinch of wind- and sun-dried, magnesium-rich sea salt (a healthier salt than refined sodium-based salt) with a full glass of water. 'Stay with me girl,' he kept repeating, 'Stay with me.'

As Bill tuned into my energy field and scanned my body with his hands, he said my nerves and adrenal glands were completely exhausted and recommended I increase my intake of vitamin B5 (pantothenic acid), which supports adrenal function. I should also get more rest. Bill gave me a homeopathic remedy, *Aurum metallicum*, which he said would help to strengthen my auric field and stressed that all would become clearer if I just gave it time. He added that if I could force myself to eat regularly, food would 'ground me' more quickly. Before I left, Bill also balanced my chakra energy centres, which he said had been blown open like a dam bursting because all the spiritual energies were flowing in and through me unrestricted.

Bill recalls, 'You were suffering from what is known as a spiritual emergency. In almost 20 years as a healer I have only seen about four cases like yours, but the number of people going through these types of experiences is growing. These experiences affect mental, emotional and physical stability, and, without doubt, many people who go through various types of spiritual emergency end up on psychiatric wards. In fact, if they could be given the correct nutrition, remedies and support from people who understand what's going on, many lives would turn out very differently indeed.'

Bill said that by being exposed to so many great spiritual insights and huge amounts of information pouring unrestricted into the brain almost overnight, it is often difficult for people to assimilate what they hear, and many go off at tangents making inappropriate statements.

I cannot help but recall Glen Hoddle the England football coach who lost his job In February 1999 after inferring that disabled people born with disabilities, are somehow 'paying' for misdeeds in other lifetimes. I believe that Glenn only understood one reality, and spoke before he realized there are hundreds of thousands of realities. But I now know that full integration of the knowledge to become a spiritual master would take a lifetime's work (see pages 270–2 for further reading on this subject).

Bill hugged me goodbye, told me to eat more, and to go with the flow – just as Bob Jacobs had recommended over Easter. He knew there was more to come. And I suppose I knew it too; it was as if I was slowly getting the point of what was happening to me, and that *something* was intangible and yet vital. I would have to wait and see. But whatever it was, it went way beyond hearing Diana, it felt as though I had to find the ultimate answer for myself – like dying – no one else can do it for you.

As I walked back down the street, for the first time in days I became aware of my feet actually making contact with the ground. I definitely felt better, and as I had this thought the sun suddenly broke through the clouds. It was if someone – somewhere was saying, 'It's all right – you will be OK.'

On my way home in a taxi I asked the spirit world, 'What is causing these spiritual emergencies?'

Instantly, I heard a reply, but this time it was a man's voice, 'The higher realms are beaming a powerful frequency to Earth. Its power was intensified by the death of the English Rose. Her death was part of a greater plan. It is time for the people of Earth to raise their vibratory rate, which will help to change the way every one of you acts, thinks and feels. But because this frequency is so powerful and is everywhere, many people who are not aware of this time of transition may have problems with their nervous systems. Hence it is imperative that every one of you should take as much care of yourselves as you can, physically, mentally and spiritually, then the transition will become much easier. There is truly no need for anyone to become ill or die as they receive this frequency, but many could unless they understand what is happening.'

Whoever was speaking, after all I had been through I knew that he was definitely not kidding.

That evening as I lay on the bed deep in thought, Stuart suggested a walk in Hyde Park. Diana was obviously thrilled as she sang in my head, 'Let's get physical, physical' – come on lazybones – the more energy you use, the better you will begin to feel.'

The energy, Diana, whoever it was, wanted to rock 'n' roll while all I wanted to do was to sleep. As we crossed into the park, it was as if she was shouting 'Yippee, I'm back.' My legs felt like wobbly jelly but her voice urged me on. I believe she was fairly obsessed by her physical body. And why not? I wouldn't mind looking like her any day of the week. As we walked past the Serpentine, I was overcome by a feeling of wanting to dive into the water. But after a near-fatal accident in my early childhood, I have always had a fear of water. I eventually learned to swim in my early forties but have never had the courage to dive or even jump into water. Was it possible that the energy or essence of Diana was truly inside my body and mind?

As I prepared for bed that night, I noticed as I looked in the bathroom mirror that my skin looked younger, my eyes sparkled and were a stunning blue grey colour. In my youth, I had spent far too much time in the sun and my chest and arms are covered in brown patches where the skin, I have been told, is irreversibly damaged. But as I stood staring at my arm, the brown patches began to fade before my eyes. It was fantastic. I determined that as soon as I felt stronger I would interview scientists and experts I had met while I was at the *Sunday Times*. Somehow I had to prove this was really happening and learn how it was possible. Also to try and prove that life after death is a fact and that I really was hearing Diana. But I had no tangible proof – yet …

She returned, 'Call Sarah, call my sister-in-law, she will help you, she will know what you say is true.' This was not funny. She, Diana, the energy, the voice, whoever it was, wanted me to call Sarah, Duchess of York and ask for her help. It seemed crazy, my credibility would be blown away. It's all very well to have an incredible experience that your immediate friends and family witness, but it's something different to contact a member of the royal family and claim to be hearing Diana. I ignored the message.

But the next day she continued unabated with the same message, 'Call Sarah – call Sarah'. It just would not stop. Diana must have been a real pain when she wanted her bidding done … OK, I would do it, but what would I say?

'Just be dramatic', said the voice. I was shaking as I rang Sarah's office. Eventually, I spoke to her private secretary, Kate Waddington, whom I had met earlier in the year when interviewing the Duchess for my column. I told her that something incredible had happened which had almost cost me my life, and I needed to see or speak to the Duchess, as what had happened had enormous implications for Sarah and the royal family. Kate was very polite and said she would get back to me. Right … I let go of worrying whether Sarah might see me or not, I had made the call.

I had had enough. I was fed up of being told what to do. I was tired of saying to my husband, to Lindsey, to Dr John Briffa, to my doctor that I had an energy in me – that 'they', 'she' or whoever had messages for the world. It all sounded so crazy. From now on, I would just say what I was thinking, I would stop all this nonsense and get back to normal.

'Are you *joking*?' said the voice incredulously. 'After all you have been through, there is no turning back now.' I had the feeling this lady must have been a hard taskmaster.

The next day, 23rd April, I kept my date with Whoopi Goldberg. I felt different, special, and I looked years younger than I had the previous day. After all, surely there could not be many people who could hear Diana? As I walked into the Savoy Hotel to meet Whoopi, I felt sad that I had left my job, but like the voice had said, I was still alive. Whoopi was fabulous, she is obviously a very 'awake' lady. She signed a copy of her book for me and I rambled on about how I was leaving my column to go and write my own book. 'Good for you' she beamed and as she smiled it was like watching the sun come out.

Whoopi has had an inner knowing that she is special ever since she was a child. I was only just beginning to feel special, but I wasn't going to tell her about Diana, so I asked her how she managed to stay so calm in all the chaos, with press, photographers and PR people all around. She looked at me with very 'knowing' eyes and said, 'When you are truly connected to the source, it is easy to stay calm'. 'OK', I queried, 'but which source?' Her PR people came up and tapped me on the shoulder. My time was up. Great.

My brain began cooking again and I went home to sit in silence. All I craved was silence. No voices, no doctors, no telephone calls – just peace and quiet.

Stuart broke my contemplation as he walked in with some tea. We put on the TV. It made me realize how much of our lives is taken up with noise, the world needs more peace. Talk about an understatement …

As we sat watching a Kim Basinger film, the red colour of her dress hurt my eyes. Red is the frequency colour for energy, and the 'energy' inside me was churning, so I suppose the last colour I needed to see was red. The pain was so severe that I was forced to close my eyes. When I looked again, to my amazement I could see colours all around the actors; reds, greens, purples. Was I seeing their auras? Maybe it was just the TV set? I turned to Stuart and I could see all the colours around his body, too – it was fantastic – I could see his aura.

For years I have known about the energy fields which surround every living thing, and had seen dozens of photographs of auras, including my own. I knew lots of people, including psychics and healers, who could see, read and even diagnose illness by 'reading' auras but I had never expected to see them myself. I was so excited that the TV screen began to fill with static, then the phone rang which really made me jump. It was my friend Dr Richard Lawrence. We had not spoken for a few days and he wanted to know how 'things' were going. We agreed to meet the next day, as I did not want to upset Stuart by telling Richard on the phone everything that was happening, and phones still made me nervous …

The energy inside me was growing stronger. Physically I still looked thin, but I had begun eating a more varied diet, and now felt completely telepathic. Richard is a great friend and over the years he has channelled dozens of messages for me from John Lennon, my mum and various spirit guides, and I wondered what he would make of my experience. As I sat down I could feel Diana asking me not to tell Richard all that had transpired, she was clear that I should not mention her name.

Richard recalls: 'Your face was being overshadowed – you had a spirit face over your own. You looked haunted and afraid of your own shadow. I felt that whatever had happened to you was not altogether malevolent, but as I did not know then it was Diana, I was very cautious. I remember telling you to eat your lunch as you were so thin, but your eyes were very dark and mysterious. In all the years we have known each other I had never seen you look so strange. I was genuinely concerned.'

But as we sat there I knew what Diana was doing, she was allowing me to experience another facet of her personality. She wanted me to know that at times she could be very calculating indeed and she had resorted on occasion to using people the way they had used her. I felt as though I was being very deceitful with Richard, but I could not tell him her name. Diana also wanted me to understand how she had felt when she agreed to give the Panorama interview – she had felt like a hunted animal. She had a deep-rooted fear that she might lose access to her sons. She felt totally bereft and desperate and felt there was almost no one she could really trust. She bitterly regretted appearing on that programme and the furore it caused, but at the time she believed it was her only way of fighting back.

That afternoon on the train back to Birmingham I began to doubt the entire experience. But the more I doubted, the more odd things would happen. I would walk past my bathroom and hear the words 'turn on your radio' in my head, and as I flipped on my transistor it would be Paul McCartney singing *Paperback Writer*, another day it would be George Harrison singing *My Sweet Lord*. And as I listened to his lyrics it was as if Diana was saying, 'Forget the Beatles, you have me instead.' It was as if she was cajoling me via the media saying, 'come on write the book'.

Suddenly I loved classical music and wanted to read poetry. Me – poetry! At school my entire knowledge of poetry was gleaned during two or three boring English classes, I never appreciated it at all, until now. A desperation came over me to read *The Lady of Shallot* and poems by Khalil Gibran. And as I read Tennyson's famous verses it was as if Diana was letting me know that she identified with the woman in the poem who lived in, 'Four grey walls, and four grey towers,' who knew that a curse would come upon her if she looked down to Camelot. But when she sees Sir Lancelot in her mirror, the temptation becomes too great and she turns to face her destiny:

…She left the web, she left the loom,
She made three paces thro' the room,
She saw the water lily bloom,
She saw the helmet and the plume,
She look'd down to Camelot.
Out flew the web and floated wide;
The mirror crack'd from side to side;
'The curse is come upon me!' cried
The Lady of Shallot

And so in loving Dodi, had Diana found her Lancelot? I read on:

Who is this? and what is here?
And in the lighted palace near
Died the sound of royal cheer;
And they cross'd themselves for fear,
All the knights at Camelot:
But Lancelot mused a little space;
He said, 'She has a lovely face;
God in His mercy lend her grace,
The Lady of Shallot.

*The Lady of Shallot* by Alfred Tennyson

I seemed to know poetry that I had never heard or read in my life. I would hear odd phrases such as, 'Though every prospect pleases, only man is vile'. It was only months later that I was to find out this comes from a wellknown hymn.

Music began 'talking to me'. My old computer had finally given up the ghost and Lindsey had bought a new one with a built-in CD player. As a gift she had given me a couple of classical music CDs. I used to loathe classical music, but as the days passed it was as though I could 'feel' the emotions within the notes. Was this because Diana became emotional when she heard certain pieces of classical music, or was I now simply more sensitive to the specific frequencies of the individual notes?

Having learned about sound therapy years ago, I know that musical notes have specific frequencies that have the ability to change our mood, to calm people down or even make them hyperactive. In fact sound therapy is often used to help autistic children. Dolphins can help to heal people because they are able to tune into the harmonic frequencies emitted by every healthy cell in the body, and to somehow 'ping' them back to us, encouraging the body to heal itself. There is now a machine that can mimic this process – called a BiCom – which has proved highly successful in treating many disorders, from chronic fatigue to certain cancers (see page 270).

In March 1998 I had interviewed Dr Horace Dobbs, a medical and atomic research scientist based in Hull in Yorkshire, who heads the charity International Dolphin Watch. Dr Dobbs spent years running a medical research laboratory where he investigated the effects of extremely potent painkilling drugs on the brain and central nervous system. But his life changed after a chance meeting with an 'ambassador' or lone dolphin off the Isle of Man in 1975. He was fascinated, but remained highly sceptical of stories claiming that people had been healed after contact with dolphins, until he documented the case of a severely anorexic woman who recovered after several encounters with dolphins.

In 1986 Dr Dobbs set up Operation Sunflower – a research project aimed at furthering our understanding of the way in which dolphins heal and communicate with humans. Like us, dolphins are warm-blooded mammals, they breastfeed their young and the bones in their flippers are almost identical to those in the human hand. On a weight for weight basis the brain of a dolphin is the same size as the human brain. However, dolphins have been on Earth 30 million years longer than we have, during which time they have evolved an extremely complex cerebral cortex, the part of the brain associated with intelligence, intellect and higher thought processes. We are not so very different from dolphins, but the potential of the human brain is far less developed. That is changing. Just as dolphins heal people, humans also have this capability.

As I sat in my office back in Birmingham reading about Dr Dobbs, I began to understand that the human brain is capable of far more than even I had previously realized. I read on. Dr Dobbs believes that dolphins can communicate via holographic sound images, methods of communication that are far more advanced than any human language. It's similar to telepathy. Imagine being on the phone to a friend, trying to explain what someone looks like or telling a long story. Then instead of using a phone, imagine being able to instantly communicate a picture or a message through your mind. This sounded incredibly similar to what had happened in my bedroom on 8th April, when I could 'see and hear' the answers to any questions I cared to ask.

Dr Dobbs related the story of a German woman with terminal cancer which had spread from her lymph glands to her breast and into her bones. Doctors gave up hope and sent her home to die. Using her life savings, the woman flew to the Bahamas and swam for several days with dolphins. She felt them 'tuning into her' and sensed strange vibrations resonating through her body. Within three months her cancer had disappeared.

I have heard many similar stories about patients who have received hands-on healing. How is this possible? The answer is through frequencies.

The medicine of the future is already here, but most people just don't know it – yet. (For more information about Dr Dobbs' work, see page 270.)

Back in April I did not fully comprehend the enormous implications of what was happening to me regarding frequencies, but in the months to come I was to hear from scientists who did …

Meanwhile, my mind was having trouble processing the hundreds of realities I was experiencing. Perhaps, if I were to have a relaxation therapy it might help to calm 'things' down. My brain had now been working overtime for almost three weeks and was in dire need of a break. I was also rather concerned, as I had read research suggesting that overuse (and underuse) of the brain could be a possible trigger for Alzheimer's disease.

I decided to visit hypnotherapist Leila Hart whom I had known for several years and visited from time to time for relaxing treatments. I made the appointment for 28th April, hoping that Leila would be able to help shut my brain down and allow it some rest.

Leila talked me through the usual relaxation technique counting 'down, down, down, going deeper and deeper into relaxation'. Whenever Leila had taken me through this procedure before I had gone into a deeply relaxed state after ten minutes. Leila would bring me 'back up' after an hour and I would feel thoroughly refreshed.

But on this occasion, the more deeply I relaxed, the stronger the spinning inside my solar plexus became. Suddenly I heard thunder outside – strange, the weather again. Everything really was a paradox.

As I left Leila's Bayswater home and walked down the road to find a taxi, the sun broke through the clouds and a hearse passed in front of me. I knew it was just a coincidence but it was as if Diana was saying, 'Yes my physical body is dead, but I'm still alive'. Suddenly, I felt lighter and began to smile. I needed more laughter in my life; laughter lightens the soul and boosts the immune system.

The sunshine was so wonderful that I decided to walk through Hyde Park back to our London home. As I strode along, I smiled confidently and said 'Good morning' as I passed people. Most reciprocated the greeting, especially the tourists, but some looked at me as though I were mad. Their reactions brought home to me how defensive we have become, how so many of us live in fear … it's so sad.

As I passed Knightsbridge barracks suddenly the band of the Grenadier Guards began playing the national anthem. I stopped in my tracks and began singing. Passers by gave me some really strange looks so I shut up immediately.

Diana began chatting to me as I listened to the band: 'Now you see so clearly how, when people are judging you, you change your behaviour to conform to what you think you should be doing. In the beginning I tried to do this and it nearly drove me mad. Remember little Daisy on Easter Sunday, remember what I said about the children. Inside you are still like a child, you need to play more and have more fun. This will help you to balance the new energies – and your life.' She was right. In my mission to try and help people to heal themselves and the planet, I had become too serious. Yes, one should be serious about one's work, but in life we also need a balance in all things, and so I would make a real effort to lighten up a bit.

As I had this thought I heard her laughing, 'Yes, lighten up, all of you and then the whole world will change.'

Then she began talking about the national anthem: 'It's the history,' she said. 'The monarchy has so much history behind it. Think of the history rather than the individuals, see the bigger picture.'

On the subject of Charles and Camilla, she said that the media and the establishment might be against him becoming king if they married, but if he were determined it would be all right. She said that Prince William is just like her, they were joined at the hip, and that he will marry for love and make a caring king. She believes that, in his own way, William will bring about changes she was not able to achieve. Diana says her son as great healing capabilities, as she had, and is able to sense when she is with him.

She asked me to try and contact Prince Charles, saying she had messages for him. For goodness sake …

It was one thing to call the Duchess of York's office, but quite another to attempt to meet the Prince of Wales. Diana said I would be seeing the Queen shortly anyway …

Not as far as I knew. I was in a daze. Suddenly the band stopped, which brought me abruptly back into the moment. I carried on walking and thought about Prince Charles. I had received numerous messages for him and wondered if there was any way I might one day pass them on. After Diana's death he must have been inundated with letters and calls from all over the globe, and I'm sure there were plenty of messages from people claiming to be 'hearing' his ex wife … I would just appear like another crank – yet I knew what was happening to me was real. The Duchess of York had still not called, but I had not really expected her to.

Life went on.

Our new home in Oxfordshire was nearing completion and on 29th April, the live-in couple were due to move in. Having arranged for their flat to be decorated and organized new furniture before Easter, now it was time to put the scheme together. With everything that was going on in my life, decorating a flat was the last thing on my mind but, as much for Stuart's sake as for my own, I needed to act as normally as possible.

Paul and I loaded the car with lampshades, kitchen equipment, sheets and blankets and set off for the country. I fastened my seat belt tightly hoping that the ginger capsules I had been taking as a remedy for motion sickness would relieve the nausea I now seemed to feel whenever I got into a car. The voice in my head sang to ease my tension, 'Nellie the Elephant packed her trunk and said goodbye to the circus …' Maybe this was one of Diana's favourite childhood songs – I had no idea. 'C'mon lighten up', she said, 'don't take it all so seriously.' That was easy for her to say …

I remained apprehensive about being in other people's company. During the past few weeks I had stayed in my bedroom in Birmingham as much as possible – this was where I had felt safe, and where the energies were pure and unpolluted. But now it was time to get back into life and out into the world. The staff flat had to be ready and I needed to prove to myself I could do it. As we drove into the grounds my solar plexus began spinning violently – now what? Perhaps if I just ignored it, it would go away. Paul and I began unloading the car and Peter Jackson, our new part-time handyman, came to say hello.

Peter, who worked as a business and technology professional for over 27 years, is someone who doesn't miss much. He remembers that day well saying, 'I was aware that you had not been well but had no idea what your problem was. You looked very thin, your skin was ashen and looked almost transparent. I asked how you were feeling and you said that you were much better and made a joke about having had a weird experience during the previous few weeks. When I asked what that was, you shrugged the comment off and said we should get on with the unpacking.

'I had spent the previous two days cleaning the flat ready for your arrival and it was spotless. But as you walked into the living room you exclaimed "What's this now?" You sounded annoyed, as if I had missed something, and there on the small coffee table was a very fine, powdery, dark greycoloured ash covering an area the size of a tea plate. There had been no fire, electrical or otherwise, and no possible explanation for where that ash had come from. I knew that I had cleaned the table because a small container of flowers had been delivered that morning and I had wiped the surface before placing the flowers there. I wondered if the ash had come from any flower pollen or if it had been stuck to the base of the container, but when I lifted it up, the container and its base were perfectly clean. I dusted the ash away and to this day I wonder where on earth it came from.'

I wondered too: but I knew it appeared whenever I became very 'hyper' and when the spinning in my solar plexus area was intense. Just then, I did not fully understand the significance of the spontaneous appearance of the ash, but I was to find out in the weeks to come.

On 1st May I opened my post for the first time in almost a month and there was a reminder from Harrods telling me that I had not paid my account in April. Harrods, how could I have possibly forgotten Harrods? Easily. It's as if I had lived in another dimension for almost a month. In my diary I noticed I was supposed to meet a friend for lunch that day. The prospect terrified me – I was so worried that ash might suddenly appear again or that something weird might happen.

'Come on,' I told myself, 'for every negative thought, replace it with a positive one. The lunch will be perfect. You can do this, you look fine, you can drive your car, you're OK …' And as I backed my car out of our driveway at exactly 12.30 pm I turned on BBC Radio 2 and heard John Lennon singing 'Imagine'. I burst out laughing, it was as if someone up there had got their claws into me, and they wanted me to know that it was time to start the book. The lunch was fine.

# 7 The Birth of a Master

**AS THE DAYS PASSED THE** ash-like powder appeared from time to time, but I did not know how to control it, it simply showed up. I had heard a great deal about spiritual masters such as Sai Baba in India who could materialize 'holy' ash, known as *vibuthi*, from their hands at will. I knew people travelled from all over the world to receive the 'divine' energy from Sai Baba and others, such as Mother Meera in Germany.

In January Lindsey and I had visited Mother Meera in Germany. An Indian lady who was recognized as being 'divine' or special when she was very young, Mother Meera receives visitors from all over the world who come to receive her energy and simply be in her presence. She literally stares into your eyes for a few seconds, pulsing an energy through her eyes into yours, but says nothing. After seeing her on two evenings I became more psychic. On the last night at the hotel the receptionist told me that Ringo Starr had also been to see Mother, and had stayed in the same room as me … another Beatle, the book was to have been entitled 'Imagine' – another coincidence? … At the time I thought it would have been great to interview Ringo for the book; after all if he was spiritually 'awake' enough to visit Mother Meera, perhaps he would have believed me if I had told him that I'd heard from John Lennon years earlier. But in the end I had decided to let the book go for a while …

Was I now like Mother Meera? Could I channel the energy continuously pulsing through my eyes to help other people in some way, or would they think I was mad? By this time, I knew that compared to most people I was definitely different.

In addition to disrupting the television, I also seemed to be having a strange effect on the telephone. On several occasions the line would suddenly go dead in the middle of a call. Initially, I blamed this on poor connections, but after being cut off several times, I became aware that it was me. It was really weird, but once I knew that I was speaking for longer than necessary, the phone would simply go dead. It was as though the energy, or something inside me – perhaps my subconscious mind – had decided the call had gone on long enough. I made a note to call Roger Coghill, a scientist with an incredible knowledge of electromagnetic energies and the working of the brain who had helped me on many occasions. Perhaps he would be able to explain what was going on.

After everything that had happened I began to think about my life and what the voice had said about 'living every day as if it's your last'. For some time, I had been toying with the idea of going to see my daughter in Australia for her 30th birthday in September. I felt I had never been a good mother and so carried a huge burden of guilt, some of which goes back to when I sent Victoria to boarding school at the age of five. I had wanted to continue my work as an air stewardess, instead of being there for my only daughter.

Mum looked after Vicki almost from the day she was born. We made a pact, I would work and mum would care for Vicki. But after Dad died, Mum was forced to sell our house in Coventry. We moved to a tied-cottage in the country near Leamington Spa on the agreement that we got the house rent-free. In return Mum worked as a cleaning lady for the people who lived in the big house up the hill. In winter that cottage was so cold we slept with woolly hats on.

The constant grind of the daily cleaning, looking after my daughter and the huge emotional loss of my father eventually took its toll on Mum's health. The doctor told me that if she was to survive I would have to look after Vicki myself and Mum would have to stop work. But my flying salary was our only income. What should I do? I remembered how much I had wanted to continue my education and become a doctor, and I was determined to give my daughter a good education. So I enrolled fiveyear-old Vicki at a local private school where she boarded during the week and came home for weekends. I bought a small one-bedroom flat, and over the months Mum slowly improved and she looked after Vicki at weekends. Whatever would I have done without my dear mum?

And as I sat in my little office in Birmingham remembering my mother and how selfish I had been in my youth and thinking of all the things I wish I could have said to her before she died – a little voice in my head said: 'Aye, Aye.' I jumped. This was the phrase Mum would use as I walked down the drive to her bungalow every Saturday during the last two years of her life. Was this really my mum?

'Pull yourself together girl, yes your dad and I are here. We have always been here. We are so proud of you.' Since my mum died in 1991, I have often imagined what she would say in certain situations and have received numerous wonderful messages that could have only come from my parents through various mediums. But in that brief moment I heard my mother speaking very distinctly – this was definitely not my imagination.

'I love you, Mum and Dad,' I said in my mind.

'We love you too, daughter,' came the reply … Tears filled my eyes.

The fax machine on my desk began ringing and shattered this magical moment. A letter appeared from someone who wanted me to write about their new slimming product from Australia. I smiled at the coincidence and as I read the letter more closely it mentioned a friend from my flying days, Linda, who lived in Sydney and who was the business partner of the person who sent me the fax. Apparently, Linda had spotted my picture in the *Sunday Times* and wondered if I would consider featuring their new product. I phoned her and we had a real laugh. Amazingly, she lived only 20 minutes from my daughter and said that they would have a drink together. Linda had not seen my daughter since she was four years old. Even though I had resigned from the *Sunday Times* I wanted to help my old friend if I possibly could, so I made arrangements to meet her partner in London on 6th May.

On Sunday 3rd May my last column that I had written in April duly appeared. As I read it I felt incredibly sad and sat in my bathroom having a really good cry … Diana came for a visit and spoke gently, 'Don't weep for what has gone when you have so much to look forward to. You are now able to see life through different eyes, you are becoming very special, look in the mirror and see me.'

My heart began pounding, what did she mean? I was rooted to the spot and felt too terrified to stand up and look into the mirror in case I saw her. But I could not sit there all day, so, very sheepishly and slowly, I moved. In the mirror I was astonished to see four irises in my eyes instead of two. I realize many of you reading this will say 'rubbish', but I know what I saw and it was no hallucination. I examined my eyes closely in a magnifying mirror. My own bluish-grey eyes looked normal, but behind them were two larger irises and their colour was distinctly different from mine – they were a beautiful, bright sapphire blue. Why was I even surprised with everything else that had happened?

On 6th May, I met Linda's business partner for breakfast to help her with the PR for their new slimming product. She watched in amazement as I ate porridge, poached eggs, grilled tomatoes and toast. I felt as though I was eating for England, suddenly my appetite was back … She wore a red jacket, and I was so sensitive to colour that I was able to 'feel' the energy being emitted – it made me feel quite hyper. Obviously, I needed to stay away from red. I felt envious that she was travelling back to Australia that night and as we said goodbye I made up my mind to visit my daughter for her 30th birthday. The moment I had this thought, Diana was back: 'I will be seeing you in Australia, something special will happen there.'

Now what?

After breakfast I went to see my doctor Brian for the results of my blood tests from 21st April.

All the tests were negative. He had thought that my terrible thirst, tiredness and cold hands might have indicated I was diabetic, but I was fine. My thyroid, hormone levels and heart were also normal. He was perplexed – he wasn't the only one.

On 8th May I went for a facial in Birmingham to cheer myself up, as we were due to go away for three days to Cliveden, once home to the Astors, which is now a fabulous hotel in Berkshire. Stuart was worn out by everything that had happened since Easter and just wanted a few days' peace and quiet. I had long since stopped telling him about the 'goings on' around me. He just wanted his normal, cheerful wife back.

As I lay on the treatment couch there was a mirror directly in front of me. The pain when I looked into my own eyes was excruciating and we took the mirror off the wall. The beautician must have thought I was very odd, but there was no way I could look into my own eyes for any length of time. I realized that the 'light' or energy coming through them was becoming so powerful that when it was mirrored back to me, it caused me great pain.

On Saturday 9th May, my trainer Al came to our home in Birmingham to give me a workout. Al is a real character. In between lifting weights he would tell jokes and I would end up dropping the weights in peals of laughter. 'What happened to the man who swallowed a Hoover?' he asked. I didn't know the answer … 'He's cleaning up nicely' … really light stuff, but it lifted my spirits. Al and his girlfriend had house-sat for us the previous Christmas, and for some reason we brought this subject up. Al said, 'I could never live in this house, there are so many people coming and going, it disturbs the energies …'

So, Al is sensitive to energies, I thought, and wondered how much I could tell him. Lifting even the smallest weights drained me and yet the little voice inside me was still singing, 'Let's get physical'. Obviously, Diana loved working out and boy did she want me to get fit again. But as I tried to lift my normal weights, I was overwhelmed by exhaustion and instinctively grabbed Al's arm.

Al later related his memories of that afternoon, 'You had lost a lot of weight, but your eyes really sparkled. When Stuart came for his workouts every week he had told me that you had been unwell and I thought perhaps you had been working too hard. After you had lifted a few weights, suddenly all the colour drained from your face and you grabbed my arm, saying that you could do with some of my energy. As your hand touched my arm I sensed a strange pulsing and after a couple of minutes I felt quite drained. Then you asked me to stand back and tell you if I could see anything different about you. I had no idea why you did this, but the longer I looked at you, the stranger your face became, so I took off my glasses (I'm short-sighted) to try and focus more clearly. What I saw was the outline of a man with a beard in a black and white robe. You were black on one side and white on the other, it was weird and yet I was not scared. I told you what I saw and you looked shaken.'

Yes, his statement really shook me. I felt sure that Diana must be with Jesus in Heaven but I didn't know why Al saw a figure that appeared black on one side and white on the other.

Diana answered: 'Because there is good and evil, black and white, dark and light in every living being – we are not what we seem.'

Al brought me back from my 'day dreaming'. I now knew that I could drain energies as well as give energy, and as I did not want to harm anyone I would be more careful in future. Whenever we finished a session Al would pop down to the kitchen and help himself to one of my homemade oat-based biscuits. That day, as he went to pick up the white biscuit tin, it turned black. He looked at his hands and saw that they were covered with a fine dark grey powder.           .

We went to Cliveden on the 11th May and as the porter showed us to our room the irony was not lost on me when I saw the plaque on our door – 'The Prince of Wales Suite'. Very funny.

The sun shone. Stuart slept properly for the first time in weeks, but Diana still toyed with me. The continual voices had stopped, my life was getting back to normal, or so I thought. I had heard mediums in the past say that you have to learn to set limits with spirit, as they have no concept of time as we know it, and they will simply go on and on unless you tell them when it's convenient to hear and when it's not. All right, I would take control. But how? Norma had told me to visualize an iron door closing in the top of my head, which had worked for a few days, but sometimes I seemed to lose it and the energy and information would continue flowing into me unimpeded.

For years, I had strived to hear spirit clearly and now that I could, I wasn't quite sure how to handle the situation. When the messages stopped for a day I would panic and think 'she' had left me, then when she talked non-stop I screamed for it all to come to an end. Typical, I thought. We want things until we have them and then we begin to take them for granted … Often we don't know what we've got until it's gone. Somehow I had to come to a compromise.

As I sat reading by the pool in the sunshine (I could now read for an hour a day before my eyes began to ache), a waitress offered me some coffee. I know purists may be horrified that a health writer drinks the occasional coffee – as more than three cups of ground coffee a day increases the chance of contracting osteoporosis by up to 80 per cent because it depletes the bones of calcium (for more details see page 270) – but, let's face it, after what I had been through I felt like I deserved a few treats. We all deserve treats, all we have to do is to stop living on them, and do everything in moderation.

As the poolside waitress made her way back to the kitchen I overheard her telling another guest that she had been off sick for a few days. When she returned with my coffee I enquired after her health. She said that she had fainted several times and the doctor had told her to rest but could find no cause for her blackouts. After a lengthy chat, I came to the conclusion that she might be suffering from low blood sugar (hypoglycaemia).

I suggested that she eat small regular meals and include more foods that help to balance blood sugar for longer periods, such as good-quality protein: chicken or fish, plenty of fresh fruits and vegetables in her diet; and to make sure she ate breakfast, especially porridge or oat-based cereals. I also recommended that she include more wholemeal bread, pasta and brown rice in her diet; that she replace sugary drinks with more natural alternatives such as diluted apple juice and that she should drink more water. I also advised her to take the mineral chromium which helps to balance blood sugar levels and also reduces cravings for sugary or refined snacks. And her name? Sabrina – the name of the film about Paris I had been 'told' to watch over Easter. Another coincidence? Maybe.

I walked towards the pool and the hotel guest I had seen Sabrina chatting with told me she had overheard our conversation. We too began discussing health issues. She was under considerable stress and wanted to know if she was taking the right supplements. It transpired that her 19-year-old brother had just been killed in Bosnia. She was heartbroken as they had been very close. I shared my belief in life after death and recommended that she read *Testimony of Light*, a magical book by Helen Greaves (C.W. Daniel) that tells the story of a nun who died and then returned by speaking through a colleague she had known for over 30 years to tell of her life on the 'other side' … When my mum died, this book gave me great comfort and I had recommended it several times in my columns.

The woman was desperate to believe me, but I could not 'hear' her brother. I suggested she contact the Spiritualist Society in Belgrave Square, London which would give her the name of a registered medium. My fellow guest's name was Diana. Another coincidence?

As I sat down to drink my coffee, the voice of Diana returned in my head, 'I miss my family too, and I want the world to know that we all go on. Here there are many realities and many dimensions. All the things you knew and could do over Easter: the healing; being telepathic; communicating with other realms; this is what happens when you become fully conscious – this is normality, not madness. I now know that you are all capable of more than most of you can even begin to imagine and you have experienced a minute fraction of these capabilities.'

I wanted to know more about her new life. 'When you come over to the higher dimensions, you see all the times that you could have given love and helped others, and if you have caused anyone any pain, you feel the pain that you caused them.

'You quickly realize that it does not matter which religion you followed, but the way you live your life that counts. It is a very humbling experience. There is truly no such place as hell – hell is created by the mind. Some people live in such terrible circumstances that people say their life has been a hell on Earth, and so it has. People say, "Why does God let people starve?", or "Why does God allow war?" It is man that creates these things – not God.'

'You keep on thinking about your experience over Easter as being 'the madness', but war, violence, corruption, greed, judgement, envy, complacency, indifference, ego, ignorance, fanaticism, the destruction of irreplaceable commodities, loneliness, ill health, starvation and unnecessary cruelty to any living human or animal – this is the real madness that afflicts you on Earth. There are souls here who have chosen to live in darkness (their own idea of hell) because of the pain they inflicted on others. You choose your own judgement but when they are ready, anyone can come into the light and there are many who help with this work.'

The information was fascinating. Yet I also longed to know about Dodi and I asked how much they see of each other. As I did so a huge emotional surge swept through my body. Diana replied, 'We are free to be together whenever we wish and are more alive than we ever were on Earth. Dodi says his father has a strong belief in life after death, but still carries a huge sense of guilt about our accident. He asks that his father should stop blaming himself. There is no point in him thinking that he could somehow have prevented our deaths. Yes, on a physical level, many factors led to the accident which culminated in our physical deaths.. Dodi asks that any further money his father is thinking of spending on investigations should go to charity, to give more children hope and help for the future.'

I tried to change her mood and asked, 'So what is your job now?' She answered, 'To continue healing where and when I can. Your book will be part of this process.'

'So what should go in the book?' I enquired.

'That there is life after death', she answered. 'That your thoughts and actions create your world, about judgement, religion, the health of the planet and the people on it. Also what will come if you don't all wake up and take more responsibility for yourselves, your lives and the health of the planet – and soon.'

She is also desperate to see the Spencer and Windsor families re-uniting to strengthen the monarchy and support her boys. She said that Charles sometimes feels 'torn in half' – as she often did in her lifetime because he is trying to please too many masters.

How could I possibly bring her wishes to fruition? I wondered. 'Learn to trust and let go', she replied. 'Help will come, contact Sarah again' …

That was the last thing I wanted to hear, and I went back to reading my book by the pool.

That night at Cliveden there was an incredible storm. The energies in my solar plexus and the fever returned. Around 2 am I got out of bed and went through to our sitting room to watch the storm from a window. As the lightning danced in front of my eyes, I felt the energies swirl around the room from the open windows. Whatever was happening to my physical body was being increased – turned up – by the energy within the storm. It was as if the heavens were talking to me. I remembered Good Friday when I had said to Robert the cook, 'I am the weather,' and wondered who the 'I' was. As I pondered this question I heard a new voice. It was all-powerful, filling my head and the room. 'I,' said the voice, 'am God.'

I was dumbstruck. And in that moment the enormity of what I was hearing was almost beyond words, it was so profound. I felt so special I swear if someone had asked me to walk on water I could have done it. My body began to feel strange and weightless again, just as it had during my visit to Bill and Celia's on 22nd April, and as I looked down at the floor my feet and legs appeared translucent – I was beginning to dematerialize. Panic rose in my throat, a thunder clap shattered the moment and I fell to my knees which I could no longer see. I imagined that any moment a UFO might land on the lawn before me and God himself would get out. My heart was in my mouth as I stumbled back towards our bedroom, and as I passed the lamp in our corridor the bulb flashed and went out.

If I had felt different before, now I felt truly special. As I lay in the darkness of our room, I remembered a message that Norma had given me during one of our meditation sessions almost eight years earlier. It went something like, 'The gifts that spirit bring are worth more than all the diamonds in the world'. Back then, I adored jewellery and wonderful clothes. 'Stuff' meant a whole lot to me because people seemed to judge me by what I wore, not what I said and as the years passed I came to equate good clothes and appearance with being wanted. How stupid I was. Today I still enjoy wearing jewellery and looking good – but I understand that such things are meaningless in the big scheme of life. Now as I lay listening to my husband breathing peacefully – I truly understood what Norma had meant. I felt different, but looked the same. I was still only Hazel, but I felt superhuman, super awake, super conscious, and fully alive for the first time in my life.

The next day thunder and lightening rumbled on overhead and the rain fell like a sheet of silent mist over the trees. Stuart left early to attend meetings and I packed our bags. My mind was full of what had happened the previous night and as I sat eating breakfast and idly staring out at the storm I accidentally cut my finger on a knife, which brought me back to earth with a jolt. The sight of blood and the sensation of pain gave me a shock, and Diana's voice returned: 'This is another valuable lesson. You must bring yourself back down to Earth, you must remember that you are only human, you are still in a physical body and in each lifetime you only get one body, so you must look after it. This is the first step to saving the planet.'

Then the strangest thing happened, within 12 hours of cutting myself, the wound healed. There was no scar, it simply vanished … How was that possible? I had no idea – but one day I would find out for sure. I have read many books saying that before you can save the world or anyone in it, you must first learn to love, and look after yourself. Everything begins with the self. I have long believed that the way to save ourselves a lot of grief and chronic illness is to take more responsibility for ourselves and our actions. Our lives would then change for the better. Don't pay attention to things that you have no control over – it just wastes precious time and energy. All you have to do is take the first step – and you begin a positive chain reaction.

Try to replace every negative, angry, jealous or judgmental thought or act with a positive, kind thought or act. Concentrate on what you can change not what you cannot. Look at your life and examine what is wrong in it. What don't you like about it? Who do you like having in your life? Who drives you crazy? Then write down three things you would like to change about your life. And do it today. If you want something badly enough, you have to be willing to make it happen.

If you are sick, buy a book on your specific condition. Book shops are groaning with highly informative, alternative ways to become and stay well. If you are suffering from lack of confidence, lack of money, low selfesteem or guilt, there are thousands of self-help books out there written just for you. I fully appreciate there are millions of people who are too sick or disabled to help themselves and who need constant care and attention, and that the great majority of those who care for these people have the patience of saints. But most of us can choose what we eat, what we do for a living and we can choose our thoughts … and our thoughts create our reality.

Diana interrupted my thoughts saying, 'You do not fully appreciate just how powerful your mind is becoming, you can indeed create what you want in your life by thinking about it, by becoming focused on exactly what you need and then taking the action necessary to bring it into being. The ring you attempted to manifest from the higher dimensions will come in time.' I blushed deeply when she mentioned this.

As I understood it, the universe, God, whatever you choose to call it, seems to want us to understand that we can all create everything that we need. Most of us believe that in order to have what we need, life has to be a continual struggle but this does not have to be so.

She continued, 'Here in the higher realms all we have to do is think of something we need and it appears immediately. You soon learn to be very careful with your thoughts and what you wish for. People from all races and creeds can read each other's thoughts instantly so there is no need for the spoken word. What we also see from here is that the majority of thoughts (energy) being emitted globally are negative.

'Thought creates… You must grasp this concept and soon. You can change your life, your health and your planet. Nothing can be created unless it is first a thought, and from thought comes action, and from action comes a result. For instance, there has been much discussion about the millennium computer bug that is predicted to cause havoc after New Year's Eve 1999. If enough people think and believe that there will be chaos, then this is exactly what will happen. Your cumulative actions will determine the outcome. Should you all choose to withdraw your money from the bank 'just in case' and to avoid flying or whatever, you will all contribute to the chaos. But if the large institutions and companies take the appropriate action to prevent this from happening, and if enough positive action and thoughts are utilized, then chaos can be prevented. It's all up to you.'

My thoughts returned to the day that I had attempted to manifest a ring and my sheer incredulity as my thoughts virtually instantly created what happened next. It was mind-blowing, but it had happened. In ten years I had read endless books advocating the belief that we create our own reality, but reading and thinking about it is not the same as knowing and experiencing it. Now I knew it to be true.

I remember being given an American magazine called Science of Mind back in 1994, containing an interview with the then Director of the Center for Frontier Sciences at Temple University in Philadelphia, Beverley Rubik Ph.D. I had kept that article thinking that one day it might come in handy, and now I know why. Dr Rubik earned her doctorate in biophysics from the University of California at Berkeley in 1979.

Since moving to work in San Francisco, she and her colleagues have shown through their experiments that there is a definite interaction between consciousness and matter. In other words, what you think about becomes your reality. In Dr Rubik's words: 'The research has shown a significant relationship between what we intend in consciousness and what we experience. Of course, if our intention is not clear, the results we get will be muddled by deeper, unconscious inclinations that may even work in the opposite direction. But when we do have a clear intention for something to occur and it is not blocked by contrary subconscious thinking or a feeling that we don't deserve it, our thoughts do tend to create the results that we desire. Thoughts matter, thoughts materialize. A clear intention will create a reality.'

The implications of this concept are staggering. The upshot is to think as much as possible about what you need in your life and stop thinking about what you don't need …

But what about the millions of people living in poverty, especially children, who are dying unnecessarily every day? To intimate they are somehow creating their reality through their thoughts is, to my mind, ludicrous. I felt Diana sigh as if to say, 'I knew this would come up some time'. She continued, 'Again there are many realities. On one level you could say that because millions are born into abject poverty all they experience as they grow up is hunger, so a lack of food and having nothing becomes 'normal' to them.

'Once millions of people think and believe 100 per cent that their lives are always going to be this way, what manifests is more of nothing and misery – remember, thoughts create. On another level you could say that while more than 350,000 children are born each day, the fact that over 32,000 under the age of five die daily from hunger, war, poverty and disease, means things have gone way out of balance. Certain countries throw away or destroy millions of tons of food every year which, if transported, could help to feed the starving. Many infant deaths could also be prevented if the mothers could receive more education on birth control.

'On another level, you might say that if people were to stop fighting over really stupid issues there would be more peace and people could settle and grow their food instead of continually being herded like sheep into becoming refugees. On a much higher level that many of you do not yet fully comprehend, many of these souls choose to come to Earth and play their part as one of these starving people to help raise the consciousness of others on the planet. If I gave you every reality on this one subject alone, it would take many days and neither of us has the time. I am only offering you a few realities.'

And I knew she was right. If you really think about it, we have by our thoughts, words and actions created almost all of our own and the world's health problems – the wars, global warming, pollution and so on.

I heard Diana again: 'Be more positive, then you can change things. So many of you moan on and on about governments, saying, "Why don't they give us more money, why can't I have this and that for free?" You act as though being given things for free is a god-given right. Again there are many realities. Yes, there are millions who cannot help themselves, the infirm, the brain damaged, the totally paralysed and those who are born with terrible afflictions.

'The way to get what you need in life is to change your attitude from, "What's in it for me?" to "How can I help?" Then everything you need will come to you. I now realize that I used to spend far too much time thinking and worrying about situations in a negative way, with the result that the situation took control over me, and my life got worse instead of better. By the time I worked out what I wanted and how to go about it, my life was running out. You all need to focus on exactly what you really need in your life. Stop wasting time on what you don't need as time is very precious.'

When I used to present lectures and advise people how to create what they wanted in their lives I used to say, 'When you go into a restaurant, you don't just say "Give me some food," you order a specific meal. Then you let go and trust it will come. You have taken the action necessary to bring it into being.'

If you are not clear on what you want, then how can it ever come into your life? To some people this sounds ridiculous. Often they will say, 'I want more money.' So I give them a 50 pence piece and say, 'here's more money'. But they frown. They want a lot more money. How much more?

'Well, winning the lottery would be great', they answer. Then I ask what they actually need in their lives. Usually, it's a better job earning more money but with fewer hours, a bigger car, house, and more freedom to do what they want.

They want everything – but all too often they are not willing to give very much to get it. 'How badly do you want these things in your life?' I might ask. Some simply shrug and look despondent but if we want something badly enough, we must be willing to take the necessary action to bring our dreams into being. Then there are those who believe that they can only ever have sufficient material possessions and money by working excessively long hours which often causes their health to break down.

Some people choose to work extra long hours because they want security for their children. It's only natural to have a desire to give our children the things we might have missed – but remember if they are blessed with good health our children can go into the world and earn their own living. I often suggest to a person whose only desire is material wealth that they should ask a wealthy person with terminal cancer if more money would help them … No, of course it won't … that person just wants to be healthy. A blind man wants to see, a starving child wants food, millions stranded among warring armies want peace. Life for so many is completely out of balance … There is so much madness, but it could be Heaven on Earth – if we want to make it that way … It's our choice.

I decided I would take my own advice. My thoughts were in total chaos after everything that had happened to me, so I would sit down and think about what I wanted, what I intended. Ever since Norma had 'woken me up' all those years ago I have kept a diary intermittently of all the coincidences, my spiritual insights, and my hopes and dreams. For example, how falling on ice and breaking my knee back in 1991 had given me the space and time to look after my mum when she was dying. That accident turned out to be a blessing in disguise. I needed to look at my hopes and my dreams.

In February 1998 I had aspired to putting together an alternative health TV show and taking my column to America. Now, I realized just how much my priorities had now changed. As I sat reading my diary – in that moment – having a TV show was the furthest thing from my mind. It's amazing how our priorities change from day to day, week to week, month to month. What matters so much one day can be completely forgotten the next. So now it was time for me to get down to basics – what did I really want in my life? I wrote in my diary:

1. To become and stay healthy for as long as possible.

2. To write *Imagine*.

3. To earn £1 million.

Diana had told me I was one in a million and it seemed like a pretty good figure with which to start a charitable foundation ... a dream of mine for almost 20 years. What the hell: I would go shopping too – I'm only human. Diana was back, 'This is great, remember what one person can do when they have a fire inside them. It may start as a spark, but one spark can light a small fire, and as it burns it grows. Remember what Bob Geldof achieved in 1985 after seeing the famine in Africa on the news, which inspired him and others to help the starving – one man's dream became a reality because he had a fire inside him, he took action and made it reality. Charles and I thought his Live Aid concept was fantastic – it really inspired us both.'

Her statement evoked memories of that warm July day in 1985 when 80,000 people in a concert arena were joined by another billion worldwide on TV. A few years later in his wonderful autobiography Is That It? Bob recalled, 'All my life I felt like I had been waiting. For what I was unsure. Things felt good or bad, but never complete. There was always something else – something specific. Not today. Had all the waiting been for this? Was this it? ... Yet looking back it is clear to me how in one respect everything conspired to bring me here ... My hand was held still in the air, stiff with purpose. There was no element of personal power. Another banal truism had been made real; at that moment there was no difference between the man on the stage and the audience, none at all. We were all part of some greater purpose, all attempting an understanding of one another and all part of something completely outside ourselves.'

'Well done, Bob,' I said to myself. Diana agreed, 'Yes, Bob made a huge difference, and let what he and others have achieved and continue to achieve inspire you now. Every one of you has chosen to be a part of today's drama, you are all needed to play your part. Inspire others whenever you can and this will begin a huge chain reaction. Above all remember that you are all one race, the human race, and in the days and years to come you will need to think and work as one to survive.'

Suddenly she seemed very prophetic. I have often thought that we need to find more in common rather than continually bring up subjects that keep us apart. I hoped I was not going to hear a whole load of doom and gloom – we already have sufficient bad news. Many 'channelled' books written by celebrities, such as *Has The Countdown Begun?* by French dress designer Paco Rabanne, foretell nuclear wars, disaster and the end of the world. But I have always believed that if enough people could change the way they think and act then many of our probable futures might be changed.

I reviewed my list. What could I do today that would begin to bring my dreams into being? I was back to eating a healthy diet, and had even begun baking my favourite carrot cake again. I was gaining weight and both Stuart and I were taking more exercise. However, my eyes were still a problem when exposed to bright artificial light, and if I was to write the book I needed to be able to see the screen properly. I would have my eyes tested.

I would also need a publisher. Perhaps the Duchess of York would help me? When I had written my first health book in 1995, a healer friend arranged for me to meet Sarah, who is keen on alternative medicine. She had agreed to write a brief foreword for me and had been truly helpful, asking nothing in return. Perhaps I could now repay that debt by giving her messages from Diana. I sent a fax to her office, remembering the phrase, 'If at first you don't succeed, try, try again.'

Diana had told me to be dramatic and so I wrote that I had some tapes that I thought might be of interest to the Duchess … It was cheeky but it was also the truth.

The £1 million would have to wait and I would trust that it would come – if it was meant to be.

When I visited the optician he could not detect anything substantially wrong with my eyes, even though the vision in my left eye was seriously blurred. Maybe 'seeing' through spirit's eyes was causing the cloudy effect. Anyway, the optician said I needed glasses for reading and for working at the screen. I ordered them, but at the same time determined to do my utmost to help my eyes by natural means, as I had often read that wearing glasses encourages the muscles to become lazier so that you end up needing a stronger prescription, and so on down the slippery slope. I promised myself I would eat more foods rich in eye nutrients – sweet potatoes, oily fish, apricots, bilberries, blueberries and so on, and I would take supplements known to protect the eyes, including vitamin A, bilberry extract (which is high in flavonoids known to strengthen fine capillaries), plus the herb Ginkgo biloba, which increases circulation.

I thought of Sheila and the healing I had given her eyes over Easter. The next day, 15th May, we returned to Birmingham and as Sheila walked into my bedroom I could instantly see that her eyes looked different. Her pupils were a normal size, not the great black pools they had been for years. I asked her what had happened. She looked reticent but told me that her field of vision had widened, she could see more clearly, and that she was not so afraid of the dark (retinitis pigmentosa begins with varying degrees of night blindness). Somewhat hesitantly, she said that she really felt as though something special had happened.

I was overjoyed, but we wanted to be sure and so I made an appointment with the eye specialist who had seen her three years earlier and taken her driving licence away. He had predicted that within ten years she would be registered blind and would only be able to see a tiny circle of light. To Sheila, a young mother with four children, the prospect of almost total blindness by 48 was a devastating blow, especially since there was no cure and no hope of one in current orthodox medicine.

I held my breath as he examined her eyes. The good news was that her condition was no worse, the bad news was that she still had the condition. Within two days Sheila's field of vision had closed in again, but I knew that her sight had improved and prayed that one day I would meet an eye specialist who could tell me what had happened. I sent out the thought and waited for help – it was to come within a month. Meanwhile, over the weekend of 15th–17th May 1998, world leaders gathered for a G8 summit in Birmingham. Clinton, Blair, Kohl, Yeltsin and many others slept less than half a mile from our home. I wondered what they were discussing … would their talking make any real difference?

At 8.30 pm on 16th May I was 'instructed' to tune into the Discovery Channel on TV. It was a programme about psychics, detailing research being done by Dr Marilyn Schultz at the University of Nevada. It featured people being tested for their powers of telepathy, and the scientist said that profoundly psychic people are currently one in a million. This was the exact figure Diana had quoted some days earlier. As I watched, I became increasingly excited as they interviewed a woman who, when out shopping, had suddenly realized that people were walking right through her – she had become invisible.

It was fantastic. It transpired that numerous scientists have located and interviewed many people like her who are having similarly unusual experiences. The whole programme was so matter of fact, it all sounded so normal. The screen filled with static. Stuart watched as I walked across the room and took a deep breath so that the programme could come back on … It was so incredible. Here were renowned scientists talking about many of the things that had happened to me. Could it have been that when the woman disappeared, she had unwittingly gone into the fourth dimension – the same dimension that 'dead' people go to? Did that mean we could go there too? 'Yes,' answered the voice in my head, 'there are many who can hear us and your numbers are growing, a few can even see us.'

As I heard this, I remembered Jacki Humphries and how she had claimed to have seen and spoken to her 'dead' son Philip. If only I could find one more person who had seen a 'dead' relative to add weight to Jacki's story, which I certainly believed. I sent my request out – and waited for it to boomerang back into my life. I did not have long to wait.

At a birthday party on 31st May I happened to be seated at the same table as Kathy Bowling, who I had met in Barbados several years earlier. As we chatted she told me that her only son Mark had been killed in a motorcycle accident on 12th August 1997 at 7pm in Kent. Just as Jacki had 'known' that something had happened to her son at the exact moment he was killed, Kathy had experienced a similar premonition. Sitting on board a plane waiting for take-off from Barbados airport, waves of nausea swept over her. It was exactly 7pm in England. Landing in London the next morning, relatives were waiting to give her the terrible news. Kathy was devastated – Mark was only 22.

Every day she would visit the morgue to talk to her son, touching his hands and his face, which looked perfect. Kathy recalled, 'He looked so wonderful – as if he were asleep – and I would sit there and stroke him and talk to him about anything and everything. As the week progressed it was as if I could hear him talking to me in my head saying, "Stop fussing over me so much, Mum". But on the sixth day, the day before his funeral, he was almost unrecognizable when I went to see him. 'Overnight his face had become swollen and black with bruises. It was so strange. I heard him say, "Enough is enough, Mum." and I knew he didn't want anyone else to see him. During those last moments I realized that his essence had finally left his body – the spark that was my son was gone and I stood looking at an empty shell. But as the weeks passed I became desperate to see Mark again. I just wanted to hold him and to know that he was all right in his new life – wherever that might be.

'On 10th September I spent the evening with a girlfriend. Her mother had committed suicide and the fact that we had both lost our nearest and dearest in tragic circumstances meant we could truly open our hearts to each other. Around 2.30 am we decided to call it a day and turned out the lights. The curtains were open and we could see residual light coming through the window from the floodlit stables below us. Suddenly we both became aware of shadows and bright lights flickering all around us in the room and the lampshades began spinning. I have been psychic all my life and was not at all afraid, but my friend was petrified. I told her to stay calm, saying that it was OK. Then my son appeared at the end of my bed. He was wearing an old tee-shirt and jeans that he loved, but I could see no colour, only monochrome. He looked solid, not at all 'ghostly'. He walked round the bed, bent over and kissed me but said nothing. I was so stunned that I couldn't move but I will treasure that moment for the rest of my life as I know my son has gone on.

'And have you seen him since?' I asked. 'No', she replied. 'But I can often "smell" him when he is in the room with me' … Diana had said that her sons, especially William, sensed when she was with them from the smell of her perfume. Many people tell similar stories and they have no reason to lie.

# 8

# The Meetings

**THE FOLLOWING WEEK, FIVE** nuclear bombs were detonated for 'test' purposes in Pakistan. People there danced in the streets with joy because they now had nuclear bombs. But what on earth was there to celebrate? Millions of people were appalled, and so was Diana, as she said: 'This madness must be stopped, it will cause terrible underground shockwaves – people must be made to understand the laws of cause and effect.'

She was right again. Just 48 hours later there was a terrible earthquake in Afghanistan, killing 4,000 people. So what might have triggered that? You don't need to be a nuclear physicist to realize that if bombs of such magnitude explode underground they are going to cause considerable shock waves around the globe. Many scientists are at last speaking out. On 14th April 1989 at a United Nations conference held in Seattle, Washington, Gary Whiteford, Professor of Geography at the University of New Brunswick in Canada presented the most exhaustive study available on the correlation between nuclear testing and earthquakes. He has studied all earthquakes this century measuring more than 5.8 on the Richter scale. In the first half of this century, before nuclear testing, large earthquakes occurred at an average rate of 68 per year. With the onset of testing the rats rose to 127 per year. Professor Whiteford said, 'The geological patterns in the data, with a clustering of earthquakes in specific regions matched to specific test dates and sites, do not support the easy and comforting explanation given by the US military of "pure coincidence". It is a dangerous coincidence.' Of course, there are other scientists who disagree – but I know what I believe.

Life went on. On 19th May I met with my public relations advisor, Ciara Parkes. Since my last column on 3rd May I had been inundated with letters asking me why I had left, and Ciara could not understand how I could have given up my page when everything had been going so well. She recalls, 'You told me you had been through an incredible experience over Easter and you looked really well considering what sounded like a terrible ordeal. During our lunch I noticed that your eyes changed colour significantly from their normal grey-blue to a pale aquamarine blue – I was fascinated. I asked whether you were aware of this physical change, and only when you looked in your compact mirror did you see it for yourself. I wondered how this was physically possible.

'During lunch you wrote a few notes and I immediately noticed that your writing was different. You talked about an energy being inside you, and during our car journey back to your home you said you would show me what you looked like when you 'let go of the energy'. I was transfixed as I watched the 'energy' drain from your face and you suddenly appeared quite exhausted and gaunt. I don't know much about spiritual happenings, but I am open-minded, and knew I had witnessed something that has no rational explanation. It made me really think and I wanted to understand what had happened to you.'

Ciara was not the only one. After she left to return to her office I went upstairs and looked in the mirror, and yes she was right, my eyes were a pale aquamarine colour, but I did not know how this happened. How could I look so well and how could Ciara say that I had put on weight when I had just been through the most harrowing month of my life and had hardly eaten at all? It seemed that I could look older or younger, thinner or fatter, just by thinking about it. It was mind-blowing. Thought creates … After being with Ciara and looking at myself in the mirror – I knew I was tapping into something very powerful but I had no idea of the mechanics of what actually made me look fatter or thinner or how my eyes changed colour.

Before Easter, when I was tired, I would look and feel awful. Now, even when I had only had three or four hours sleep, I was full of energy. Where was it all coming from?

During the previous few weeks some friends had given me hands-on healing, while others, including Dr John Briffa, Bob Jacobs and Richard Lawrence, had all given me lots of advice on what to do. But now the journalist in me demanded some kind of rational explanation.

In February I had interviewed scientist, Dr Serena Roney- Dougal, who has a PhD in Parapsychology, a Bsc Hons in Psychology from University College London and 25 years' experience of research into the power of the mind, telepathy, life after death and psychic phenomena. I remembered how her knowledge (and her book, *Where Science and Magic Meet*) had greatly impressed me and I had asked my editor if I could devote an entire page to her work – it was to have been entitled *The Meaning of Life* …

Now I decided I would go and see her, tell her my story and trust that she could suggest some rational explanations for everything that had happened to me. She agreed to see me three weeks later on 10th June at her research centre in Glastonbury.

In the meantime, following my resignation from the *Sunday Times*, I asked Lindsey to cancel all interviews that I had agreed to carry out for my column. There was no point in wasting people's time if I was not going to write about them. But two people wanted to meet me anyway, so on 20th May I went along to the Hale Clinic to meet the first, healer Kelvin Heard. We had never met or spoken before. Kelvin was pleasant enough but seemed to be looking all around me instead of at me, and I realized he was reading my energy field. He said, 'The spirit world apologize for what they have done to you, but I am here to help you.'

I smiled nervously …

Kelvin said there was a fantastic amount of energy or light coming into my body, and that the shock of what had happened to me had taken its toll. How could he have known? I was fascinated. It was one of those moments when you instantly 'gel' with someone. We both intuitively knew that there was a purpose for our meeting and yet I did not tell him my story. After all, we had only just met and I wasn't sure whether I could trust him or whether he might think I was crazy. As I lay on his couch feeling the warmth from his hands, Kelvin suddenly said, 'Spirit are saying you need to go to Australia, especially the Blue Mountains.'

Suddenly he had my undivided attention. Just one week earlier I had finally booked our flights to Sydney to see my daughter. When I asked Kelvin where the Blue Mountains were, even I was astonished when he said, 'Oh just a couple of hours' drive from Sydney.' Australia is a very large continent and the Blue Mountains could have been anywhere. Another coincidence? Why was I supposed to visit the Blue Mountains? My intuition told me I would be seeing more of Kelvin.

That evening Stuart and I went to friends for dinner and as I chatted with a well-known photographer I found that I could 'read' some of his thoughts. When I told him that I used to write for the *Sunday Times* I intuitively knew he was thinking, 'She only wants to know about all the famous people I have photographed.' OK, so I would only talk about him. The energy inside me grew stronger, my eyes began pulsing energy. He knew that something special was happening, but I was confusing him, so I stopped. I decided that from then on I would only pulse the energy into the eyes of people who understood what was happening.

I glimpsed a flash of light outside the window. At first I thought it was a camera flashing, since there was a hotel next door where lots of well-known people stay, but when the second and third flashes came I realized that there was an electrical storm right overhead. The energy inside my solar plexus seemed to accelerate whenever I was near a storm … I made a mental note to ask Serena about storms and their electrical energy.

That week, the Festival of Mind, Body and Spirit was taking place in London. I thought about what Kelvin had said about me, that I had a lot of light coming into my body. Perhaps if I had my aura photographed I might be able to see some tangible evidence of this light and so better understand what was happening. I could compare it to the one I had had taken earlier in the year (before Easter had now become BE and everything after that date was AE!).

I sat and stared at the camera and then waited to see the results. There were several specialists on the stand interpreting the photographs, but I was in no mood to be 'interpreted', I just wanted to see the picture. Finally, it was handed to me and I saw that the main colour surrounding me was purple, while on my left-hand side there was a mass of white light. As I was leaving one of the specialists pulled me aside saying, 'I need to see you, let me look at your picture.'

I felt almost hounded. Did I have a sign emblazoned across my forehead, saying 'I'm weird'? Yet I wanted to know why the young man had approached me, so I gave him the picture. He looked into my eyes and I didn't say a word, but he knew that I was special. 'Would you like to tell me what has happened?' He asked. 'Not really.' I replied. Then I succumbed to verbal diarrhoea. I told him that I had almost died over Easter and related how I had 'seen' another person's death through their own eyes. He smiled.

I didn't think it was very funny.

'You have had a walk-in,' he said matter of factly.

'A what?'

'A walk-in.'

'What's that?' I wanted to know.

'You have been possessed.'

We went for a cup of tea. His name was Anton Simma-Arjuna and he explained there are quite a few people experiencing 'walk ins' at this time. I wondered if that meant that hundreds of people were also hearing Diana. I had no idea. I felt extremely self-conscious chatting with this stranger and yet he wanted to be with me, and I knew why. He wanted to receive the energy pulsing through my eyes into his. I have heard the phrase 'seeing the light' many times in many situations, now I felt as though I was the light. The light was inside me and it was coming out through my eyes. And as I sat with him, I knew it was time to choose. I realized I could have power over people and it was time to examine my motives. I knew I had become a more fully conscious being with seemingly amazing powers – I simply hadn't yet figured out how to control these powers. My mind was still in turmoil but I knew that I was becoming some kind of a spiritual master.

The energy pulsing through me became so powerful during that afternoon, I felt that at any moment my solar plexus would burst into flames. I feel sure this is how spontaneous combustion might happen. Anton, a spiritual counsellor and qualified Ashtanga yoga teacher, said he could have stared into my eyes for hours. He recalled vividly the day we met when I saw him again in June 1999, saying, 'As soon as I saw your eyes I knew you were carrying a lot of light and your energy fields were extremely unstable. From the huge amounts of blue and purple in your aura photograph I knew you were experiencing an enormous influx of spirit. You were literally being washed with divine energy from the higher realms and the white-bluish glow on your left-hand side indicated even more incoming energy, showing me that you were receiving direct guidance and assistance from spirit. Your light told me that in that moment you were like a spiritual master, but your body and mind were having trouble processing the enormity of what you were experiencing, which is why I offered to help you. 'You believed that I wanted the energy from your eyes and I did, but in return I was trying to ground and anchor you with my eyes, to help prevent your spirit from leaving your body. You were on the verge of overload; your nervous system could no longer handle this level of divine current. You desperately needed help, but I knew that because I was a stranger you were too afraid to ask.'

But in that moment my solar plexus was spinning and my head was pounding. And as I sat pulsing the energy into Anton's eyes, another voice came into my head. 'I am Sananda – Lord of Light and Keeper of Time.' Now what?

It was time to go as I had to get to a meeting. I walked outside into torrential rain. We seemed to be having some very strange weather lately …

I took a cab across town to meet Diana Cooper, the UK's leading authority on angels. A pretty way-out subject to be an expert in, but after she talked about angels on TV's *Good Morning* with Richard and Judy, over 100,000 people jammed the switchboard wanting more information. Diana and I had met briefly at a health show that April and I had promised to write about her work in my column. When Lindsey had rung to cancel the interview Diana had said we should meet anyway.

Over coffee we chatted about guides, angels and the higher realms and I asked Diana about her own guides. She gave me several names that I had never heard of before, but then there are millions of guides – the same as there are millions of people on Earth. No one can know everyone, or everything. I asked her if she had ever heard the name 'Sananda' …

'Oh yes,' she smiled, 'that's the modern name for the spirit of Jesus.'

My mouth fell open …

My mobile phone rang. It was the Duchess of York's office – she had agreed to meet me for 30 minutes on the 4th June. Talk about everything happening at once.

I burst out laughing. This must be Princess Diana's way of keeping me on my toes. I had no idea what I would say to Sarah, but I had set something in motion and it was too late to pull out now.

My gut was on fire and my solar plexus was spinning out of control. I needed help, and quickly. I called Kelvin who sensed that something special was happening and said we must meet immediately. When we met Kelvin looked into my eyes and examined my energy field. He said the energy inside me had become so powerful that if I did not learn to control it, I could die.

I was already carrying two tectonic plates around with me, which helped to ground me and I had also eaten sugary food – what else could I do? Kelvin told me to start meditating as this would help to calm everything down. Meditation switches the brain from its normal beta (busy) state to an alpha state in which it can completely relax. Because the mind controls many bodily functions, meditation also helps to slow down the heart rate and lower blood pressure. I readily admitted that my mind craved silence, but that life kept getting in the way. I resolved to make more time for some solitude.

I am well aware that the brain is both a receiver and a transmitter and that when we are in a highly relaxed state it switches to an alpha state that makes it more receptive to subtle energies. But I had not meditated once during Easter and beyond. All the mediums I had met told me that to 'hear' other realms it was important to meditate.

In the days that followed I tried to work things out. I had become some kind of a medium as I had been able to hear Diana and my mother so clearly, but things had gone way beyond my simply being a medium – I was beginning to feel like some kind of spiritual master. But even having that thought seemed too ridiculous for words, and yet I knew it was true and Kelvin believed this too.

Kelvin also felt that I needed more specialist help and gave me the number of a woman in Australia called Meg who he said had a greater understanding of unusual spiritual happenings.

I needed to think clearly. If people travelled from all over the world to receive the light energy from living masters such as Mother Meera and Sai Baba – and I had heard Jesus, who was also a master – then I, too, must be carrying a divine energy.

It was this energy that was pulsing through my eyes.

Diana had said that she carried a special energy but had not realized this until she 'passed' into the next dimension. I thought of my trainer Al, and how he had seen a man with a beard overshadowing my body at Easter – Jesus – the son of God, so he also carried a lot of divine energy. The voice at Cliveden had said to me, 'I am God.'

That night when I finally sat down at my desk, quietly I whispered to the walls, 'Am I god too?' I needed answers. Eventually, I got through to Meg in Perth. It was time to trust. I told her my story to date, keeping it as short as I could. The phone began buzzing because I was so excited. Meg seemed to understand everything that was happening to me. She told me that Diana's unique frequency was sitting just under my heart, hence the reason for my solar plexus spinning out of control. She predicted that once I got used to and integrated the energies, the spinning would stop.

'And what about living spiritual masters?' I asked.

Meg said that they all have their own individual styles and ways of teaching, and that they have have access to 'all' knowledge from the highest spiritual levels. Most can appear and disappear at will and some can appear in many places at once. Some manifest ash through their hands, others work simply by pulsing the energy either through their eyes, or their hands. Some are born with an inner knowledge that they are masters, others become masters in later life.

Meg told me that masters are very special because they channel a huge amount of pure divine energy which they have integrated into their physical bodies. In other words, masters are in control of the energy, rather than, as in my case, the energy being in control of them. It is because they are in complete control of this perfect divine energy that they can effect physical miracles.

My mind was reeling from the implications of what I was hearing. 'And how many of these masters are there alive at this moment?' I asked. Meg said that there could be many masters but that she knew of only 12. She told me they are spread around the globe and that people would know them by their teachings, by the way they live their lives, and by their motives. She also warned me that there are many 'wolves in sheep's clothing', people who become masters to varying degrees but who abuse their powers.

Suddenly she asked, 'Who are you working for?'

Like an automaton I replied, 'I am of the light.'

What she said next astounded me.

'From all that you have told me, it is possible you could be number 13.'

The bulb in my desk lamp shattered, my computer crashed and the phone went dead.

'Calm down, calm down,' I shouted to myself. 'You can deal with this. Maybe Meg is wrong, maybe she's not, but you are still only Hazel. Just keep calm.'

But at that moment I really felt special. Thirteen has always been my lucky number… Eventually I called Meg back and over the following weeks we spoke quite a few times. She helped keep me sane in some of my darkest moments.

As the days passed, I changed a great deal. I had always felt like a 'light worker' or a 'musketeer' as Richard, John and I used to call ourselves and I knew I had been granted this experience for a greater purpose than simply saying I had heard Diana. For much of the time I felt as though I floated above everything, not literally; it was just that I felt more 'up there' than 'down here'. The only way I can express how I felt was that I had trouble remaining physical – all I wanted to do was become a being of light and float away. It was fantastically blissful. And when it came to speaking or dealing with others, I suddenly had untold patience.

The old Hazel had had very little patience at all. Everyone seemed so child-like to me – not in a patronizing way – I simply felt that most people were children who were half awake and half asleep. I judged no one. I gave advice that I knew would help, but it was up to the individual if they chose to take my advice. When people asked me questions, I already knew the answers. I seemed to possess incredible wisdom that went way beyond anything I have ever known or experienced. It was as if I had access to the wisdom of Solomon. I did not have to think about what I would say, wisdom just came through me, seemingly from nowhere.

Sometimes, I would ask a person, 'What do you think your purpose is?' And they would tell me this and that. But I was able to 'see' into their very souls and observe the truth. No one could lie to me, it was very powerful. I intuitively knew when to offer the pulsing through my eyes because I would be drawn to a person at a party or a gathering and so would discreetly take them aside and pulse the energy in silence.

Friends told me I looked different, that my eyes looked different, that I had a different aura about me. Some even said that my skin looked transparent and suggested I get some sun. I would just smile. I was automatically drawn to people who had an ailment and when I touched them I knew where their pain emanated from before they told me. I felt benevolent, powerful, authoritative – like some kind of super human, and yet unbelievably humble. I knew I had to share my light with others. That was all I wanted to do. Nothing else had any meaning for me any more. I ate because I knew this was necessary for my physical well being; I got dressed and put make-up on; I went out and did the jobs I needed to do as a wife. But I had no interest in these things. All I wanted to do was to sit somewhere, anywhere, in silence and pulse the light through my eyes to help people. But it was not meant to be.

The Universe and Diana had other plans in store for me.

# 9

# The Duchess

**I WAS DUE TO MEET THE** Duchess on 4th June and since I looked a total mess I went to see my hairdresser, who happens to be French. As he worked on my streaks I began speaking to him in French … He looked startled – he was not the only one. As I walked home, I thought maybe Diana had been helping me, although I had no idea whether she had spoken French. Then I was overcome by an absolute knowing that all knowledge is out there somewhere and somehow I had tapped into an incredible mind or memory bank that holds all knowledge from the beginning of time …

I went along to the Capitol Hotel in London to meet Sarah, the Duchess of York. It took enormous courage on my part to face Sarah and yet as I sat waiting for her, I felt so in charge, so on line, so powerful. I was aware that Sarah has a knowledge of spiritual issues, but the press have given her a rough ride and I knew she would be very wary. As far as Diana was concerned I was only being allowed to know what I needed to know in the moment that I needed to know it, and I had to trust that the right words would come. I could only tell Sarah the truth and trust that she would believe my story. I had heard nothing from Diana for some days but in my heart I felt that everything would work out. If she had got me this far, surely she would not abandon me now?

Sarah arrived in a rush, she was running late. She only had 15 minutes. OK, what did I need to see her about?

For a few seconds I was the old Hazel, I panicked and went blank. Then I took a deep breath and began.

I asked her, 'How do I look?'

The Duchess was taken aback, but said, 'You look fine.'

'Do you think I look any different from when we last met in February 1997 when I interviewed you for the *Sunday Times*?' I enquired.

'You look younger', she said in an exasperated tone, undoubtedly wondering where I was going with these seemingly stupid questions.

I explained that I was going to tell her about something; something special that had happened to me over Easter and I asked her to be patient. The energy began pulsing into me, and the more I spoke the stronger the energy became. To use up some of the energy that was spinning in through the top of my head and down into my solar plexus, I paced back and forth across the room and the words tumbled out like a dam bursting.

For about 20 minutes Sarah listened patiently. Then as I stood in front of her, she watched with incredulity as my face and manner changed. I knew I was being overshadowed. I felt so strong, as though I was capable of anything, and the voice/energy channelling through me became more authoritative. Diana wanted Charles and Sarah to become reconciled, saying that life is so short. She wished that she and Sarah had made up their petty differences before her death. She had watched Sarah visit her coffin in the chapel at St James Palace and had shared Sarah's grief – they had been such great friends and had come through so much together. The press had been eager to judge them both and they had both suffered tremendous anguish from so many harsh words.

They had both made mistakes but they had paid dearly for them. Diana wanted Sarah to give her sons a huge hug on her (Diana's) behalf. And as

Diana spoke through me, about her sons, the emotion became too intense to bear and tears poured down my cheeks. When I had first begun my story, Sarah had looked extremely sceptical, but as the voice spoke through me about the boys, Sarah too broke down.

Diana told me that Sarah had already received messages from her through another medium and Sarah confirmed this was indeed true. She told me to tell Sarah about the films *Fluke* and *Sabrina* which I had been instructed to watch over Easter. Sarah smiled through her tears and confirmed they had been great favourites. I realized Diana was trying to lighten our mood. She began talking about Kevin Costner and said she would have loved him to have been her bodyguard. It was too late now, but she hoped he might make a film of this book. Excuse me …? Now I was in shock.

Suddenly the telephone rang, which instantly disconnected my link with Diana. It was Sarah's secretary, telling her it was time to go as they were running late. Sarah asked what I wanted from her. My head was reeling, I had to force myself back into the room, back into the moment, back down to earth.

I had to think … I asked if she would be willing to introduce me to her publishers in New York because Diana had said I must go to America. Sarah knew what had happened in that room, she had known I was not acting or joking. She knew it was real. Sarah looked at me long and hard and said that she would make that call. As she left I sat and took a deep breath. If Sarah was willing to make the call, it meant she had believed me. I could not remember everything I had told her, but some things must have struck a chord, otherwise she would not have offered to help. My hands were shaking as I signed for the tea we had shared. Everything was happening so fast. Diana was cracking the whip at my heels.

She had already asked me to contact Prince Charles and I had written to my friend, Lord Feldman, who has contacts at the Palace, in the hope that he would act as a go-between and request a private meeting with the Prince of Wales. But Basil had said that unless I was willing to give a written statement of exactly why I wanted to see the Prince, the situation was fairly hopeless. I could hardly tell Basil the whole story, so I simply told him that something incredible had happened which had enormous implications for the future of the monarchy and that I needed to speak to the Prince personally. Basil said he would speak to the Prince at a garden party in July and promised to do what he could.

When I returned home to Birmingham that afternoon and switched on my computer to begin the book, the energy inside me was so powerful that it caused my computer to crash again. I needed to calm down. Diana was back: 'There could come a time when electricity will be of no further use. You can already see how your energy affects electrical equipment. The time is fast approaching when millions of people will begin to encounter some of what you have experienced, and electrical equipment could be rendered useless on an enormous scale. Hence the urgent need to write all this down, so that people will know what's happening. The changes now affecting you and the Earth can then become a gradual transition instead of a terrible and sudden shock.

'New energy sources will be found, ones that do not harm you or the planet. Many of these are already available but are being suppressed by large corporations who wish to continue earning huge profits instead of helping the Earth. I have told you that everything comes full circle – in cycles. Every 28 days there is a new moon and every 28 days women have their monthly cycle. Every 24 hours the Earth orbits around the sun and so on. But now a new cycle or circle is beginning. Breaking away from old ways of thinking and behaving will be very hard for many people and great events are being set in place to force you to re-think your lives. World changes have been coming in slowly – the changing weather patterns, the financial crashes, the violence, but with my death, this process has been accelerated. When you are forced by circumstances beyond your control to let go of something that is precious to you, you feel as though you are spiralling into chaos.

'Our "Intervention" in April caused you to leave the *Sunday Times*. You and your husband felt that your world was collapsing – and yet you are both all right. Now you know a little more of what human beings are capable of, and these abilities will help people in the future. From your chaotic experience has come order. Many people will predict that the end of the world is coming, but this is not so, unless of course some idiot goes off the deep end with their nuclear arsenal. Choices … try making more right choices.

'Each and every person has to do what they can to help clean up the mess. Millions are already thinking differently and this is helping to change consciousness. But the scales are not yet balanced, millions more must change and soon. Time is of the essence.'

But Diana had not given me any specific insights regarding the future, and yet she had said I would come to know these in time. I was ready and waiting to hear …

# 10 The Predictions

**ON 17TH JUNE I RETURNED** to the Hale Clinic to see my new friend Kelvin for more healing. I asked Kelvin when he had first begun to hear the higher realms. He told me that at the age of 24 he had contracted post-viral syndrome, also known as ME (*Myalgia encephalomyelitis*) and chronic fatigue syndrome, which had forced him to leave his job in the City of London. He was so debilitated that for almost two and half years he was bedridden. As a last resort he tried spiritual healing. The healer asked Kelvin what he would do once he became well, and Kelvin said he wanted to return to his job in the city, but the healer predicted that Kelvin should begin giving healing himself.

It's amazing how many people I have met who now practise as alternative practitioners. People from all walks of life, from bankers and lawyers to chefs, who after healing themselves or experiencing a traumatic event turned to alternative medicine and therapies, just as I had done. 'But when did you first begin to hear spirit?' I asked. Kelvin answered, 'In February 1995 I went to see a clairvoyant who told me I would play an important role in helping to raise people's awareness of healing. At the end of the reading she told me that one day I would be able to hear spirit.

Within four hours of that reading I could clearly see and hear people who were 'dead' in physical terms. If I had not visited that medium, I firmly believe I could have ended up in a mental home. Instead, after training for two years, I began working as a healer – and in the process my own health returned to normal.'

I still had not felt able to share everything that had happened to me with Kelvin and I certainly had not mentioned Diana's name. But as I walked into the Hale Clinic her voice returned, 'People who work for the light are like a huge team, and you are being brought together to help move new energies around the world. Until now you have for the most part worked alone, but over Easter you needed your friends. We all need help now and again. You and many others like you agreed to carry more light before you entered this lifetime and now you are becoming like a special task force. A light frequency is being beamed to Earth and we need as many people as possible to anchor and hold the light before it can do its work. You must become keepers of the light ...'

For almost ten years my neighbour Norma had begun our meditations by asking me to imagine that a beam of white light was entering through the top of my head. She said that the more light we could hold the more we would be able to 'hear' spirit and open our intuitive sixth sense. As I sat with Kelvin I felt as though my whole body was made of pure white light and I began to feel very 'light' again, as if I might simply float away. I felt myself gripping my chair.

Diana's voice returned, 'We want to change the way people think. We want them to know that there are six billion people on Earth who think trillions of thoughts every day. Thought is energy, thought creates ... and if you can change the majority of your negative thoughts to positive ones, then the health of the planet and the people on it will improve dramatically. Positive thoughts and actions have the ability to change all your futures.' As I sat with Kelvin, I could see that he was 'reading' my aura again and as I watched, his eyes grew wider and wider. He beamed triumphantly and said,

'You are never going to believe who is standing behind you.'

I had a fair idea – but remained silent.

'My God,' he cried, 'it's Diana, Princess of Wales'. I caught my breath. Was I at last to 'see' her as Kelvin could? I was incredibly nervous as I slowly turned around, but I could see nothing. Yet Kelvin could not have known about Easter, only I knew the whole story. Neither Lindsey, John nor my husband had ever met Kelvin. I now felt that I could trust him and so told him more about Easter and about how Diana had promised I would come to know about certain world events that she had said were set in stone but I had heard nothing specific.

'This is incredible,' said Kelvin. 'Yesterday I channelled many predictions from the spirit realms about what's coming,' and he laid out a huge map of the world on his therapy couch. Another coincidence! Diana's voice was back, 'On Earth you wish for things to happen and then you try to "make" them happen. But when you let go of the "where and when", if whatever you wish for is right for you, it will come, often when you least expect it.'

No kidding …

She continued, 'You are already aware of a few of your possible futures. There are many who are already working for change but your numbers need to be increased. Talk is cheap.'

Diana was obviously fed up with people who said they would do things. She was more interested in the people who were actually 'doing' and therefore making a difference.

Just after Easter, she predicted chaos in Russia and floods in Bangladesh, and of course these events happened. She also warned that insurance companies and national economies could collapse if we stayed on our present course. Cause and effect. It is well known that corrupt dictators and governments are stealing huge sums of money that should be directed into helping their fellow countrymen. This will all come back to haunt us. We must now begin thinking in global terms rather than thinking of 'them and us.'

Diana continued, 'The weather is only part of the awakening process, for the moment the changes will remain gradual, but they will become more persistent until you take notice and begin doing something about it. Also as a health writer you are acutely aware of just how much people could prevent and cure many of their illnesses by changing their diet and lifestyle. Well the Earth is alive too, and it desperately needs some help.'

I know, I know … the Earth has been abused for too long. Over the past 200 years it has been exposed to with more pollution than in the previous two million. Because we have not taken sufficient notice of the planet, it will go on reminding us until we all listen and start taking steps to protect it.

Diana interjected, 'When tidal waves, earthquakes and hurricanes hit, neither they, nor the man-made poisons that cover the planet, will differentiate between rich or poor, black or white, Moslem or Catholic.'

Every one of us is responsible – we can all make a contribution. A time is coming when profit can no longer be the only motivating factor.

We sure have a lot to consider don't we? Saving the planet, our home, is a big job – and yet we still go on fighting each other. We are just like children squabbling over who gets the biggest lollipop. Well it's time for us to grow up.

After everything that had happened to me, I suddenly felt more grown up, I felt as though I was thousands of years old and a man's voice inside my head said, 'You are …'

Kelvin could see I was far away and he gently brought me back into the moment, as he wanted me to look at his map. He said, 'As things stand now, some of these events are, as you say, set in stone, whilst others are only probable futures. The higher realms say that it will take a huge shift in the way we think to stop these events, but we all have the freedom to choose, act and decide …

'The strange weather patterns continued this year with the ice storms in Canada, and the bombs in Pakistan could have triggered the earthquakes in

Afghanistan. There is already terrible pollution in Asia, Indonesia, the Philippines and Thailand, much of it caused by last year's forest fires. But unless urgent steps are taken to clean up these regions by the year 2006, hundreds of thousands will have died from conditions associated with the lungs and cancers. This will all contribute to more financial crashes.

'If we stay on our present course, there will be civil war in Africa, and massive unrest when a world leader in South Africa dies. In October/ November 2002, Nigeria and Ethiopia will be hit by severe drought – as will many other African states. These countries must stop the fighting or millions will perish. Extreme storms will hit the east and west coasts of America between 2002–2004 and many grain harvests could be wiped out by insects that are mutating as a result of genetic engineering and overuse of chemicals.'

I kept being reminded that we have all contributed to what is happening and we can change these futures if we act very quickly. As Kelvin continued to speak, it seemed as though no one would be left unscathed …

'In 2005, a possible evacuation could occur in China, along with civil unrest. This might be due to a nuclear leak. There is a nuclear plant hidden under Beijing and there will be an earthquake which could trigger a nuclear accident. In the UK there have been severe radiation leaks at Aldermaston already but the public are not being told the truth.'

I heard that one before about BSE …

Diana was back, 'Perhaps you can begin to understand the urgency of the situation, many scientists and environmentalists have been sounding the alarm bells for years – now it is truly time to listen.'

Kelvin also warned of a huge refugee crisis in Europe before the millennium. When I heard this in 1998, it sounded crazy and yet a year later one million people have been displaced by conflict in the former Yugoslavia, and so the madness goes on. Kelvin also predicted a possible pole shift in 2010.

As Kelvin continued with his predictions, I asked Diana if these events are set in stone.'Some of them are, unless of course you all choose to change and take action overnight. If you don't heed the many warnings that are being given around the globe, then the pole shift could happen. It is incredibly sad, but it seems from here that when a few thousand people are killed in an earthquake or flood you don't take much notice. Only if millions were to die in a few days would you really sit up.'

A pole shift occurs when the axis of the North and South Poles moves, by as much as 180 degrees. Weeks later I unearthed some research on possible triggers for a pole shift. In 1986, the President of Japan's Tokai University along with Yoshio Kato, head of the Universities Department of Aerospace, concluded in a joint published paper that: 'Abnormal meteorological phenomena, earthquakes and fluctuations of the Earth's axis are related in a direct cause and effect to testing nuclear devices. Nuclear testing is the cause of abnormal polar motion by the Earth. By applying the dates of nuclear tests with a force of more than 150 kilotons, we found it obvious that the position of the pole slid radically at the time of the nuclear explosions ... Some of the sudden changes measured up to one metre in distance.'

Scientists have different opinions as to what might trigger a pole shift but many believe that one occurred around 10,000 years ago. In his book *Pole Shift*, John White tells of the hundreds of thousands of animal carcasses found in Alaska. The stomach contents of these animals were so deeply frozen that scientists could have thawed and eaten them – yet many of the carcasses were 10,000 years old! He goes on to say that the food found in their stomachs came from a temperate climate and yet they had been frozen solid within six hours of eating their food, which was not fully digested. So one minute they were eating in relative warmth and within a few hours they were dead and buried under mountains of ice. One theory is that this may have been caused by a pole shift ...

If a pole shift were to occur today, we would be in deep trouble. Enormous tidal waves would roll across continents as oceans became displaced from their basins. Electrical storms with winds in excess of 100 miles per hour would sweep the globe. Volcanoes would erupt, their lava burying entire cities. Climates would change instantly. Not a scenario we would want to invite. Diana said that our transition could be gradual or cataclysmic. She is serious. More importantly she said that this predicted pole shift could be stopped – by the way we think, behave and act, we can change our world.

Many months later I met Professor Bill McGuire, a scientist who heads research at the Benfield Greg Hazard Research Centre at University College, London. I wanted to try and verify some of Kelvin's predictions. Professor McGuire stated, 'As far as I know there is no consensus of opinion that the Earth has ever undergone an instantaneous shift on its axis. The magnetic poles switch sometimes, the last time was 700,000 years ago. We can measure the magnetism in rocks and we know there were no mass extinctions at that time.

'Regarding the weather, it is thought that through our actions – mainly emissions of carbon dioxide from burning coal and forests, emissions from power stations, cars and vehicles – the Earth's temperatures are indeed warming. We are already seeing more weather extremes, and we will see more hurricanes, droughts, floods and temperature extremes. The ice caps at the Poles are beginning to melt and they hold sufficient water to raise global sea levels by as much as 65 metres, but we don't know how fast they are going to melt.' (For more information see page 272.)

Professor McGuire believes that the effects of global warming could be reversed but that it would take at least 50 years before any improvement could be felt, and that's if all carbon dioxide emissions could be substantially reduced today …

As I listened to Bill, I thought about the 4.5 tons of carbon monoxide being produced annually by cars in Britain alone. And how, during school holidays, asthma attacks are significantly reduced as there are fewer cars on the road. Research from Holland shows that asthma attacks and breathing difficulties are 139 per cent more likely to occur when pollution from motor vehicles is at high levels. We either need to cut down the number of vehicles on the road, or we need to build environmentally friendly cars.

Scientists have forecast that within 50 years a man's average weight will increase by 20 pounds to 14 stone and a woman's, by 17 pounds, to just over 12 stone. Thanks to new labour-saving devices we already do a third less exercise than we did a generation ago. In 1998 the National Health Service announced that heart disease was Britain's biggest killer, costing the NHS £10 billion annually. If children could be encouraged to walk whenever practical, perhaps to and from school in groups, there would be fewer cars on the road. Fewer cars, cleaner air, and healthier children who would find it easier to breathe and have a reduced risk of heart disease in later life. It's all a chain reaction and we can change our futures ...

To many people, all these problems seem too huge and remote, and yet if we could just become more aware, every one of us could make a contribution, and others would be inspired and take notice. Everyone can help. Diana was only one person and yet three billion people took a great deal of notice when she died. Diana chirped up again, 'As I have already told you, my death was meant to bring feelings to the surface – and it did for a time ... Bob Geldof's Live Aid did too ... but we need a general raising of consciousness all the time.'

How short are our memories. One week a big story is in every newspaper every day and the next it becomes boring and is dropped. Months later someone will say, 'Remember so and so and that awful scandal', and you think, 'Oh yes ... I wonder what happened to them? ... I haven't heard of them lately.' Out of sight out of mind.

As I walked home from the Hale Clinic I thought about that terrible week after Diana died. But on a higher level I now realize it wasn't so terrible.

Yes, she had died tragically, but we saw strangers chatting openly and sharing their feelings. There was a sense of caring and sharing and compassion. Doctors even reported less sickness that week, especially from stress-related conditions. They said this was because people who usually bottle up their emotions, which can eventually trigger numerous health problems such as heart attacks, strokes, stomach ulcers and so on, were releasing them by crying openly and sharing their feelings.

There were fewer burglaries and muggings. We also saw people power. When sufficient numbers of people joined together and made their feelings known about the lack of a flag at Buckingham Palace, and the lack of Royals in London, the powers-that-be eventually bowed to accumulating public pressure. It shows that when enough of us care enough about something, together we can bring about change.

In the spring and summer of '99, there was a similar outcry against genetically modified foods, which I pray will continue …

In the aftermath of Diana's death, many of us stopped thinking of ourselves, and instead thought of Diana and what she had achieved. We were thinking of something other than our own problems and our own lives. We hugged each other more and appreciated each other more, and she loved that. And the events of that week certainly made most people think … I imagine it must have been the same during both World Wars, that people would have come together to share, to cry, to pray for an end to their nightmare … So why is it that we are not learning from our experiences?

'Absolutely,' Diana's voice was back. 'This is one of our aims, to try and recreate that feeling of friendship and joining together all over the world, but without the need for such devastation. There are far more good people in the world than bad, but a few control the majority. Unfortunately, we see that more and more people are thinking, "The world is going crazy – where will it all end?" And if enough people think this way that is exactly what will happen – more craziness.

'It is vital that anyone who cares about their own health and that of the planet should begin to think more positively and take positive action, then the world will change for the better. You could all be happy, healthy and well-fed and you could even have the money you need. But at this moment, the scales are badly out of balance, and only you, every one of you can bring them back into line.

'The feelings that were vented after my death and the deaths of John Lennon, Martin Luther King, Mother Teresa and President Kennedy were mostly positive emotions of love and caring, and these need to continue all the time. You don't have to die for your dreams to come true, but if you do not listen millions could die.'

This statement reminded me of a vivid dream I had almost ten years ago; I was in San Francisco and had been shopping all day. My hotel room was full of goodies and I was in heaven. Then the room began to shake and I stood under a steel door frame in the hope it might protect me from the earthquake. But the building started crashing around me. I watched as all my shopping fell through the floor, suddenly owning 'material goods' lost all meaning. I watched in horror as my husband and daughter fell into the void. I screamed, and as my moment came and I fell to my death, the last thought that went through my mind was 'all that really matters is love, nothing else matters – nothing' and then I woke up in a terrible sweat.

Would my dream now come true, all this doom and gloom. What about some good news, Diana?

'Remember cause and effect, you can choose', she answered. It's not too late. Some things are set in stone, but you can repair some of the damage if you act quickly. We still want you to have fun, because laughter helps to raise the vibratory rate on the planet and you can still shop, but think before you buy. Has a child, an animal or the planet been harmed needlessly in the making of what you buy. Buy consciously ...' I pictured the new clothes, handbags and shoes in my wardrobe. Did I really need so many? I thought about the millions of newspapers and magazines we read every day and the huge amounts of junk mail that the majority of us simply throw in the bin. All those trees. I realized that most newspaper organizations make sure trees are replanted to sustain the natural balance, but many other forests are being burned down deliberately to clear land for farming. And what about cosmetic and food packaging, bin liners, plastics and disposable nappies?

All the stuff that we throw away. Where does it all go? Mainly to incinerators that emit toxic chemicals such as dioxins. And these persistent chemicals fall on the Earth and enter the food chain, and more cancers and mutations appear in animals and humans ...

I vowed to do what I could to reduce this terrible load; before we moved I would make sure that I gave away everything I no longer needed. I would re-use plastic bags, I would flush the loo less ... Every one of us can make a difference: all we have to do is to become more aware and then make a start.

Meanwhile life began to get back to normal.

On 8th June Stuart and I attended a charity concert organized by Cameron MacIntosh to benefit the blind. Our hosts rang on that day to say, 'Don't forget Stuart has to wear black tie' and when I asked why, they said, 'Because the Queen and Prince Philip will be there.'

Diana had said I would see the Queen. I laughed. That evening, as the Queen entered the theatre I felt a surge of emotion in my chest. Diana was saying, 'I did not hate my mother-in-law, who was always gracious towards me, but there was never any real warmth between us. She has done an incredible job for her country but she was brought up with very rigid protocols and I did not agree with a lot of the things she said and did.

'Millions of daughters-in-law know just what I mean ... and we certainly had a few tense and frosty moments. Emotions were always supposed to be kept private and I rocked the boat rather badly.'

At the time of her divorce, Diana felt that to strip her of her title, HRH, was spiteful. Now, she realizes that titles don't make a person, it's what they do that counts. Diana made light of this incident, but deep down it hurt her very badly. However, she is pleased that her death has encouraged the monarchy to be a more 'feeling' institution.

She said she would love it if they would treat Sarah, Duchess of York more kindly, especially at Christmas. Diana said she humiliated Sarah (she would not tell me how, where or why) and now only feels remorse as Sarah was, 'More like a sister to me at times than my own sisters.'

At times Diana used very colourful language but it was strange because as the weeks passed, whenever her comments became too personal or irritable, communication between us was 'cut off'. It was as if some 'higher' force only wanted the important information to get through – I was to find out why very shortly …

# 11

# The Scientist

*9th June – Glastonbury*

**ON 9TH JUNE, THE DAY** before our early meeting with scientist Dr Serena Roney-Dougal, Lindsey and I travelled down to Glastonbury. As we wandered around the ancient town, I read in one bookshop of a legend that the young Jesus had once visited Glastonbury with his parents. Such tales encourage more visitors and the town was thronging with Americans, Japanese and hippies from around the world.

We walked up the Tor and around the town, stopping at the Holy Well to drink the iron-rich, red-coloured spring water that runs down from the Tor. As I sat in the magical Holy Well garden listening to the birds, a softly spoken man's voice echoed in my head, 'I did not visit Glastonbury but my brother and son did. I did not die on the cross, I lived a full life, I married and had children of my own. I, too, was only human.'

Now I claim nothing and can only tell you what I heard. The voice continued, 'There is plenty of proof for those with eyes to see and ears to hear.'

'And where would I find this proof?' I asked.

'In the Vatican vaults, and in ancient scrolls that are now becoming more widely available. Much of the information in your Bibles and holy books is incorrect and much has been misinterpreted. Many religious scripts were rewritten by men who wanted power and wished to control others. They removed much important information because they did not want you to know the truth, which has remained cleverly hidden for centuries. Some so-called 'holy men' had their own agenda, which was to prevent humanity knowing the truth about how powerful you all are.

'In this way you have been controlled like sheep. Over the centuries we have watched with great dismay as millions have been slaughtered in my and other's names. So many of you are imprisoned by religious teachings that are all too often taken literally. Many stories in holy books and manuscripts are more symbolic than strictly truthful and some contain important codes for those who are ready to understand certain ultimate truths.

'One day, humans will come to know the ultimate truth and there will be great confusion when you finally realize just how much of your so-called "true" history is false.'

I have never been a 'bible basher' and I am not affiliated to any religion or sect. I find people who try and ram their religion down other peoples' throats rather irritating. We all have to find our own truth. As I listened to the voice, the information 'felt' correct and incredibly profound. Lindsey sat quietly looking up at the sun with her eyes closed – she looked totally at peace.

So, I asked the man, 'Are you really the spirit called Sananda, or are you Jesus? Why have you got two names if you are the same person?'

I looked at the people walking past me in the park, wondering how they might react if they knew who I was talking to … I too closed my eyes, looked up at the sun and waited for an answer. It only took a few seconds. 'You are not so much connecting with the spirit of a single man, you are connected to the consciousness that I and many other masters represented and channelled through us when we were in a physical body. Sananda and Jesus are one and the same, it's just that you like to give everything and everyone a title or a name. It is hard for you to think of us in bigger terms and we concluded a change of name might help to bring our original teachings up to date.'

This was amazing and he continued, 'Do not concern yourself with understanding all realities – simply listen.'

I shut up.

'Again I say many truths are being hidden from you. On Earth when I came as Jesus I was special. I was one of the lucky ones who became enlightened but you can all be like I was: you can all be special. I was whole – you now call this "Holy" – but you all have the ability to be whole.'

Well, I would leave all that to the scholars. The last thing I wanted to do was to get into a heavy religious debate, I already had enough on my plate. The voice faded, but as it did so I 'saw' a white rose in my mind's eye, and the voice whispered, 'The English Rose is working with us in the higher realms. You cannot comprehend it now, but she has saved your life.'

'How?' I asked – but the voice was gone …

The next morning as I pondered the enormity of what I had heard the phone in my room interrupted my thoughts. It was the Duchess of York's secretary. Sarah had kept her promise and called her publishers, who had agreed to see me in New York on 23rd June, the day after we were due to move from our Birmingham home.

Stuart probably wouldn't be pleased because of the chaos we would be in, but as Sarah was also going to be in New York on that day, it was time to put up or shut up. I made up my mind to go. But I had not written a single word and it was already 10th June. Everything was happening so fast. Diana was driving me onwards.

Meanwhile I hoped that Serena would have some answers. She and Lindsey listened patiently for over an hour while I told my story. When I finally finished I broke down; it was such a relief to tell the whole story to people who appeared to understand. Serena gave me a big hug and congratulated me on coming through my ordeal saying: 'It's all right, you have done well.' I was taken aback and asked, 'Do you mean you have seen others like me?'

'Not in the flesh,' she replied, 'but I have heard of cases similar to yours.' Hearing this made me feel almost normal again and it was great to discover that there were others in the same situation. But I wanted to know how they coped.

Serena smiled and said, 'Sometimes when the experience is spontaneous as yours was in Harrods, it literally blows people's minds and can prove fatal. Many end up in psychiatric homes or hospitals.'

'So, what happened to me?' I asked.

'You have had an incredible experience. Every experience is valid. The explanations we put on that experience depend on the person and the culture they come from. In the West some people might say you had gone crazy, some that you had suffered a nervous breakdown. Others would say that you had become a medium and that you had connected with the spirit of Diana and that she was speaking through you. In tribal Indian cultures they would say that you had undergone a Shamanic initiation; that you had walked between worlds, connected with spirit, and come back into this world. The problem is that your experience has been so huge that there could be 50,000 different explanations or realities for it.'

I felt as though I had been through every one of them during the previous few weeks. Serena said she would give me various explanations to help me to understand. 'Let's begin with a typical near-death experience. Someone is on an operating table, everything is going wrong and the surgeons are losing them. At this point of near-death, the person steps out of their physical body and sees the mess below them on the table. The person can see and hear the doctors but no longer has eyes or ears in the physical sense.

'Some people then decide to leave the dreadful scene in front of them and go off down some kind of tunnel. Almost everyone who has had this type of experience tells a similar story; they pass into another reality which they describe as being blissful, peaceful, joyful and they don't want to leave it because it feels like home. Often they meet relatives and friends who they knew in their earthly physical life. Then they are told, 'Sorry, you cannot stay, you have to go back,' and before they know it these people are back in their hospital beds being fussed over.

'From the huge number of documented cases, we now know that the conscious "me" or mind can look back on the physical body, but is separated from it. The essence of a person is able to leave the physical body and go on to experience other realities or realms.'

'In other words,' I said, 'when I "witnessed" the car crash in Paris I did not see through my physical eyes which were closed, but a part of my mind that can see other realms?'

'That is correct', Serena answered. 'The mind can be anywhere. I am sitting here with you, but I can close my eyes and "see" a place that I visited ten years ago, as clearly as if I am actually there. An out-of-body experience usually occurs when the person's physical body is in a half resting state, but the person's mind experiences being in another place and is able to see, hear and feel what is going on at that other place.'

This sounded rather like remote viewing, which is when a highly trained psychic is able to close their eyes and in their 'mind's eye' travel to specific destinations and 'pick up' specific information about what is happening in those places. This phenomena has been well researched and practised in America, Russia and Israel by intelligence agencies. Remote viewers are asked to concentrate on secret installations and to remember what they 'see'. When they bring their mind back into the room, they are able to give incredibly accurate details of these sights.

But in my case I had been in bed and therefore I presumed I underwent a spontaneous out-of-body experience? Serena told us that research has shown that approximately one in five people will have an out-of-body experience at some point in their lives.

So if there is a part of us, the conscious 'me' that goes on, how do people who are physically dead 'see' themselves – as Diana had told me she had seen herself on the operating table.

In his book *Recovering The Soul* Larry Dossey tells the story of a patient called Sarah who 'wakes' when her heart stops during a gall bladder operation. Later she could recall 'a clear, detailed memory of the frantic conversation of the surgeons and nurses during her cardiac arrest; she knew the operating room layout, the scribbles on the surgery schedule board; and she even noticed that the anaesthetist was wearing odd socks'.

There are hundreds of such cases documenting the resuscitation of clinically dead patients who are able to recall these types of details, but the difference in Sarah's case is that she had been blind from birth … I thought about this and asked Serena, 'So, did I see the crash scene in my mind's eye or had the conscious "me" left my body as in an out-of-body experience?'

Serena smiled at my deduction, 'In your case it could have been either. The mind's eye is often called second sight which is related to our 'third eye'. Research suggests that this 'third eye' has a physical location in the pineal gland, a pine cone-shaped gland situated neither in the left nor the right hemisphere of the brain and yet in the centre of the two.

'Descartes, the French philosopher, called the pineal gland the seat of the soul and we now know this is a very important gland indeed. It produces two very important chemicals within the brain called melatonin and serotonin. If a person is under a great deal of stress this can trigger an imbalance in the production of these chemicals, which can lead to depression, seasonal affective disorder and manic depression. But the pineal gland also makes pinoline, a chemical which is thought to be involved in our dream experiences every night.

'Excessive stress has been known to trigger experiences that are similar to waking dreams.

I consider that there are some dreams that become out-of-body experiences in certain people, especially those who are psychic. Amazonian Indians use a plant extract called *Ayahuasca*, which has a similar structure to pinoline, to induce various spiritual states of heightened awareness.'

But I had not taken any mind-altering drugs. I thought I must have had an out-of-body experience during the early hours of Easter Saturday and a near-death experience on Easter Saturday afternoon, because I had been shaken awake moments before I 'saw' the crash, so I had definitely not been dreaming.

But what was Serena's opinion? 'Your entire experience seems to have been a culmination of many factors and in my opinion you have had what is known as a Shamanic initiation. In Native American culture a Shaman is a revered medicine man or prophet who can move between realities. Dreams, out-of-body experiences, psychedelic experiences and Shamanic initiation are all different aspects of the same basic process and they are all interrelated. These experiences usually happen to young people, often in their teens or early twenties, but can come later. The person becomes incredibly ill, to the point where they may almost die or even appear to be dead for a short time.'

This is exactly how I remembered Easter Saturday: somehow I felt I had passed from this world into another, and come back again. I remembered John's tears as he sat by my bedside and wondered how people are normally treated when they go through this type of occurrence?

'If it happens within a tribal culture then the person is nurtured and looked after by the whole community. Only in the West is this type of experience thought of as a sickness, and it is usually labelled as schizophrenia, a nervous breakdown or manic depression. In most other cultures it is seen as a major transformation or initiation. After it is all over, some are chosen to become a Shaman's apprentice. The training takes many years, sometimes as long as 20 years during which time they learn how to hold the energy, so that they can move out of their bodies at will, which takes great skill and much practice.

There are many people in the West, especially men, who are now claiming to be shamans or spiritual masters, but the majority are not. Others who have undergone similar experiences to yourself become aware of all they are capable of – the clairvoyance, the healing and seeing auras – and their egos begin to take over. This is when it can become dangerous. They go too far, too fast, without proper training, and either the mind or the physical body breaks down. Some go mad, while others suffer physical symptoms, such as a heart attacks or strokes.'

As I sat taping Serena's words, I was suddenly reminded of the tapes I had made over Easter and recalled that I had believed something weird was happening to time. When I spoke with John Briffa or Lindsey I kept demanding, 'How long do you think we have been speaking?' and they would say ten minutes or whatever, but when we looked at the clock, 30 minutes had passed. I asked Serena to check the tapes in case anything had happened to time during the incident.

It transpired they were normal, but Serena said, 'Einstein explained time very succinctly. Time is relative because an hour spent with someone you really want to be with seems like ten minutes, but an hour sitting on a hot stove would feel like a lifetime. Time is actually very elastic. If you had a twin sister and she stayed on Earth, and you went off in a rocket travelling half the speed of light, 93,000 miles per second, your time would slow down immensely.

'When you returned, you would only have been gone for a week in your time, but your sister would be one and a half weeks older. If you travelled at the speed of light, 186,000 miles per second, no matter how long you were gone, you would not age at all. So if you were gone two years, your sister would be two years older, but you would be the same age as you were when you left.'

How fabulous, no longer to age …

As I thought about this the voice of Diana returned, 'Serena is right, in our dimension time is different. I have been here for many months and yet it only seems like a few weeks to me, just as during your experience you felt as though you had lived many lifetimes in only a few weeks. In the higher realms where great energies, angels and masters live, time does not exist as you know it. Here you can choose your age. When older people come over they are able to choose the age they wish to appear to others – once they realize they are free to make this change, they usually revert to how they looked in their prime.

'But if another relative comes over and they want to appear to that loved one as they did before they left Earth, they can. When babies and children come over they carry on 'growing' up just as they do on Earth, and they are loved and cared for by relatives on this side or by other helpers who are dedicated to children. It has been a great joy for me to discover this new reality and I still visit as many children as I can over here. Many who arrive suddenly after an unexpected accident or whatever are often impatient to go back, and they continue to grow until suitable 'parents' are found on Earth.

'Once it has been decided that someone is going back (re-incarnating) then the spirit can enter its new body either at conception, just prior to physical birth or it can enter its new 'body ' during the period between conception and actual physical birth. This is why we do not view physical death as being so terrible from here. We do not judge. When the child is re-born, some remember who they were in another life, others remember for a short time and then forget, and most eventually forget.

'But in the coming years more and more children will remember who they are and why they have chosen to return. You will have far more control over your own bodies through the power of your minds. You all have this capability, you just don't know it yet.'

I have long believed in re-incarnation, so most of this information came as no surprise.

When I asked Serena for her views, she told me that in America Professor Ian Stevenson at the University of Virginia Medical Centre, Charlottesville has done huge amounts of research with young children who remember previous lives. 'From his work we know that some children, once they begin talking fluently from around the age of two, have recall of other lives to the point where they give names and addresses of where they lived, which check out as being correct. These memories usually begin to fade when they reach eight or nine years old.'

I remembered a book by Roy Stemman entitled *Re-incarnation – True Cases from Around the World* (Piatkus), and recalled reading about a case that caught my attention, it stated that: 'Teenage rebellion is a well known social phenomenon in most societies, but in children who remember past lives a refusal to conform can occur a lot earlier, sometimes when they can barely speak. Imagine the distress Dilukshi caused when at the age of two, she refused to call her parents "mother" and "father". Instead, she insisted on addressing her mother as "clooche" which means "aunt" in Sri Lanka. She demanded to be taken to her "real" home in Dambulla, which was over 62 miles (100 kilometres) away.

'Her parents tried to dispel her "fantasy" but Dilukshi was adamant. She told them that she had once drowned in a river near Dambulla. Troubled by these persistent statements about a past life, they decided that the high priest of the Dambulla temple might be able to help, which he did. He told a feature writer, I. Abeypala, on Weekend newspaper, who gave the story maximum publicity. This was not as irresponsible as it may sound. It meant that there was a written and published record of Dilukshi's statements about her former life before any attempt was made to corroborate them.'

The story goes on to tell how a couple read the story which reminded them of their nine-year-old daughter Shiromi who had died in September 1983, one year before Dilukshi was born.

The reporter was present when the families met for the first time and he was astonished to see the little girl greet every member of her large 'old' family by name. The little girl went straight to her 'old' colouring book, which the parents had kept, and proceeded to complete a half-finished drawing. Dilukshi then led the entire group down to the river and told of a footbridge near where she had fallen into the river.

The footbridge had gone, but it had been there at the time of Shiromi's death. Now how could a two year-old have known so much?

# 12

# The Long Road Home

**MEANWHILE, MY NEW FOUND** capabilities were slowly disappearing. I was no longer creating the ash-like powder, nor was I telepathic, spirit bodies were no longer overshadowing me, nor could I see auras. When all these things had been happening I just wanted to be normal, but now these abilities had gone I desperately wanted them back … and as we sat in our hotel in Glastonbury overlooking a beautiful garden I asked Serena wistfully, 'Why have they gone?'

'Because to hold the energy and knowledge in the physical body you would need years of training. You are very unusual in the sense that you held the energy for over two months. Millions of people are now having spiritual experiences but mostly to a much lesser degree. Many scientists and people are at long last realizing we are much more than just a body and a mind – we are also spirit. One of the most popular ways of waking up the spirit within us is simply to sit and meditate every day.'

As Serena said this I knew that I was virtually back to square one again. I could still 'hear' the voices, but now the words had become more a feeling in my head than different specific voices all the time. I knew I would not be spending 20 years as anyone's apprentice, not in this lifetime anyway. It was as if the universe had given me an incredible 'taster' of what the human mind is capable of, and now I would have to go back to meditating – I felt crushed.

Serena continued, 'Sometimes when a person has a spontaneous "awakening", when they feel they have all knowledge, it is very fleeting – it might last 15 to 20 seconds or even several minutes. Some Eastern masters have spontaneous awakenings and are able to integrate the energy from day one, but this is very rare indeed, and they have usually trained for many years. Everyone's experience is unique. How someone copes with their experience also depends on the state of their general health, stress levels and brain chemistry.

'Many people have no help, and if they come from a broken home, have been abused or have taken drugs that alter the brain's chemistry, then this can prove a dangerous experience, because they sometimes hear a voice telling them to do damaging things. Basically, if the person is violent or aggressive before their awakening, then when they begin to hear voices, their underlying personality does not change. It is these people who can become dangerous.

'Look at how your experience affected your brain. Imagine what it would do to a person who is not happy or well-balanced and already has multiple problems, or is mentally disturbed ... The problem at this moment is that western orthodox medicine is simply not aware of spiritual emergencies. You have done well to hold the energy for as long as you have.

'Jesus did not become a master as such until his late twenties or early thirties, possibly after a lengthy training within the Essene community. Buddha meditated for many years before he became an enlightened soul. Even present-day masters, such as Sai Baba in Southern India who is now 73, has had to contend with his own parents and other villagers thinking he was possessed. Yet Sai Baba today and Jesus 2,000 years ago regularly taught that what they could do (which we call miracles) we all can do, and now you know this is true.'

She was right. I had certainly felt like some kind of a master for two months. I could feel the energy intensifying inside me as I asked Serena 'But am I a master still?'

Serena's smile was full of compassion – but she walked closer, held my shoulders and her manner became very serious as she looked deep into my eyes and said gently 'No, **you** are simply Hazel again. Do you understand ?'

I nodded meekly.

'If you could have been taken for training , yes, you might one day have become a master, but as you cannot control the energy, it could easily cause you to burn out'.

As she said this something inside me died. I could still hear spirit, the energy was still pulsing through my eyes, but in that moment it was as if the energy was turned right down, and my solar plexus stopped spinning.

'So where did the energy in my solar plexus and the pulsing energy that came through my eyes originate from? Is this the same energy that healers use?' I asked.

Serena replied, 'Perhaps the energy came into you from an external source and perhaps some of it was already inside you.'

'But where does it come from?' I persisted.

Serena looked philosophical, 'I don't know, these are questions that people have asked for thousands of years.' The man's voice that I had heard in the garden the previous day returned, 'The energy emanates from the beginning of time, it has always existed. Energy never dies – it is only transformed.'

I frowned. This subject was immense. I asked Serena about my eyes changing colour, the levitating, the ash appearing, my appearing younger at various times. 'Was there any scientific explanation for these phenomena?' I enquired.

'Sadly, none that I know of at this moment', she replied, 'although we are aware that people have these experiences. However, research into mediums has shown that when contacting the spirit of a dead person some people can take on the physical appearance of the person they are channelling, and are also reported as being able to speak with their voice.' 'What about the mothers I met and interviewed who 'saw' their dead children again?' I enquired.

'There is evidence to suggest that when someone dies, the energy that leaves the body can be seen and photographed as light energy. The same has been shown for out-of-body experiences,' replied Serena.

A pity I had not had a specialist camera ready on Easter Friday. But I remembered what the voice had said about every one of us emitting our own unique frequency – a frequency of light (spirit energy) which carries information – and I believe it is this part of us which goes on, allowing us to take our knowledge with us.

The man's voice returned, 'Always remember you are light energy encased in a physical shell.'

Back to energy. Electrical energy can harm and it can heal. Food can harm and heal. Everything has a good and bad side, and everything is a paradox.

'But what about my hearing Diana?' I asked.

'A good medium is able to put aside their own personality and go into a trance-like state. This enables the energy or essence of the person who has "died" to be "channelled" through to whomever is listening. Quite often, as in your case, the medium or channeller cannot remember everything that the spirit communicated while they were in trance,' said Serena.

As I listened I realized that to the average person all of this would sound too incredible for words. Many would be frightened by the word 'trance', thinking that in some way I might have been hypnotized, but Paul McKenna the hypnotist had once asked me, 'Have you not occasionally driven from A to B and not remembered the journey upon arrival?'

In fact, there were many times that this had occurred, and in other situations, too. For example, after doing my Jane Fonda exercise tape, I often had no recollection of carrying out the exercises once the tape had finished – my mind had been 'far away on other things'. Paul reminded me that these types of experiences are forms of trance.

I wondered if I would ever have absolute proof that I had heard Diana. Having personally received numerous messages from my mother via mediums which could have only come from her, I have a personal knowledge that life after death is a reality. But many people have no belief in any form of life after death, while millions of others remain sceptical. And yet there is such a huge body of evidence that our mind, or essence survives physical death, for those who care to read it with an open mind.

Research into mediumistic phenomena has been going on for 150 years. Serena told us about the work of Dr Alan Gauld, a psychologist based at Nottingham University, who has been fascinated with the concept of survival of the mind for many years. Months later I spoke with Dr Gauld. It transpired that in 1958, he had heard of a couple living in the Cambridge area. The wife was a medium and during weekly sittings held from 1937 until 1964 when they moved, the couple with various friends who joined them, received unusual and fascinating information from total strangers.

When a medium receives specific information and evidence that no one in the circle nor any of their relatives or friends have ever heard of, this is known as a 'drop-in' communication. When the couple eventually moved house they gave Dr Gauld hundreds of transcripts full of facts from their sittings and, most importantly, details of their 38 'drop-in' communicators. Over the next ten years Dr Gauld worked his way through their transcripts and through painstaking work managed to verify 11 of these unknown 'drop-in' communications.

Fourteen of the 'drop-ins' gave insufficient evidence for Dr Gauld to verify details as being correct, and 13 he termed 'wafflers'. Dr Gauld says he carried out very careful research in case the medium could have somehow read about these 'drop-ins' in local papers, but he found this extremely unlikely as most of the communicators were people who had not lived locally. After exhaustive research Dr Gauld was unable to locate any evidence that the 'drop-ins' could have previously been known to the medium.

In several cases Dr Gauld was only able to verify facts given by certain 'drop-ins' after eventually tracing their relatives. Dr Gauld said that all the cases he verified were amazing considering the messages came through a medium who could not previously have known of these people's existence.

He also told me about a spirit named Harry who had communicated between 1950 and 1952. Harry (I have omitted his surname to protect relatives who are still living) 'told' the circle that he had been a second lieutenant in the the Tyneside Scottish battalion of the Northumberland Fusiliers and that he had been killed on 14th July 1916. Dr Gauld verified his death from war office records but these stated that Harry had been in the Irish, not the Scottish, battalion.

However, when Dr Gauld checked further, it transpired that the information given by Harry to the circle was indeed correct, since just before his death Harry had been transferred to the Tyneside Scottish – a fact that had never found its way into the public records. Harry also supplied personal details and information about his university education that were later confirmed by relatives. There are hundreds of such reported cases every year, and anyone interested in Dr Gauld's research papers should see page 270.

Ever since Norma 'woke me up' to the concept of life after death nine years ago, I have received dozens of messages from friends who have 'passed over'. Some have been vague, others totally precise and exceptional. As I sat holding my mother's hand on 24th May 1991, praying for her to die after her six-month battle with cancer, she slipped into a coma – yet her eyes remained partially open. When she took her last, long breath while I held her tightly in my arms, I whispered to her to look for the light and a single tear fell down her cheek onto my arm.

Memories like that remain with you for a lifetime. I was alone in that room with my mother and yet a year later a medium related this incident, and how my mother had watched it from above her body. No one knew about that tear – only me. I remember a talk given by medium Stephen O'Brien in which he said, 'The last breath you take here is the first breath you take "over there".' And Diana had also told me this was true. She had also given me a considerable number of small personal details, but how would I ever verify them?

Meanwhile, in Glastonbury it was time to take a break. Serena showed us around the majestic ruins of Glastonbury Abbey and as we walked in the glorious sunshine, I heard the man's voice back in my head, saying: 'The English Rose was far more important than even you can realize at this time. She carried the ultimate Mother energy. For over 2,000 years the Earth has been dominated by male energy, but with permission from the highest source, many of us – male and female – in the higher realms have joined together to beam a new frequency to Earth.

'For too long many men have believed they are superior to woman – this is not so. You are all equal. This frequency will pulse through everyone, no one can avoid it, and as the months and years pass it will increase in intensity. It will act as a perfect balance of male and female energy and will cause gentle but noticeable changes. Some of you will have problems with your sexuality as the frequency pervades your bodies. It is important during these times not to judge a person's sexual preferences, there will be much confusion, but it will sort itself out in time.

'The Ultimate Source that you call God is not a man or a women, male or female, mother or father, it is a great consciousness or creative force that is beyond your comprehension at this time. You are all from one source and go back to one source.'

I sat in the abbey making notes while Lindsey and Serena chatted. Somehow, I had to think things through. Yes, Diana was a great mother and everyone knew how much she loved her boys. And Mother Teresa was a great mother and her 'children' were the sick and dying of Calcutta. But there are millions of other great mothers, and fathers too.

Diana was back: 'Don't try too hard to work things out, just accept what you have heard and find your own truth. But I agree that too many women have remained in the shadows and millions still suffer terrible oppression.

Many times I was made to feel inferior by the grey men, always men. But now I truly see that we are all equal, we are from the same source. The new energy being pulsed to Earth is made up from equal amounts of the two frequencies that represent pink and blue. Pink is for the female and blue for the male energy – they have been fused into one all powerful frequency of the colour purple.'

I smiled. Talk about coming full circle yet again. I thought of the purple flowers that I had given to Whoopi Goldberg. Purple is a powerful and indeed spiritual colour and is one of my favourite colours. I have also noticed how many people are having problems with their sexuality, but again there are many realities. Perhaps we place too much emphasis on sex. There is so much pressure on the young to decide what their preferences are and because many are confused we are now seeing more transsexuals.

You could also say that the millions of tons of hormone-disrupting chemicals from pesticides and herbicides that are being released into the atmosphere are adding to our problems. Cause and effect. You might also say that if a person has repeated lives as one sex, they may have difficulty in reincarnating as the opposite sex.

There really are so many realities. Back in April 1998, Diana had also predicted that men would one day be able to become pregnant and that we would evolve over the next few hundred years into more androgynous beings. I remembered laughing out loud at her statement: it seemed so ludicrous that I didn't even bother to add it to my notes. And yet in April of 1999, scientists stated that it was feasible for men to carry a foetus to full term before undergoing a Caesarean section.

Back in Glastonbury, after our walk we shared a pot of tea at the hotel and I continued to question Serena. 'What about the storms that seemed to turn up the energy inside me? Why can't we all see people who have died?' We laughed; once you begin on this subject you realize there are a million more questions you need to ask.

Serena continued, 'Diana is the same as anyone else who has died. She does not have a physical body any more, and this is a physical world. But many scientists like myself believe that light energy or electro-magnetic energy, is the halfway house between the mental, psychic and spiritual worlds, and the physical world. This is why when you see an apparition, or people see the Virgin Mary or whoever, what they usually see is a nebulous (unclear) light. There is a large body of evidence showing that these incidents appear to be connected to the Earth's magnetic field. When there is a thunderstorm – this electrostatic, lightning type energy, acts like a trigger, so you are more likely to have apparitional or visionary experiences during a storm, especially if you are a 'sensitive'.

'There are sacred sites all over the world, such as Glastonbury in the UK, Jerusalem in Israel and Delphi in Greece, that have this magnetic field energy to a greater extent. These are places where visions tend to appear, especially to children, who have more open minds, or to those who are sensitive to energies.'

And so, over Easter, was I right to eat the jam sandwiches that Norma had suggested? 'In a way yes,' said Serena, 'because junk food grounds you very quickly. But another good idea would have been to lay on the ground or hold onto a tree when you had the feelings of extreme lightness because this would also have brought you back down to Earth naturally.'

So instead of eating jam sandwiches and sitting on a tectonic plate I would have been better to lie on the lawn or hug trees … Oh well, I'll know better next time …

'So, death is not the final end that most people think it is?' I asked.

'No, death is an intimate part of life.' Serena replied. 'We are wrong to try and ward off death at any cost. If you look at plants, every winter they die in order to be re-born. Some plants are weak and die, while others are strong and survive. It is the same for us. Some people die young because things go wrong physically, or accidents happen, and we go back for re-cycling. The best evidence we have from research into mediumship, re-incarnation, out-of-body and near-death experiences, ghosts and hauntings suggests that we all go back into some kind of pool of consciousness.

'However, people who are reborn again very quickly with vivid memories of a previous life do not appear to have left the Earth's sphere. In the same way as a ghost or haunting, the spirit seems to hang around and then often return close to the original family or home, often within 20 miles. Generally, for 40 to 60 years after a person passes over, they can retain their own individuality, so your mum would be able to give you specific information that only you and she knew. She could talk to you through a medium or channeller, or you could tune in and talk to her yourself. After a certain amount of time the soul can then go on to join a huge pool of consciousness. When this happens the individual is then no longer a separate entity; the unique drop of the spirit energy merges with the whole.'

'So what you are really saying is that we really are all one?' I enquired with amazement.

'In essence, yes,' Serena answered, 'but there are still many realities. For instance, I am often asked, "How is it possible that so many people still see Roman soldiers on the Fosse Way after 2,000 years?" This is the spirit of an empire that still lives on. Yes, odd souls hang around the Earth plane for a long time and some are seen as ghosts if perhaps their deaths were shocking and they have not moved on into the world of spirit. But generally, people who die seem to move on into the larger pool of consciousness after two or three generations. This is why we are all everything – we all contain every aspect of the "whole".'

What she was saying was just too huge for me to take in, but I recalled an interview I had read with actress Demi Moore who had said, 'I somehow believe we are all one' and the interviewer had called her 'gloopy'. Well, I don't think she is gloopy at all.

Serena smiled and told us the following Sufi (a follower of a Muslim mystical sect) story to illustrate her point. 'A stream runs down from the mountains and through the meadows until it reaches a desert – then the water just sinks into the sand. It cannot get across the desert. So the sand says, "well go with the wind, wind can cross the desert". But the stream says, "No, I am water, I don't want to be part of the wind. I will lose my identity and I won't be water any more, I don't want to do that." In the end, the stream is persuaded as it realizes it has come to a dead end in the desert. The stream evaporates into the air and blows in the wind. It is no longer water. It crosses the desert in clouds and, because air has to rise to cross the mountains, so it becomes water again, falls as rain and the stream is born once more.'

As I sat with Serena I had a thousand questions running through my mind, and I wondered if Diana would ever be coming back. She replied instantly, 'Not for a while, as I want to watch over my boys and see them again one day.'

Meanwhile, everything that Serena had shared with us felt 'right' to me. Essentially, Serena agrees that we are all one as we all emanate from one source. I remembered Diana saying to me, 'that we are all everything,' and she would explain later.

Diana returned, 'Everyone has every aspect of the whole inside them, good and bad, light and dark, all knowledge is inside you. All you have to do is to connect to it, either through meditation or by doing good deeds. You now know a little more of what the human mind is capable of when it "wakes up" – and the more you all tap into the sleeping giant that lies dormant within you all, the more you will be able to achieve.

'I know it's hard for you to understand, but you are getting there. Think of it this way: the ultimate source that you term God is the whole pool of consciousness: it is also perfect. We all carry a spark of this divine energy or perfection inside us when we are born in a physical body and we never lose this link. Some people carry more of this light energy than others. I now know that I carried a lot of light, but I did not fully understand this concept while I was alive.

'Jesus carried a lot of it, so did Mother Teresa, so did Buddha and many others. Those who have an inner knowing of this are those who become special in other people's eyes. Now I am living in the light and watch as it is beamed back to Earth in order to open your minds. Light carries information.'

Mediums had always told me that it is easy to 'hear' someone who has passed over if you know how to tune into their frequency. Now I truly understood this reality. The part of us that comes in when we are born, our spirit, and leaves when the physical body dies, is a frequency of light.

'OK, so we all carry a part of God inside us?' I asked.

'Yes, yes, yes – you are part of God,' Diana said excitedly. 'I am part of God. Jesus was called the Son of God, but you are a daughter of God. And all of us together make God. We just don't fully comprehend this truth. We are all from one source – we go back to that one source.'

Over the years I had heard people such as Dr Deepak Chopra espousing the theory that we are all one and that God is within us all, but reading it and knowing it are totally different. I looked at Serena and Lindsey and flushed red, saying 'Does all this mean that I'm part of God too?'

Serena smiled and said. 'Yes, you've got it at last.' I could see and hear Diana and the man called Jesus in my mind's eye, and they were both clapping. Diana continued, 'All of you carry the light, and we are sending more. When you live your light by helping others, you receive more light and begin to "shine" in other people's eyes. All humanity needs to wake up the light within them and open their hearts to receiving more, then the world will truly change for the better.'

'And what is this light?' I wanted to know.

'It is the frequency of unconditional love, this is what God is,' replied Diana. 'Some people will think that what you say is mad, but it is the truth.'

'And have you seen this energy?' I asked.

'I have visited the highest realms and seen beings of great light. As I speak I am with the energy that was known as Jesus and I am in a heavenly place.' Diana answered. 'But when one enters the presence known as the Ultimate Source, the light is searing beyond your comprehension, human eyes would instantly be blinded. In fact, the divine frequency you were given in Harrods was 'toned down' by me. I was used like a transformer or conduit to lower the vibratory rate at which the energy entered your body, otherwise you could have died. You were filled with light, you became the light, you became an enlightened being. You know this to be true.'

I had certainly felt omnipotent, and above all I had felt as though I had come home after an incredibly long journey. I had felt full of love, healing and patience, and had an inner knowing beyond anything I could ever imagine learning from books. I had lived it, and it was an experience I would never forget. I had felt whole – holy. But it was not me as such, I was simply a vessel for the divine energy that pulsed through me.

Being 'ordinary' Hazel again felt boring beyond words and I knew that for the rest of this lifetime I would have to strive to attain even a tiny fraction of what I had been able to do and know for two months.

For weeks various voices had said, 'Everything is perfect.' Now I understood, truly understood that if we want to become as perfect as we can on a physical level, barring accidents (genetic or physical) over which we have little or no control, then we must choose.

I felt as though I too had now come full circle. I was back to being totally normal Hazel Courteney, health writer – and like millions of others I know why this Earth is not a perfect place. Because too few right choices are being made …

Then there's free will. The great majority of us have the freedom to choose. So if we continue eating too much junk food, using harmful chemicals in our homes and on our foods, depleting raw materials such as oil and trees and so on, then the world is never going to be perfect. It is the accumulation of all our actions that has caused the problems that we face today.

We are all one race, the human race and we all live on one planet. Earth is a living entity and we have got to change our attitude and stop taking it, and each other, for granted. Serena agreed, 'Research into psychosomatic medicine has shown that a person with a positive outlook is less likely to become sick and if they do become ill, they are more likely to recover more quickly because of their attitude.

'Conversely, people who are angry and negative are more likely to become ill. There is now no doubt that the way you think affects your health – the mind and body are one. You can hypnotize someone and tell them you are putting a lighted cigarette on their skin. The skin blisters but there is no cigarette. You can hypnotize someone and then operate on them and they feel no pain. There are also plenty of trials where patients are given placebo tablets instead of a real drug and some get better, because they believe they are taking some fantastic new drug that is making them well.

'How are these things possible? Through the power of the mind. Mainstream medicine and science is only just beginning to work in this area. New research suggests that if people believe 100 per cent with their conscious and subconscious mind that they will get well, for the most part they do. Miracles can and do happen. Now that you are back to normal you can spend the rest of your life knowing that you are capable of socalled miracles, and if you want to be able to do them again, you are going to have to meditate every day. Practice makes perfect …'

Right …

So there it was, I could have talked to Serena for days and it did not take many hours with her to realize that I if I were to write of every reality, this book would be many volumes thick. But now it was time to go home. For details of Serena's fascinating book see page 270.

# 13  The Journey Back to Chaos

**IN THE CAR ON MY WAY** back to Birmingham I mulled over everything Serena had shared with us. I recalled a comment that she had made about a good medium making a great bereavement counsellor. Then I thought of the angry letters I used to receive when I wrote about life after death, saying it was evil to speak to the dead. But we have been talking to Jesus for 2,000 years and that is not considered evil.

Four years earlier I had received a moving letter from an elderly man whose wife had passed away after 40 happy years of marriage. He wrote about how much he missed her and how he felt suicidal but was too afraid to kill himself. I rang him immediately and suggested he go to his local spiritualist church so they could give him the name of a reputable medium.

Several weeks later I received a second letter which was quite magical. The man had received specific information from his wife, even telling him where she had left her last shopping list, which he subsequently found exactly where the medium had said it would be. Via the medium his wife also congratulated him on the building work he had completed in their home. This 'sitting' gave him new hope because his wife had said she would be waiting for him when his time came and that meanwhile he should get on with his life. Three weeks later their daughter told him that she was expecting her first child. Suddenly, the man felt as though he might be useful again – he had a reason to live and was no longer afraid of death.

I realize there are good and bad mediums, and that some so called fortune tellers do more harm than good. But this goes for all walks of life.

When you go for a reading or sitting with a psychic, you soon know whether the information you are being given is correct or not. And always remember that 95 per cent of your future is not set in stone. For example, if someone foretells a car accident or an illness, by all means heed the warning by driving more carefully and taking precautions against illness by eating the right food and taking exercise – but don't invite unwanted situations into your life.

Don't 'magnetize' what you don't want … only what you do want and remember that your thoughts create – so be very careful what you wish for. In 1991, I remember whining to my housekeeper Sheila that I was fed up with commuting to London twice a week and how wonderful it would be just to live in one place for a few months. Three weeks later I slipped on ice, fell under a stationary train at Euston station and broke my knee, which soon put an end my commuting …

I was more careful with my thoughts after that. And yet the six months I spent on crutches gave me the time to visit my mum every day while she was dying of cancer. Initially I thought that breaking my knee was a tragedy, but it actually gave me precious time to sit and chat with Mum as she lay dying and in the last moments when I held her in my arms – I was able to say goodbye.

Yet again, everything had turned out for the best. We have to look back and see what we learn from situations or experiences so that we become wiser as a result … sometimes it may be hard but there is always another lesson to learn.

I had felt very despondent when saying goodbye to Serena as I was still desperate for irrevocable proof that I had truly been speaking to Diana, but the little voice in my head was laughing, 'You have still not learned to trust. When the moment comes, the information and help you seek will come. You are so impatient, you are like a child who wants to do everything at once. Patience was not one of my greatest virtues and it has certainly never been one of yours. We all come with a purpose and we come to learn various lessons, so for the moment, learn to be patient.'

I felt like screaming, 'But why don't you just give me some proof, and then everything will be perfect …'Yet I had realized some weeks earlier that Diana would only tell me what she wanted me to hear and no more.

As I sat in the back of the car speeding back to Birmingham, I wondered what I would say to Sarah's publisher in New York. Would they believe me?

On 12th June, as I sat at my desk ready to begin the book in preparation for my meeting in New York, I was 'told' to call Sarah again. The command came out of the blue and was so strong that I dialled Sarah's number. A man answered and since I thought it might be a butler, I asked when the Duchess would return, explaining that I wanted to send her a private fax.

The voice replied, 'This is the Duke of York speaking, and I can assure you your fax will be safe with me.'

I was so taken aback I said I would call back. As I put the phone down it was as if Diana was playing with me by offering me a one-off chance to speak to one man who might have helped me – Prince Charles's brother. But in that brief moment of opportunity I had panicked and said nothing. Now I wondered if I would ever have a private meeting with Prince Charles. Lord Feldman had already told me categorically that unless I could give a full written account as to why I needed to see the Prince, there would be little hope of my seeing him.

Yes, I had received minor private details, such as the fact that Prince Charles had received messages from his uncle, Lord Mountbatten, through a medium in Scotland but I knew he would never tell me if this was true or not. I knew how I came by information I had never previously known, but proving it to anyone else would not be easy. Even if I did meet Prince Charles and he believed my story, what could he do? He could never help with such a book. Cynics would say he had stopped talking to his plants and was now chatting with his dead wife … which would not really help his credibility. Oh well, I would leave it to fate.

On 14th June I received a fax from a friend in America asking if I was ever going to be on his 'side of the pond' would I care to come and present an overview of alternative medicine in the UK to a new taskforce at the University of Pennsylvania in Philadelphia. Another coincidence! I would be in New York for just one day within the week – and Philadelphia is only one hour away by train … My original motive for writing had been to help awaken people to alternative medicine and encourage them to help themselves. I made my choice. I would meet the publishers in the morning and travel to Philadelphia in the afternoon.

I needed to start writing, and fast. My eyes were now almost back to normal. I had my new prescription glasses, but was determined not to wear them unless it became absolutely necessary.

I also needed to help with the packing, since the removal men were due to arrive at 8 am on Monday 22nd June – the day I was to fly to New York. Everything was chaotic. There was no longer time to sit in silence and listen to Diana or anyone else. As I emptied dozens of cupboards I realized just how much 'stuff' most of us tend to collect over the years.

I sent three van loads to Oxfam, and then moved onto my clothes. I thought of Diana getting rid of most of her formal wardrobe for charity, and remembered that Barbara Streisand had 'downsized' and sold many of her possessions to simplify her life. I thought of stars such as Demi Moore and Madonna who are becoming more spiritual. They have realized that having material possessions and money does not guarantee true happiness and, like millions of others, they are looking to the realms of spirit for answers.

Diana whispered in my ear, 'By all means get rid of all the things you no longer need, as this will help others, but don't give everything away –

otherwise you become part of the problem instead of part of the solution. The universe wants you to be happy and it's not wrong to appreciate and own quality possessions, but it's great when you decide to help others by giving away the belongings you no longer need.'

In giving away a third of my wardrobe it struck me that if every one of us could clear out our homes and wardrobes every year or so, we could help to raise more money for those in need.

'You are right', Diana said, 'we in the higher realms are desperate to encourage everyone who has a good standard of living to share something, anything, no matter how small, with those who have little or nothing. We have already told you that we are sending a special energy to Earth, an energy of pure love. The more people that offer to work for and hold the light, the sooner many of your problems on Earth will end. From the neighbour who offers a friend a cup of tea and a shoulder to cry on, to the millions who give to charity, every single time someone offers to help without thinking, "What is in this for me?" their inner light will become brighter and help will automatically be given to them.'

'Don't waste time being jealous of those who have more possessions than you, this is just a waste of energy which you could redirect to 'do-ing' so that you can earn sufficient money to cover your needs. Actions always speak louder than words. Happy accidents happen too – like a lottery win – but don't envy the winners, all they did was to buy a ticket. What goes around comes around … and this is happening faster and faster … what you give out you get back. The chaos that Kelvin and many others have predicted does not have to happen. The transition that is now upon you could become far more gentle if you could all become more open-minded and realize just how much you can achieve if you choose to.'

'So, what do you think of the charity set up after your death?' I enquired of Diana.

There was a very long pause and I felt I had touched a raw nerve. It was as if she was debating whether or not to comment. I will not use her exact words because they would upset a few people, but Diana feels that some of the people running it are not particularly spiritual and that they are treating it as a business rather than giving from their hearts. But I don't know the full circumstances and I do not want to enter into any feud on this subject. I am simply a messenger.

I left the packing cases in the hall ready for the removal men the next morning and wished my husband luck for the move. I was painfully aware that my timing could not have been worse, but the Duchess of York had organized this appointment and I was not going to miss this window of opportunity.

As I backed out of our drive for the last time, I was both happy and sad in the same moment. Sad to be leaving my neighbour, Norma, who had given me so much spiritual advice, and my housekeeper, Sheila, since together we had come through so much during the years. Memories are precious gifts, and they would remain with me forever. But there was no turning back now. I was heading towards a new chapter in my life and I was going to New York. Butterflies fluttered in my tummy with anticipation. It was as if Diana was thrilled that I was going to America, she had really loved and treasured her visits to the States. She liked Bill Clinton, saying that he was 'a real charmer' and predicted I might meet him one day. I'm not holding my breath on that one ...

# 14

## Return to America

**AFTER A TWO-HOUR DRIVE** to London, I strolled by the Serpentine in Hyde Park to stretch my legs. I watched as a teenage nanny allowed her two young charges to throw their empty cans into the lake and, as I retrieved their rubbish and placed it in a nearby waste bin, the nanny flushed and the children looked bewildered. I did not need Diana to tell me what she was thinking, as I was having similar thoughts ... What hope is there if we do not teach by example?

On 22nd June I flew to New York. Diana had told me to trust and to let go, and as we climbed through the clouds into the sunshine I felt as though I was travelling more on a wing and a prayer than trust.

During the flight I began chatting to the gentleman next to me. I had to contain my astonishment when he told me what he did for a living – he was a Queen's messenger, one of the many trusted couriers who take Her Majesty's private and sensitive correspondence to other countries ... I could not help but smile inwardly ... it felt like a nudge from Diana and yet it was just another coincidence. It took all my willpower not to tell him a thing or two ... To while away the hours, I watched the film Contact, written by scientist Carl Sagan, starring Jodie Foster. The film was about a scientist who contacts a non-human intelligent species, but is unable to prove it to the masses … and yet the scientist had known her experience was real. The irony was not lost on me.

Within a few hours I was in the 'Big Apple' and the next morning I went along to see Sarah's publishers. Although they were convinced of my sincerity they felt that the public would only be interested in intimate and revealing details of Diana's personal life and not her messages for humanity. I knew this was not the book that Diana had in mind and left, resolving to write it my way.

On the train on my way to speak about alternative medicine in Philadelphia, feelings of despondency overcame me but Diana's voice in my head was philosophical. 'What did you expect? The media contributed to my death and still they think they can ask for more. Their arrogance is almost beyond belief and yet it no longer surprises me. What they do not seem to comprehend is that you can only write what I am willing to share with you and I am not willing to give any more intimate details – enough is enough. They hounded me when I was alive, and now, Hazel, you must trust me. No one ever promised that this process would be easy and you came here of your own free will – you chose to come.'

If she could have appeared in front of me, I might have been tempted to use a few expletives.

As I had this angry thought I suddenly 'felt' her sad emotions within me as she began talking about the media again. 'Yes, I courted the press, especially in the beginning as I desperately wanted to be loved and to please Charles. But instead it made him furious and as the years passed I realized I had gone too far. Once the children were born I needed more privacy and thought the press would respect that, but it was too late. There were many occasions when confidences were broken and I often felt violated. For people who have never experienced such intrusions it is hard for them to truly understand.'

As I sat looking out of the train window on my way to Philadelphia I felt really sad for her, and her voice came back, 'Lighten up, for goodness sake.' She could be so authoritative when she chose to be.

'Don't fret for me. Apart from leaving my sons, I'm glad to be out of it all. I planted a seed in William who is incredibly sensitive. I advised him to help people as much as he can and, as you write, your words will plant a seed in those who are ready to wake up. After all, the Prince of Wales' motto, 'Ich Dien', means 'I Serve'. Charles has helped many people and since my death this has become more widely known and I wish him well. During my last few months we became friends again but I pray that the 'grey men', the establishment, do not try to repress William's sensitive side, which can easily be closed down unless it receives regular doses of inspiration. This is why I took both my sons to hospitals and to centres for the homeless – it helped to wake them up ...'

On 24th June I flew home. We were due to move into our new house in Oxfordshire the next morning. Over Easter, Diana had said I should go to America and I had made this happen, I was indeed creating my own reality. During the flight, I recalled a meeting months earlier with the dancer Michael Flatley who had said we should all have a dream, and if we really wanted our dream badly enough we must be willing to make it happen. I met him after he had torn a ligament in his leg during a show and specialists had said that he would not be able to dance for at least six weeks. But they had not understood Michael's resolve, or the power of his mind. He received lots of hands-on healing, spent many hours quietly imagining and visualizing that his leg was healing, and six days later he went back on stage. He made it happen. Now I would have to do the same.

Circling over Heathrow, I felt her voice whispering in my head: 'You have done well to get this far, we will do what we can to help you, but Charles is creating his own reality. He is in charge of whom he sees and has many sycophants around him. You may never meet him, but keep going, don't stop now and don't give up hope – we are with you always.'

It sounded as though she was saying goodbye. She continued: 'Tomorrow you will be in chaos and as the days and weeks pass you will find it harder to connect with us. We are always here, but now that you are truly coming back down to earth, your mind will be on many other things and we will find it harder to get through. But you have learned and heard much from us, all you need to do is remember – the words will come – do not doubt, and when you are ready we will be back.'

'What?' I cried. I had almost died, lost my job, used my savings for the trip to New York and now they were leaving me? I began to panic. The voice returned as we taxied to our stand at Heathrow, 'Don't worry, help will come when you need it, you are never truly alone. Trust, let go and get on with your life, and keep your promise to write the book.'

And she was gone. I burst into tears. I felt desolate and alone and in that moment all the money and possessions in the world would not have consoled me.

But life goes on, I had to learn to take one day at a time, and simply to live for today. There was no point worrying about a future which did not yet exist ... until I created it.

OK, I would not give up. I would go and see Sarah and trust that in the moment that I saw her again, Diana would return and tell me something very specific, something that only the two of them had known. Since 10th April I had been able to 'hear' Diana almost at will, it was as if we had a hot-line telephone. I had written notes when I could, even sitting on the loo, in the car and at my desk. But as the days passed and I truly accepted that I was actually hearing Diana, I began to presume that I would always be able to hear her clearly, that I would go on being telepathic, creating the ash and giving the divine light through my eyes, and so I stopped making notes all the time. The summer holidays were looming and I knew that Sarah would be going away with her daughters. I also knew I was indeed heading into chaos, but I hadn't realized just how much chaos.

# 15

**The Move**

*Thursday 25th June – Oxfordshire*

AS I DROVE DOWN OUR newly laid driveway and looked through the trees at our new home, I had to pinch myself to make sure I was not dreaming. I closed my eyes and remembered the little girl in the back streets of Coventry, where my mum was a cleaning lady and our toilet was a corrugated metal shed at the bottom of our tiny garden, our bath a tin tub in front of the fire.

I remembered how Mum nursed me and my brother through scarlet fever, measles, German measles, chickenpox and a dozen ear infections, not to mention my breaking my arm, my jaw and twisting my ankle or wrists every other month – and how I had cried at night when she gently fitted callipers on my spindly weak legs to try and straighten them out. Tears sprang to my eyes as I realized what an easy life I had enjoyed compared to Mum and how she and Dad would love to see me now.

And in the second that I had this thought, I heard my mum's voice in my head, 'We are so proud of you daughter, who would have guessed that our little girl would one day live like a queen and write a book about a Princess, don't worry about us, we are fine. It's you we worry about, you take care running up and down those stone stairs …' This brought a big smile to my face and I drove on into the courtyard.

Sheila and Lindsey had agreed to come from Birmingham to help me for the first two days. There must have been 20 workmen in the house, desperately trying to complete their work. Wires jutted out from unpainted walls, tiles were missing, toilets were without seats. To say we had a few teething problems is a huge understatement. The house was far from ready. But we could all only do one job at a time, and as we scrubbed, unpacked, dusted, washed and attempted to file all my research papers and books hour after hour I soon realized that we had become slaves to a building and to our possessions.

When Saturday came and it was time for Sheila to say goodbye we hugged each other. I was still concerned about her eyes and desperately wanted her to get better. Over Easter I had known with my whole heart that when I had looked into Sheila's eyes and said 'they were perfect' that her sight had improved. It was only when the eye specialist had told her that she still suffered *Retinitis pigmentosa* that her vision had closed in again. And as we said our farewells I promised to find her an answer. It was to come sooner than I expected.

The experience of moving reminded me just how much most people dislike change. Diana had said many times that from chaos comes order, and that when the world plunges into chaos (which it could unless we change the way we think and behave) we would all wonder how to manage. Saying goodbye to Sheila I realized that I was wallowing in my own chaos and that Sheila was also apprehensive about her future. But none of us is indispensable, life goes on and we learn to adapt to our new life or situation or we move on – we choose. But as the weeks passed my self confidence began fading. I had given up my column and even if I were to write about my experience who would ever believe me? But it had happened, it was real and no one, no one, could take that away from me. Diana had told me to get through all my personal 'stuff', (an ongoing angst about why she would choose me to channel through), to clear the chaos in my mind and my new home, as soon as possible so that I could continue with my purpose.

On 9th July I attended a conference on light and colour at Reading University. The invitation to cover this event for the Sunday Times had arrived months earlier and though I had meant to cancel my acceptance, my instinct told me to go. Among the experts were orthodox professors such as George Brainard from Philadelphia who advises NASA on using light therapy to keep astronauts alert in space, along with other less conventional specialists from Russia, the USA, Ireland and the UK who use various light frequencies and colour techniques to heal conditions including anxiety, depression, learning disorders, coordination problems, hyperactivity, some cancers, multiple skin disorders and even epilepsy.

As I wandered from lecture to lecture it was like preaching to the converted. I have written a great deal about the importance of full spectrum light, which contains seven colours, and how, if the body is deprived of any of them for a prolonged period, we become ill.

As I sit writing another 'coincidence' occurs – outside my study window a magical rainbow has formed. The marvellous clarity of the colours – purple, indigo, blue, green, yellow, orange and red – is a graphic reminder that these colours are around us all the time, but we can only see them with our physical eyes when there is a rainbow. Like spirit and the infinite number of frequencies that surround the globe, just because we cannot see them all the time it does not mean they do not exist …

For weeks I had sent out the thought that I would dearly like to meet someone who could help me to understand what had happened to my housekeeper's eyes. By another coincidence, the organizers of the conference had arranged for me to meet Dr Jacob Liberman from Colorado, who just happened to be an optometrist, an eye specialist with almost 30 years' experience. As we shook hands and I looked into his sparkling blue eyes, I knew instantly that he was an 'awake' soul, that I could speak freely and he would not think I was mad. I was able to 'see' the light in his eyes, and I realized we were of like minds.

After I related a fraction of what had happened to me, Dr Liberman smiled knowingly, and shared some of his story. Until 1976 he had worn glasses for almost nine years, for driving and most other activities. He was nearsighted and suffered a significant amount of astigmatism, which causes objects not only to appear blurred but also distorted.

A keen advocate of meditation, it was during a session that he had an experience that was to change his life. With his eyes closed, he suddenly realized he was outside his body and was able to observe his physical shell sitting meditating. His 'vision' from this new viewpoint was not only crystal clear but also holographic in nature, in that he felt he was seeing from everywhere simultaneously. This sounded like a classic out-of-body experience which lasted for only a few minutes, but when Jacob opened his eyes, he was able to see clearly without his glasses. Needless to say, he was dumbfounded. After examining his eyes Jacob found that although his eyesight had improved more than 200 per cent, the optical measurements of his eyes remained the same.

In other words, the change in his vision occurred without a reduction in his eyeglass prescription and he realized that although his orthodox colleagues would state that he still needed glasses, Jacob knew this was not the case. He was very confused as his medical training had taught him this was impossible. Yet it was happening to him. Since that day he has taught thousands of people, including fellow medical colleagues, how to 'see' clearly without their glasses. As we chatted I understood that he had experienced a spontaneous healing – a moment of absolute knowing that his eyesight was perfect.

I thought about what had happened to Sheila. When I had looked into her eyes, I had 'known' 100 per cent they could be perfect and had told Sheila that they were. The moment was so intense that Sheila's sight began to improve. Then we saw the specialist who told her that she was still suffering from retinitis pigmentosa and the next day her vision deteriorated again. I had pulsed divine energy from my eyes to hers, and Sheila and I both realized that something special had happened which had triggered an improvement in her eyesight. Was the improvement sparked by her belief that her eyes were perfect? Had the healing energy I had pulsed into her eyes somehow triggered Sheila to help heal herself? Or was it combination of the two?

I received many letters from readers whose doctors had told them that their conditions were 'to be expected at their age' and that nothing could be done for them … and when a person believes these statements and accepts them as being true, what happens? The illness becomes that person's reality and they get worse. They believe wholeheartedly what they are told and are therefore not surprised as their condition worsens. The power of the mind again …

I asked Dr Liberman about Sheila's eyes and he said, 'I have found that when you introduce a person who is chronically ill to someone who has healed themselves by whatever means, it gives hope to that sick person and it gives them a licence to become well. You gave Sheila a licence to heal her eyes and to totally forget that she ever had the problem in the first place. She had a spontaneous remission. But then you took her to a doctor, an expert, who told her she was still suffering from her condition. I call this a lethal diagnosis and hence it does not surprise me that her symptoms returned within 24 hours.'

As I sat listening I realized that taking Sheila to the specialist to see if I had somehow initiated a miracle was my biggest mistake. Dr Liberman smiled, understanding that I felt guilty.

'Don't worry, you could not have known at the time. You were going through an incredible experience and most people would have wanted to seek out some kind of proof. But many times I have found that it's not the disease that kills a person, it's the diagnosis. Tell a person they have cancer, even if they don't, and the effects can be incredible. Ask anyone who has been misdiagnosed. They prepare for their funeral, say goodbye to their relatives, take to their beds and become really ill, all because they have been told by an 'expert' how ill they are. The power of the mind is incredible.'

The good news is that as I sit writing this, Sheila has now read Dr Liberman's books and has begun taking 15,000iu of vitamin A daily (but if you are pregnant take no more than 5,000iu), as recent research from Harvard Medical School has shown that this dosage helps to maintain useful vision for several more years than would normally be expected. I also gave Sheila other nutritional supplements to help her eyes … and I wish her luck on her journey.

But what about my eyes? I told Jacob about my not being able to see properly over Easter and believing for a short time that I might be going blind. Again he smiled knowingly. 'But what were you able to see without your physical eyes?'

Now it was my turn to smile, I had been able to 'see' and understand other realities clearly … 'Exactly, real vision, the real knowing, the keys to the universe come from the seeing part of our consciousness, which activates when people connect to a universal source – not through our physical eyes.'

'So, have you seen many cases of spontaneous healing?' I asked. I had heard of this phenomena many times and interviewed several people whose illnesses had literally disappeared after receiving hands-on healing, swimming with dolphins, or experiencing a moment of 'absolute knowing' that they were cured – and then they were. They literally switched off their illness.

Jacob told me that he had received thousands of letters and calls from people who, after attending his lectures, claimed that their eyesight and other problems had magically disappeared. Although he has personally experienced the physical effects of many different types of extraordinary healing he feels that the most powerful effect we can have on others is through the degree of our presence. He explained, 'The more we are a living example of what it means to be fully human and fully conscious ... [as I had been during April, May and June] ... the more we contagiously empower others to fully expand to their maximum potential – physically, emotionally and spiritually, for wellness is much more contagious than disease.'

Well said ... Jacob is a truly magical individual and I could easily have sat and chatted with him for hours, but he had to go and present his lecture.

Before we parted he gave me copies of his two books, and if anyone would like to know more about his incredible work I recommend you read them (see page 270).

The success of healing is often derided, but there are hundreds of documented cases including those of numerous babies and animals who are not aware they are being given healing and yet many become well.

Seka Nikolic, a healer based at the Kailash Centre in North London, was born in Sarajevo, and realized in her early childhood that she could heal people. Without ever being taught that every healthy cell in the body emits a harmonic frequency, which alters to a disharmonic frequency when we become ill, Seka intuitively knew that she could tune into an individual's unique healthy frequency and send it through her hands back into the patient. Just as the woman who swam with dolphins felt them 'pinging' her with an energy that helped her to become well.

As I have said, some people can hold and channel more of the energy, and healing works for some people and not for others (for more information see page 270-2).

As I drove home from the conference I mulled over what Jacob had said about becoming a fully conscious being, and I thought about how I had felt during those precious months. Diana predicted that the day would come when people who are 'fully conscious' will have far more control over their bodies than they realize.

When this day arrives, women will literally be able to 'choose' when to become pregnant or not, there will be no more 'mistakes'. We will also be able to heal injuries and illnesses at will, and this will include growing extra limbs and nerve endings through the power of our minds.

Diana had predicted that what we now term miracles will become everyday occurrences. I recalled asking her whether Christopher Reeve, the actor who played Superman, would ever walk again. She was obviously a fan of his and said: 'Christopher had a terrible accident and has endured much heartache but he has done an awesome job of helping to raise the consciousness of the way people view severely handicapped people. And yes, one day others like him will walk again.'

How wonderful it would be if this prediction were to come true, I thought. Surgeons are already working on stimulating nerve endings to re-grow by using electrical stimulation (frequencies again, everything keeps coming back to frequencies) and this technology is being tested on humans. Alternatively, there is a psychic surgeon in South America, Joao Teixeira da Faria, who has helped some people with Christopher Reeve's type of injuries. This healer works in a tiny village called Abadiania in central Brazil where he is known as Joa de Deus — Man of God. Every day hundreds of people gather from all over the world to be 'operated' on by this amazing healer. (For more details of his work, see page 270.)

Years ago when I first began researching alternative health I had taken my doctor Brian MacGreevy, to watch the UK's leading psychic surgeon Stephen Turoff at work. Even for an open-minded person such as myself, the experience was incredible. Stephen told me my pancreas wasn't functioning properly and we watched as he plunged an instrument deep inside my body. There was no pain, but I could feel his instruments inside me, and I burst into tears. Why? Because I thought that if someone had their hand inside my body surely I should feel pain? But there was none, all I could feel was his hand and his instrument rummaging deep within me. Mind boggling. I was left with a small, raised red scar on my upper abdomen but this disappeared after two days.

Slowly but surely I was now beginning to understand how this 'miracle' surgery is possible. Spirit vibrate at a much faster rate than we do, which is why they are not normally visible to the human eye. Psychic surgeons, therefore, with the assistance of spirit are able to go beyond the normal physical laws to affect physical matter.

Science has never been my speciality and so to better understand what had happened to me during April and May I rang Roger Coghill, an eminent UK-based scientist who has worked in the field of bioelectromagnetics research for 10 years. Again I shared only a fraction of what had happened to me, but Roger seemed to understand perfectly saying, 'Today there are more and more people like you who are becoming electrosensitive, both passively and actively. This means that some people can affect electrical equipment as you did, while others become sick from over-exposure to electricity, either from overhead and underground power lines, excessive electrical equipment in the home and workplace or mobile phones and so on. There are even societies in Sweden and the UK formed by people who are affected by electrical equipment. If large numbers of people were to become like this, it could cause serious problems.'

As he spoke, I recalled Diana's prediction that electrical equipment could be rendered useless. Imagine all the chaos that would cause …

Roger continued, 'It is essential for people to fully comprehend that the human body is made up of billions of electrical circuits encased in a physical shell. Therefore we emit electric fields from low to very high frequencies and their field strengths vary depending on the person's mood. For example, if I were to test the electrical field of a highly emotional or stressed person they would give off a high electric field that might affect equipment and the people around them. Electricity can be used to harm or heal and it is a wonderful technology, but we have to take into account that nature rarely bestows a riskless benefit. At this moment in time, over-exposure to power lines, photocopiers, satellite dishes, household appliances, VDU screens and mobile phones is undoubtedly doing us more harm than good.'

During my experience I had 'seen' energies around people, plants, trees and animals, but as Roger spoke I realized that if we could also see every artificial frequency pulsing from and into man-made objects such as TVs, mobile phones and computers we would realize that there is hardly a square foot anywhere on the globe that is not affected.

Why is this?

As I have already said we all emit our own frequencies and if these are upset in any way by negative frequencies (from junk food or from external pollutants such as mobile phones etc) then our healthy frequencies are disturbed and we become ill. The great pyramid at Giza was constructed in such a way that waves of electromagnetic radiation could not permeate the walls. It seems the ancients knew more about this problem than we do.

For years, Roger and many of his colleagues have believed that a large proportion, perhaps as much as 30 per cent of cancers, depression, ME (chronic fatigue) and other modern illnesses are triggered as a direct result of electrical pollution.

'Twelve years ago', Roger said, 'scientists at the Brugemann Institute in Germany developed a machine called a BiCom which is able to differentiate between a patient's harmonic healthy frequencies, emitted by healthy cells, and their disharmonic frequencies, emitted by diseased cells, diseased groups of cells (such as the liver or kidneys) as well as viruses, fungi and bacteria. The machine is able to amplify the healthy, harmonic frequencies back into the patient to speed up the healing process.'

Many healers, spiritual masters and dolphins have been able to do this for years! But I wanted to see the machine in action for myself and several months later went to see Peter Smith at the Hale Clinic in London to be tested on the BiCom. The concept is amazing. Peter took a full medical history and then began testing to see which diseases or traces of disease I still held in my body. For example, in my teens I had contracted glandular fever and this had caused ongoing chronic fatigue which has plagued me for most of my life.

Peter took a phial containing Epstein Barr, the virus that causes glandular fever, and placed it in a metal dish attached to electrodes. He then pulsed the frequency of the virus back into me and was able to see from his readings that my bodily fluids tested positive. Peter said that although the virus itself might be dead, my fluids still carried the memory of the specific frequency of Epstein Barr, which would disrupt my normal harmonic frequencies, thus affecting my energy levels for years.

To destroy the memory he inverted the frequency of the virus and pulsed it back into me so that the stored frequency of Epstein Barr was cancelled out. In this way Peter is able to 'neutralize' viruses, bacteria, fungi, and many more illnesses and their symptoms.

Before we parted he amplified harmonic frequencies back into my body to strengthen my natural body processes and I must say for a few days afterwards I felt more energized. For years Peter has used his machine to 'pulse' himself with the frequency of vaccinations, so that he does not need to have a physical injection. 'New age' energy medicine, such as the BiCom machine, is now entering mainstream medicine and will undoubtedly become a major force in health treatment. For those needing further information, see page 270.

Back to Easter. I had 'known' that the energy coming through my eyes was very powerful, invisible, carried huge amounts of information and could heal people. In short, it was a combination of perfect frequencies. So when I pulsed people, I introduced more perfect frequencies into their energy field, which in turn aided healing.

And I had felt this divine energy's 'thoughts' – it has a conscious mind, but not in the physical sense. It is this energy that healers pulse to a greater or lesser degree (depending on how much they can hold or channel) into their patient's energy field. It was this energy that 'hit me' during that split second in Harrods.

But what did Roger think had happened when my legs had begun to dematerialize at Cliveden? He reminded me of the top secret Philadelphia experiment, code-named Project Rainbow that took place in 1943. 'The US Navy was trying to make its ship, USS Eldridge invisible to radar. Scientists installed equipment to create a huge electromagnetic field around the ship with the idea of bending radar and light, but it all went badly wrong. What actually happened was that the ship and its crew disappeared for almost four hours.'

I had often read reports of this experiment stating that when the ship reappeared, some of the crew were found embedded in the deck, others were on fire, some were repeatedly materializing and dematerializing and many were never seen again. I now understand they had moved from our normal third dimension into another dimension and that's what I had begun to do at Cliveden. But I had not been part of any experiment and I wondered how I had achieved this partial dematerialization of my own accord. I was soon to find out. Serena had told me I was lucky not to have gone mad and thinking of those poor men back in 1943 I realized just how fortunate I had been to come through in one piece.

I then asked Roger about the day back in May when I had held my fitness trainer Al's arm, and consciously withdrawn energy from his 6ft 2in tall, 17-stone frame, while I watched the energy drain from his face and body.

'This is a basic law of physics. If you were to plug in a kettle to boil, the energy that it takes to boil the water comes from somewhere. You needed more energy to run your physical body, therefore when you grabbed Al's arm it was as though you acted like the kettle using Al as the mains, you drew electrical energy from him to give yourself more. We are all capable of draining people's energies, because we are electrical beings, but you can also be with people who energize you. Whenever people meet and interact, there is an exchange of energy.'

For years I had written about how our thoughts can affect our health and I had noticed when I was with certain people (especially angry or negative ones) they 'drained' my energy. Lindsey, my PA, had shown me how to protect my aura, my energy field, so that this no longer happened, and it had worked. All I had to do was to visualize myself as being surrounded by a bubble of white light encased in a reflective glass bubble, so that whatever thoughts (energy) people were sending out that drained my energy, would automatically ricochet back to them. I realize this might sound bizarre, but it worked for me.

If you are in a room with someone who is really angry, you will know it, even if they do not speak. You will easily sense the atmosphere as being unfriendly just as if someone loves you and is your true friend you can sense their love and affection. The energies we all emit have the potential to harm or to heal: thoughts affect us emotionally. Above all during April, May and June I knew that people who live in constant fear emit the most negative energies, and I realized that it's the accumulative effect of so many negative thoughts that is contributing to many of the world's problems.

Everything seems to be linked to energy and frequency so I asked Roger, 'If we are all made up of energy, what happens to us when we die?' He was totally unfazed by this question saying, 'Matter cannot be created or destroyed, so everything that dies is just changing into a different material form. That material form itself is composed of energy. As the physical body decomposes, the spark or essence of life leaves. Where it goes has been asked since humans first lived on Earth.'

What about my skin regenerating, my being able to look thinner or fatter at will, had my mind instructed my cells to regenerate? I had thought at the time that because I was somehow possessed by Diana, she was making me look younger, but I now knew this was only when I was being overshadowed. At the height of my experience I had believed that ancient parts of my brain were 'waking up', but Serena had told me that CT scans show we already use every part of our brain.

Diana had subsequently told me that although the human brain might be fully utilized, mankind is only using a minute fraction of its potential capability. She told me that currently most people use only around five per cent of their potential capability. Even at the height of my own experience, I was only using around 15 per cent. My mind boggles at what we might be capable of when we learn to maximize our mind's potential to 100 per cent …

What I do know is that what I went through is based on science. I did not go mad – the experience may have frayed my nerves to breaking point – but I don't believe I had a nervous breakdown. I also now knew for sure that for a brief moment I had moved between dimensions. If you want to know more about how energy fields affect our health, I strongly suggest you read Roger's books, see page 272.

And then came another incredible coincidence. Weeks earlier Diana had told me that there would come a time when new energy sources would be found that would not pollute the planet. After ending my conversation with Roger I began sorting through my post. A blue poster sent on to me from the *Sunday Times* caught my eye. It advertised a lecture that Dr Brian O'Leary, a former Apollo trained astronaut and physicist, was to present that very night on Free Energy. Could this be one of the energy sources that Diana had mentioned? 'Yes, Yes, Yes,' said a voice in my head. I had to laugh, spirits have a magical way of making sure that their important messages get through.

Weeks later I read Dr O'Leary's book, *Miracle In the Void*, which explains the concept of free energy, and how many scientists around the globe have independently found that occasionally they tune into frequencies which produce more electrical output than input. Machines using this free energy are now being tested in India and Japan … Could this be the very same energy that had pulsed through my eyes? A perfect range of frequencies that supplies all our needs?

Roger's words 'Energy can neither be created nor destroyed' evoked memories of a wonderful dinner I enjoyed with the late Michael Bentine, a founder member of the Goons and a great personality. Michael had used the same phrase over dinner while trying to explain that we all come from, and return to one source. Michael had been very patient and explained his concept saying, 'Imagine that the universe, God, whatever you want to call it, is a gigantic ball of energy rather like the sun – only much bigger. Now, imagine that every soul that ever was or will be resides in that central sun, and within the sun there are many levels. Liken the core of that sun to the centre of a huge wheel. And when you choose to be born, when you re-incarnate you become another spoke emanating from the wheel. But you remain attached to the wheel all your life by an invisible spoke or cord, and when you die, the cord breaks and you return to the wheel for it to be repaired, and so we all get re-cycled. Every living being comes from one source and returns to that source.'

It was a great story and I never forgot it. At the time I had thought Michael to be rather eccentric, now I don't. And so I sat at my desk pondering the fact that energy cannot be created nor destroyed. This must surely mean that everything that is, was or ever will be, has always existed? Think about it. Everything truly is a paradox.

# 16

## Return to Mother

**BY LATE JULY, THE WORKMEN** and mess in our new home were driving me crazy – the dust, the drilling, the smell of paint, the lack of any peace and quiet. I simply could not cope with their energies and my thoughts dragged me into an abyss of depression. How would I even hear spirit again in such chaos? I felt totally drained and despaired of ever hearing Diana or anyone else again. Mediums had always told me that if you want to tune in to the spirit world, you need silence and, of course, experience helps.

Some people become aware of their psychic abilities after having lessons from psychic teachers such as my friend Dr Richard Lawrence, who says it's easy once you know how. Others never hear a thing as they think anything to do with spirit is evil. It's only evil if your intention is evil in the first place. Knowledge is neutral, it's how you use the knowledge that counts. In my case I have been slightly psychic all my life – but I had never been able to hear as clearly as during the previous three months. I was also worried that I might no longer be differentiating clearly between my own thoughts and those of Diana. After all, my total experience of hearing her to date was a little over three months and I knew that if it were going to continue I would need the help of a professional medium.

As I went about my daily tasks, waiting and hoping to hear again from Diana, I was desperate for credible proof. I simply wanted something, anything that would prove categorically that I had heard from the spirit of the Princess Of Wales. I needed some silence and soon – my soul was crying out for a little space and time to think.

I recalled Lindsey's and my visit to Mother Meera in Germany in January when we had found two days' peace to think about our lives. Now Lindsey was soon to move on to another job back in Birmingham. Perhaps if I were to return to Germany I would hear Diana again. I was willing to try almost anything in order for that to happen. And so on 26th July Lindsey and I returned to Thalheim, a tiny village in the German countryside outside Dusseldorf, to pay another visit to the Indian lady affectionately known as Mother Meera. Every weekend hundreds of people congregate from all over the world simply to look into Mother's eyes and receive the divine light that pulses through them. Some come for healing, others hope that somehow by receiving this light, their lives will change for the better, others, like me, are simply intrigued.

On my first visit I had thought the entire set-up bizarre to say the least. A healer friend had told me about Mother and I had arranged the visit out of curiosity as I had thought that seeing her might make an interesting feature for my column. On our first evening, Lindsey and I had been dropped by the hotel bus in a sparse, windswept car park in the centre of Thalheim and at 6.30 pm, one of Mother's followers had come over to collect us.

Overseas and first-time visitors were invited to the front of the queue and we followed the young man in a convoy of silent anticipation across the sleepy German village green to Mother's white walled home. At the door our names were ticked off the booking list and we were asked to remove our shoes. Around 300 people filed respectfully into Mother's large living room to sit on the rows of white plastic chairs. When chairs ran out, devotees sat on the floor. Not my idea of being in heaven, but if you had seen their faces, they would have sat on hot coals in order to be in that room. Instruction packs were on each chair.

We were to sit in total silence. When mother entered the room, we had to stand. When she sat, we could then sit again. Like being in the presence of the Queen I thought.

As each person felt the need, we were to make our way down the narrow aisles between the chairs and wait in line on our knees until it was time to go forward and kneel before Mother. We were instructed to lower our heads so that she could touch our temples for a few seconds and then to sit back on our heels so that Mother could look into our eyes. When she blinked the ceremony, known as 'darshan', was over and we should return to our seats.

We were requested to wear clean socks and to wash our hair before each 'darshan'. Fair enough, after all who would want to touch 300 greasy, dirty heads and have smelly socks in their home?

As I watched the diminutive figure of Mother walk into the room to take her seat, I sensed the energy change to one of reverential, hushed expectancy. Personally I wondered what all the fuss was about, she looked very nice, but quite normal. I'm not sure what I had expected. As we all sat in silence I craned my neck to see what happened as Mother stared into each person's eyes. It seemed perfectly ridiculous to me that anyone should treat another person with such deference and so much reverence. I have never been one for religious rituals but by 8.30 pm almost everyone else had been up to Mother and I had to make up my mind.

I decided that as I had come all this way, I might at least discover what all the fuss was about. So, I too, went forward. I felt embarrassed in case I did anything wrong with so many people watching, and as I looked into her eyes, I saw and felt nothing.

After the ceremony we were allowed into a tiny anteroom to buy Mother's books and various memorabilia. While chatting with strangers I discovered that most people had booked to receive 'darshan' on four consecutive evenings. If it had not been for the fact that we had booked for two nights and the hotel and air tickets were already paid, I would not have returned for my second 'darshan'. After returning to our hotel at 9.30 pm that first night, as I lay listening to the wind and rain lash my windows, I could only imagine what Ringo Starr had experienced during his visit.

But as I read her books I discovered there was a child-like simplicity to them. They were made up of the most commonly asked questions from people around the world, and as Mother does not speak during the ceremony this was her way of helping people to understand what she does.

Why do people have to kneel? Because Mother is so tiny that otherwise she could not reach people's heads if they were to stand.

Why do people worship Mother, when she is like the rest of us, simply a human being? She does not ask them to worship her, they simply choose to. True. I hadn't worshipped her.

Also, 'darshan' is free, there is no charge whatsoever. Back in January I had thought, well, she must have something special, otherwise why are all these people here?

On that fateful second evening I decided to use the two hours of enforced silence to meditate and ask for what I really wanted in my life. I prayed to become more psychic and for an acceleration in my spiritual journey.

Now on my second visit, as I sat in silence on a warm July evening watching Mother pulse the energy into people's eyes, I felt sure that my prayers had been answered in a more fantastic way than I could ever have dreamed of. I also knew that for almost three months I had felt the same as Mother Meera and realized why people worshipped her. Because in their eyes, Mother and many other enlightened souls, such as Sai Baba, are believed to be God on earth and they are. But as we watched people hold their hands in prayer and worship Mother, Lindsey and I felt strangely detached – not through any disrespect for Mother, more from an absolute knowing that we are all part of God – that we all carry a unique light, but some carry more than others.

As I sat looking at Mother it was possible to see an aura of white light around her body. It's no coincidence that many saints and people such as Jesus are portrayed in paintings as having halos of white light around their heads – this is their aura. And in enlightened beings this light is often so bright that it can be seen by sensitive people.

That's why my eyes had hurt so badly. I was so full of light that when I looked in a mirror the light energy reflected back into me, but I was already full to the brim. I was overflowing with light and didn't need any more, just as you feel bloated when you have eaten too much food.

The difference with Mother is that she has lived her light all her life. Luckily others had known she was special and kept her apart from everyday life. During April and May I had realized that if I could have been left in total silence then I too could have continued to hold the frequency, which would have enabled me to go on giving 'darshan'. But that was not my purpose. I also came to understand why Mother works in silence.

During my experience I had 'known' hundreds of realities. There are six billion people all thinking different thoughts who have their own realities and opinions on situations and life, and as I sat in the room with Mother I realized that if she were to try and answer everyone's questions, she would never have any time to herself. After all, what makes sense to one person is totally unacceptable to another, and one word can have so many meanings, depends upon who is hearing or reading the words.

Mother simply acts as a channel for the divine light to pass through her and into others to enable them to find their own truth. For two months I had needed nothing other than simple foods, water, silence, and to give the light from my eyes. I had become a being of pure love – unfettered by judgement or interest in material wealth – and for a brief moment I too had felt like a master.

Now as I knelt before Mother Meera and looked deeply into her eyes, it was like looking into a mirror. She was pulsing a little more of God's unique frequency into me, but I was already full to the brim …

As we left on that Sunday summer's evening, I met a young man from Glastonbury who, like me, had begun giving 'darshan' through his eyes and he too was hearing Jesus. I ruined his day when I told him that we all have the potential to carry this energy, and that he is not the re-incarnation of Jesus, he is simply carrying the same divine energy.

Masters carry and hold more divine energy than the rest of us, but everyone has the potential. Most people do not realize this, they worship others and look for answers outside of themselves, but the light and knowledge is inside us – all we have to do is to know this.

As I watched people kissing Mother's feet and holding their hands in prayer I recognized that the second 'darshan' the next evening would be my last. But I now know that when we are in a master's presence, we pick up some of their energy, which helps to raise our vibration and increase the amount of light we are able to hold. Back in May, as I had walked in Hyde Park with Stuart, he had asked why we both had so much energy when we had hardly been sleeping (for weeks I had been waking him up when the voices came at night as I scrabbled around writing messages in the dark). I had turned and said, 'Because you are with me.' Now I truly understood why I had said this.

During the silence on the Monday evening I simply enjoyed being in the presence of Mother's magical energies. I asked to remember all the information that the spirit of Diana had shared with me during April, May and June.

When the time came to leave and as I put on my shoes, it evoked memories of Easter – when I had begun to remove my shoes and slippers before entering my bedroom. I knew that the soles of our shoes carry negative energies from outside, and I wanted the energies in my bedroom to remain as pure as possible. As our hotel bus left the car park and sped back down the lane into the sunset, I whispered goodbye to Mother and thanked her for sharing her light with me which I believe contributed to what had happened to me over Easter.

The next morning before finally leaving Thalheim, Lindsey and I trekked up the 'Hill of Miracles', a large promontory overlooking the village. As we puffed and panted our way to the top, Lindsey made light of our struggle saying it must have been called the hill of miracles because it would be a miracle if we ever made it to the top without having a heart attack from overexertion. We laughed together, and promised that we would make even more effort to become fitter.

At the top of the hill is a tiny church built in the 9th century which is still in use today. We sat quietly with our thoughts, and I felt sad that I could no longer hear Diana and wondered if I would ever have absolute proof that I ever had. In that moment the word 'trust' popped into my head and then I faintly heard the words, 'We have already told you all you need to know for now – don't panic, the proof will come – you will hear again when the moment is right. Meanwhile, please stop talking about writing the book, just sit down and do it …'

I laughed out loud, she was reminding me to practise what I preached, to become a 'doer', instead of just thinking and talking about doing …

As I sat making notes on the flight back to London I berated myself for not writing down every single word that spirit had said to me. Then again, this would have been a physical impossibility as the information had come faster and faster in the weeks after Easter. If only I had not taken my new gifts for granted – if only I had carried on writing notes – if only.

Meanwhile it was time for Lindsey and I to say our farewells. As we hugged goodbye I hoped with all my heart that one day we might work together again.

Stuart and I were due to leave for Australia on 9th September, and I was really excited at the prospect of seeing my daughter Victoria again. I was also intrigued to know what the special event in the Blue Mountains might be. I felt like a child waiting for Christmas morning – patience, as always I needed more patience.

# 17 The Memories

IT WAS AMAZING HOW much Diana's mood had changed from one of anger and despondency to one of pure love and joy as the weeks went by. It was as if she had allowed me to feel the multitude of emotions she had felt in her own lifetime. But by the end of July my emotional roller coaster was almost over. I was eating normally, exercising normally, and could sleep without interruption – except that I now lay awake into the wee small hours asking to 'hear' clearly again. The words 'trust', 'let go' and 'you create your own reality' had become like a distant memory.

The aluminium tectonic plates which I had used to 'ground myself' during my experience, I now place under my food to help 'raise' its vibration, which is what these plates are normally used for. When I felt myself becoming 'light' in every sense of the word during April, May and June, I would stand or sit on the plates and almost immediately I could feel energy running down from the top of my head down into the grounding plate which helped me to feel less 'strange'. Food emits energy just as we do, and the tectonic plates help to raise the energy within food, which in turn gives the body more energy.

I had gone through phases when I knew that I was acting like Diana, and there were many occasions when I had felt that I no longer had total control of my own mind.

There had been periods of desperate negativity when I had craved ice cream, which I rarely eat. I began mimicking people on the spur of the moment. I never mimic people, but I think she did, and I believe she was rather good at it. If I walked near water I would have an almost uncontrollable urge to dive in, but I don't dive. I developed a craving for spicy food and for cleaning my teeth four or five times daily, and for carrying a toothbrush everywhere. And I desperately wanted to dance. My apprehension about talking on the phone remained for many weeks … So many things that were simply not like me.

When I had first heard Diana and seen pictorial flashes of her last few hours and felt her emotions, the intensity of the experience was immense. The depth of her anger and feelings of frustration were incredible. She had felt that no one truly understood the level to which she had been followed, harassed and chased. And her despair immediately after her physical death was appalling. I remembered shouting her words through my tears when I was alone in the bedroom on that Easter Saturday afternoon: 'They never really wanted me, they only wanted me to produce children for them … there was a stage when everything I tried was cut from under me and Charles and his flunkies tried to poison almost everything I did …'

She never truly found peace within herself except when she was with her own and other children who gave her so much love, but without wanting a piece of her. So many people wanted a piece of her … She had never truly understood what unconditional love meant when she was alive, but she knows now. She resented 'dying' just as she had found happiness with Dodi. He had become one of the truest loves of her life – and was willing to devote his life to her. And he has.

When I had asked her very personal questions she could be fairly abrupt. She was evidently tired of all the inaccuracies that had been written about her. When I asked if she had had other affairs, she had said, 'Yes – for the warmth.' And she sent her 'eternal gratitude' to those who have kept her secrets. She had not been pregnant when she died – she said she 'wasn't that stupid'. Yes, she had known that Dodi's father was 'using every means at his disposal' to encourage their relationship, but he became like a surrogate father to her. She said that he has done many wonderful things that the public have never heard about, and that he is not as black as the press paint him.'

And what about Henri Paul, their driver on that fateful night, ?

She told me that Henri Paul had been beside himself with feelings of guilt when he passed into spirit. He was inconsolable at the enormity of the part he had played, not only for himself, but for the family he had left behind. For many weeks Diana and Dodi had found themselves unable to visit him as they were dealing with their own grief at the loss of their families. But after a few months (in our time) they had finally understood and accepted that their deaths had been 'set in stone' and that if they had not died in that car, they would have been killed shortly afterwards. There had been no way out for them – no escape – this was their destiny. Her message that we 'all choose our own judgement' became Henri's reality as he refused to enter the higher realms of light, choosing instead to stay in the darker realms where he mixed with others who were punishing themselves for their actions on Earth.

As time passed, Dodi and Diana's emotional turmoil had lessened and they were taken to visit Henri. She had told me that the realms of lower vibration are dismal indeed, they are on an even lower vibration than the earth plane, and everything is dense, heavy, shadow and darkness. Henri had held his hands over his eyes as they approached. Diana said, 'My heart went out to him and I gently moved his hands from his eyes so that he could be warmed by our light. Initially he was very emotional and kept apologizing over and over again, but we explained that he must forgive himself. Eventually I gave him a big hug and we cried together. Hazel, forgiveness is a wonderful therapy – letting go of all my resentment and anger helped me to move on.'

From the levels of lower vibration, Diana and Dodi had taken Henri Paul into the higher realms where she says he is now being trained to give counselling to others who choose to remain in the shadows, so that when they feel ready they too can move into the light. She had told me that certain souls who have caused suffering to others on Earth often stay in this place of darkness for centuries, but always at their own choosing. When finally they feel they have paid their debt, they can then move into the higher realms. No one who asks for assistance is refused.

Again Diana reminded me that there are thousands of realities. She also said that certain people who live only for material wealth and power find it very hard to move into the light. Many of these souls often linger on an astral plane close to the Earth as they hate leaving their possessions and position behind, while others feel guilty and are desperate to return to apologize to those they hurt, especially those who take their own lives. In these cases when earthly mediums sit in groups known as 'rescue circles' they are often contacted by these souls and are able to help them make the final transition across to the higher realms. Others are cared for by volunteers who help newly arrived souls deal with their guilt and negative emotions.

During her physical lifetime Diana felt that much religious teaching was hypocritical and became very disillusioned with people who taught one way of life while living another, away from the public eye. She felt disenchanted with the bureaucracy, in-fighting and petty power struggles of churches, governments, institutions, and people in power. She too fell into this trap especially with the press, but now realizes that ego and judgement hold so many of us back. We waste so much energy and time on things that don't really matter. Hence her admiration for Mother Teresa and others who work for good causes who truly lived and live their light.

As July turned to August I heard nothing from Diana. At the new house we were still overrun with workmen and I despaired that we might ever find order. The Duchess of York was away until September, and then we were off to Australia. So another meeting would have to wait until late autumn … The days passed, I typed up my notes and tapes, and I waited … I desperately wanted to call my editor at the Sunday Times and plead for my column back, but by then I knew that if I went back to working 60- odd hours a week, writing the column and answering hundreds of letters, the book would be put aside again. It was now or never …

On 12th August, to cheer myself up I dragged Stuart along to see the film Armageddon starring Bruce Willis. It tells the story of a huge chunk of space real estate that is heading destructively towards Earth. Of course Bruce gets to save the world. It was a similar story to the film Deep Impact, the other big disaster movie of the summer. It was all great fun with fantastic special effects, but it certainly made me think. And as we walked back across Hyde Park towards our home, we sat down by the Serpentine to watch the sun set and enjoy the moment. I looked around at the trees, the wonderful colours of the flowers and the sky, and realized just how much we tend to take our home – our planet for granted.

I felt suddenly despondent, as if the job I had been asked to do was quite simply too big and totally beyond me. In despair I looked at the sunset and whispered to the sky, 'Where are you Diana? Why can't I hear you any more?' In a flash her exasperated voice was there again in my head, 'For the millionth time,' she cried, 'I'm in another dimension and you are trying too hard to hear me. This is preventing me getting through.'

Her voice was so clear, it was incredible, it was just as though she was sitting next to me. I felt totally confused and asked how this communication was possible?

'Because you are relaxed and you asked for help without ego,' she replied.

'But I wasn't relaxed during April, May and June and I could hear you all the time then …' I retorted.

'But during that time your vibration was raised tremendously,' said Diana. 'You were on our wavelength, now you are really back down to earth and we are finding it hard to get through, as your mind is rarely still. For us to operate in your dimension it's like swimming through treacle but as more people open to and anchor the light, either through meditation or doing good deeds, then the vibratory rate on Earth will rise. Eventually every one of you will be able to communicate with the higher realms more easily.'

'So, do you communicate through many people?' I enquired.

'Yes, I'm coming through to quite a few mediums (channellers) around the world, but only those I can trust.'

At this statement my chest puffed out with pride, but my mind went blank. We started talking again. Had she seen the film too?

'Yes', she replied. 'I was able to watch it in the cinema with you. It was great. We wish everyone would go and watch films such as these in the hope that it might shake them out of their complacency. They should never take their lives for granted, but live for each precious moment and have some fun and laughter along the way.'

Diana suggested I close my eyes and imagine that I had one day, week or month, left on Earth. What would I do? Where would I go? How would I feel? Who would I say goodbye to? Who would I share my last hours with? She recommended that we all practise this exercise more often to focus on what and who we really want in our lives. Yes, we must all have our hopes and dreams and become 'doers' so that our dreams can become our reality on a day-to-day basis, and my dream in that moment was to be able to prove that I was really hearing Diana.

On that note, 'What about a little more specific information for Sarah, Duchess of York?' I asked … It was amazing, although I could not physically 'see' Diana, I felt as though I could. She seemed irritable. She said that she loved Sarah, but on several occasions had been 'driven to distraction' by her sister-in-law. But Diana wished they had made up, they had truly been like sisters for some years until a third party had made things worse between them. Diana tried to recall a few incidents that had occurred and I scribbled them down on a note pad that I now carried everywhere 'just in case'. I would tell Sarah when I saw her in the autumn and prayed that it would be sufficient information to prove my case.

'How do you feel about Charles now?' I enquired. Again I felt a huge surge of emotion in the centre of my chest and I 'felt' her smiling. She loves the new relationship he has forged with their sons 'it has warmed her heart' and she asked me to remind her boys that they were born from love. Like any mother she is concerned for their welfare and never a day goes by when she does not visit them. She said that Charles and her sons, especially William, have sensed her, sometimes by her perfume, and at other times by simply knowing that she is there. She had given private messages to Charles through a medium on two occasions …

Night was falling over the river, and it was time for us to walk on. Stuart was content to walk in silence as he could see I was deep in thought.

'So, how do you appear now? Do you eat, sleep?' I wanted to know all about her new life. Diana laughed at my impatience. She told me that although she has lost her physical body, she now has an etheric or spiritual body which in her dimension enables her to appear the same as she did here. She is also able to overshadow people during sensitive moments. This is what she had done during my meeting with Dr Lawrence and the Duchess of York back in June. She had overlaid her energy field over my body so we became as one during those brief moments.

In her dimension she will not age, and she told me that there will come a time when all humans become fully conscious, that we will be able to choose our age and regenerate our bodies at a cellular level. We will all have more energy and need less sleep. As she said this I remembered that hysterical hour back in May when every thought had an immediate effect on my physical being, and how I would look in the mirror and see my eyes changing colour, I could look thinner or heavier, and I could appear younger or older at will.

I now knew that spirit had wanted me to experience as much as my mind could assimilate so that I would know that Diana was telling me the truth, and that the seemingly impossible is possible.

Her world appears as solid as ours, but there are a huge number of differences. Everyone in her dimension has to work for the good of the whole. There are no wars, no weapons. Sure people still have 'words' with friends and loved ones, but there is an unwritten law that no one can harm another.

Diana went on to say that they can 'speak' with their thoughts. Once in the spirit world they can also eat and sleep if they wish, even though their spiritual bodies do not really need food or sleep. Their food is light energy and she predicted there will come a time when we on Earth could also be able to live on light if we chose to, but this would not be possible until we become more spiritual. She also said that one day we will all be able to travel between dimensions at will. When that day finally comes we will know for sure that there is no death, as we will be able to 'walk between worlds' and take our physical bodies with us.

When I first heard this information I thought it sounded impossible, but I had met Kathy and Jackie who had 'seen' their children again in a solid form, even though their physical bodies were 'dead.' I had also watched as my legs disappeared at Cliveden. They were still there – I just couldn't see them. I know it's hard to comprehend, but I know all this to be true.

At this point in our evolution the physical body is made mostly from food molecules and when we 'die' the physical shell rots. But what if the light energy that had pulsed through my eyes is also a type of food?

After all I knew it was an incredible source of information, healing and free energy …

As I pondered this question a few weeks later, a further coincidence happened when a friend invited me to attend a lecture in London given by an Australian lady called Jasmuheen, who claims not to have eaten any appreciable amounts of food since 1992. She was monitored by doctors for two years during which time she ate virtually no solid foods, and drank only juices and fluids. Jasmuheen looked incredibly youthful for her age, worked out regularly, and told us how she literally lives on divine energy – the same energy that I had pulsed through my eyes.

She told us that she hardly needs any sleep and is full of energy, just as I had been, except that during my experience I had not even conceived that it might be possible to live without the need for physical food which is why I lost so much weight. When tested by doctors Jasmuheen's nutrient (vitamins, minerals, essential fats etc.) levels were found to be perfect. I thought of all the doctors and nutritionists who would be horrified at her story, especially given the growing numbers of anorexic young women. And yet I know that this divine source of energy is perfect in every way.

Scientists now know that every nutrient in food emits its own frequency, and that when you pulse a patient who has, for instance, low magnesium levels with the unique frequency of this mineral, the levels will rise in the body.

So what if you received a perfect spectrum of frequencies at all times? Would you then be perfect? I wondered. Think about it. Although this may sound amazing – light, colour, vibration and sound are set to become some of our medicines of the future. But by far the most important healing tool will be an awareness of the enormous capability of our own minds …

Jasmuheen told us that many children are being re-incarnated at this time who do not require much food. These are children of light, who come remembering what their purpose is, and carry the knowledge that they are a divine spirit encased in a physical body. She warned parents that any child who persistently refused food should be checked by a doctor, as the light children would always appear healthy and happy whether they ate or not. However, others who have allergies or other physical ailments will become sick and lose weight if they are not eating the right foods.

The lecture was like something out of a science fiction film, and yet after all that I had experienced I knew that what she was telling me was true. At the end of the lecture she was bombarded with questions and I asked Jasmuheen if she could dematerialize at will. She smiled graciously and said: 'this is easy when you work with the light …'

I have heard of people who are able to do this, but they are very rare. I had never previously met anyone who could do this at will. Jasmuheen has 5,000 followers who claim to live on divine energy (and liquids) alone, and the results of medical trials are due to be published shortly. But it takes special training to achieve this state of living purely on light, and I love my food too much. Perhaps in my next life time I might give it a try.

But if the medical trials corroborate what Jasmuheen has already proved to herself – that the divine energy source carries everything that we need for survival of our physical bodies the implications are staggering. For anyone wanting details of Jasmuheen's work, see page 270.

For the foreseeable future however, in order to become and remain as healthy as possible and to delay the ageing process, we need to eat more of the right foods, take regular exercise, reduce our stress and pollution levels, think more positive thoughts and have more fun on our journey. In fact, Diana had told me that if every person on the planet could somehow be synchronized to repeat and believe completely in the words, 'Everything is perfect' for 10 minutes at a pre-agreed time, then all the negative aspects of Earth, including pollution and sickness, could disappear.

In this way, fantastic though it may sound, she also said that some of the more severe weather changes could be calmed considerably. Diana said she knew that the majority of people would laugh at this suggestion, but had warned that unless we started to listen there could come a day when this might prove our only option.

A few days after hearing from Diana during August, my ex-secretary Lindsey called to say she had dreamt again of Diana.

'What happened in the dream?' I asked.

'Well,' Lindsey replied, 'It will soon be the first anniversary of her death and she is desperate for people to think positively on that day and says that it is a wasted opportunity if people become distressed or think negative thoughts.'

Another coincidence? I know that spirit often find it easier to contact us when we are asleep as the brain is more receptive. It was as if I was receiving confirmation that what I had heard was truly from Diana and Lindsey's dream lifted my spirits no end ...

I also thought how great it would be if I could meet a scientist who could explain in scientific terms how it is possible for us to move from one dimension to another at will.

I didn't have to wait long. Just two weeks later I went to London for a meeting with my TV producer friend Joanne Sawicki, as Dr John Briffa and I were working on a TV show concept. As I arrived at Jo's home, she was running late in another meeting and introduced her guest David Ash. We chatted amicably for a few minutes and he gave me his book, *The New Science of Spirit*, to look through while I was waiting. I had nothing else to do and as I flicked the pages, I was astounded when my eye caught sight of the words 'physical ascension'. I needed to talk to this man ...

My TV idea was forgotten for a moment as I shared with David and his nutritional physician wife, Lisbeth, some of my story. David nodded and smiled and interjected with quick-fire questions: 'And how did other people smell over Easter?' he asked with a wicked twinkle in his eye. I laughed, thinking 'he's my kind of scientist'. I remembered the smell in our home in April. I was so sensitive that I could easily 'smell' and 'feel' negative energies. Of course Stuart and his mother were frantic with worry, so were Dr Briffa and Lindsey ... The smell in the house had been their negative thoughts.

On Easter Saturday when I had 'died', our bedroom stank of physical death, but once we had opened the windows and Sheila had changed all the sheets and towels the sickly sweet, putrefying stench had disappeared. However, to me, the rest of the house still smelled – it was my heightened senses, as no one else could smell a thing.

David said, 'Our third dimensional world is so dense that to a person experiencing an ascended state as you were, negative thoughts and emotions would literally stink.'

Here was a truly enlightened scientist who has spent 30 years working on the theory that energy forms matter by spinning. I remembered how for weeks my solar plexus seemed to be spinning out of control to the point where I thought I would surely explode into flames. How wildly it had spun on that afternoon when I had almost managed to manifest a diamond ring from nowhere. So where would the ring have come from? 'Does this mean that ultimately it is possible to manifest any physical object at will?' I asked.

David explained: 'Thoughts are matter on a higher speed band of energy. So, with the ascended powers that we all have access to, but just don't know about, it is scientifically possible for objects to appear in our world seemingly from nowhere – this is what Sai Baba in India is able to do.'

'So, how could my legs have begun to dematerialize without the help of any physical equipment and how could my skin begin regenerating?' I enquired.

'That's easy,' was his reply. 'The energy within your atoms began moving faster than the speed of light: this could happen to part or whole of your body. In this case it happened to your legs, causing them to disappear out of physical space time and to enter another dimension. If the whole of you had disappeared, once outside the physical space time continuum, you could then have re-entered our world at any point in space and time.'

I knew it. There was a point back in May when I had known that I could access the past and many of our possible futures in this way, but had been too nervous to experiment with this knowledge. This was why it had been so easy for me to 'see' people's immediate futures.

David continued, 'With this possibility of involving the physical body in time travel, it is possible to reverse the ageing process and bring about a physical rejuvenation. Because your body was shifting in and out of the dimensions, you would have seemed younger at times. It has been well documented that spiritual masters can achieve this at will and from what you are telling me, you became a master, an enlightened being, a fully conscious soul for a short time. In our world everything is relative to the speed of light, other dimensions are on a higher speed band, they are created out of vortices of energy that move at much faster speeds than the speed of light. They have their own space and time. Their world is as real as ours.'

'But where is this world?' I wanted to know.

'It's everywhere,' David answered. 'What separates us is not space and time, but the speed at which the energy is travelling.'

David chastized me for continually talking about frequencies saying, 'The context in which you talk about frequencies is totally wrong from a scientific standpoint. It would be more correct to talk about 'energy patterning'. Frequency is a measure of waves and on every level you have a full electromagnetic spectrum of waves, but it is the underlying speed of the energy that matters. Many worlds, dimensions, speed bands, whatever you choose to call them, overlap, so that when you felt Diana inside your body and heard her voice she simply overlaid her speed band over yours. You became as one.'

'So, why did so many realities come into my mind? How come I was inundated with new senses and new knowledge?' I asked.

David continued, 'Aldous Huxley explains this concept brilliantly in his book Doorways of Perception. On an everyday level everyone's brain filters out tons of information, but your filters were lifted and you suddenly had access to unbelievable amounts of information and realities that understandably freaked you out.'

'And what about the ash that manifested from my hands or simply appeared in the room when I was present?' I queried.

'Ash, such as the 'vibuthi' which Sai Baba in India manifests, is atomic matter from another dimension', replied David. 'It is able to manifest through enlightened masters into our world as the energy within it slows down to the speed of light. Matter is simply energy within atoms which has slowed down. Atoms lock together through chemical bonding to create the illusion of solidity in our world, in fact our world is nothing but force fields created by the movement we call energy.'

'But why did ash appear when I would have much preferred the diamond ring?' I joked.

'Because, in the East, devotees burn incense sticks in their temples and the ash that collects from these is considered sacred. Sai Baba's 'vibuthi' is this same sacred ash, so while it does not mean much to people in the West, in the East it means far more than diamond rings!' I felt suitably humbled.

# 18 The Higher Realms

**DIANA HAD SAID THAT WHEN** people first pass over into the next dimension, most are shocked when they realize that there is life after physical death. Apparently, she says, when we let go of our heavy physical bodies it is a joy to feel so 'light'. But death does not change the underlying personality of an individual. Whatever the person's state of mind when they die, this creates their first impressions of their new world, which is why it is so vital to help people to pass over in a loving way. She related how a being of light (an angel), a trained helper, or a loving relative who has previously passed over, is always on hand as a soul moves into the next dimension. No one is left without help who wishes it.

Diana has become painfully aware of just how many people kill themselves or others in 'a moment of madness' and begs all those who are in the depths of despair to talk to someone and let all the pain out. She talked about how she too had tried to take her own life in a desperate cry for help, but now realizes just how precious physical life is and is aware of how most people who commit suicide deeply regret their actions and the hurt felt by their loved ones after their death.

This reminded me of sentiments that Dr Deepak Chopra had shared with me during an interview in 1997 saying, 'There are millions of people out there who are literally dying, because they cannot get things off their chest.' He recommends that anyone who is at the end of their tether should make a space and time between what stresses them and their reaction to it. To go somewhere, anywhere quiet, and think about life. Wisely he then advises people to open their hearts and tell someone what they are going through. Friends and family are not psychic, and if you don't tell them, they will never know the state you are in. Chopra says the secret is to remain open-minded so that you can recognize the signals and situations before it is too late. If we could all do this I believe that many illnesses, arguments and even suicides might be averted.

Diana had agreed.

'But what about pre-meditated murder, rape and all the people who make it their mission in life to bully others?' I had enquired.

'On Earth you worry about punishing people who have done wrong or committed a crime, but you have to realize that this is the old style of 'an eye for an eye'. When I was on Earth, I often said and thought dreadful things about quite a few people, but I now see that it all came back to me. It is imperative you start seeing what good can come from even the worst situations – what you learn from them,' she said.

'We realize that society still demands punishment for certain crimes and see that schemes where criminals have met their victims have often proved successful in helping offenders realize how much hurt and anguish they have caused. Sometimes they choose to make amends. This is wonderful. There are also fanatical and angry people from all walks of life, religious fanatics or cult fanatics, who want to try and persuade everyone to see their point of view. They often resort to violence which makes no difference to the 'bigger picture', it only hurts the innocent, which is a tragedy.'

She had said that even if criminals are caught and punished during their physical lifetime that they have automatically broken universal laws and will feel the pain they inflicted on others when they move into the higher realms. But if they genuinely, and with their whole hearts, ask for forgiveness, they can make amends by helping others, some of whom were their victims in their physical lifetime. But again their 'punishment', their atonement is always of their own choosing.

She had said that if a person died in a state of fear, because they were murdered, starved to death or whatever, they carried their fear over with them. These souls are looked after in really loving halfway homes until they understand that there is no longer any need for fear. Diana said that fanatics with closed minds, religious or otherwise, get the biggest shock of all when they realize that no religion is better than another, and that the only thing that counts is how you live your life. She sees how some religious fanatics rule through fear and claim to be 'the true voice of God' by making predictions and then resorting to force to ensure their dire 'predictions' happen.

Again Diana cautioned about the many different realities, saying, 'Yes, some people are beginning to realize that they are indeed part of God, that you all carry the frequency of God within you. But you now know what an incredible baptism of fire this can be, and unfortunately many do not come through the experience with their feet firmly on the ground as you have done. Some have unbelievable delusions of grandeur and their ego grows and grows, and because they speak with such conviction, those who are vulnerable believe them. But as you have already pointed out, if and when a person has this awakening, their underlying personality does not change, and some will use their newly discovered powers for negative purposes. Others are simply con men who have climbed on the bandwagon for money or to boost their ego.

'Some want power over peoples' minds and actions. Others are mentally ill and need medical attention. This is why it is imperative for people to find their own truth. When you were a junior master for those few weeks, you knew that living masters such as Sai Baba, Mother Meera, Swamiji Satchidananda in Virginia and others including Jesus, Buddha, Mohammed,

Krishna and so on lived and still live by example. They do not ask to be worshipped, or for people to be killed in their name. These are and were people that truly worked for the light – for the Divine energy source that you call God. Any person or religion that teaches through fear, coercion or bullying is definitely not working for the light. On Earth many people are seeking a new messiah, but there are quite a few masters already here and you will know them by the way they live their life. These masters are here only to help you to wake up the master within each and every one of you, not to be worshipped.'

'All this master stuff is very heavy, could we lighten up a bit?' I asked.

Diana began repeating herself. 'In the higher realms everything is done for the good of the whole. There are great places of education just as there are on Earth, where everyone is taught the meaning of life and shown how they can help. We don't need money as we can manifest our needs through our minds. There are great and wonderful gardens here just as there are on Earth, and for those who do not wish to live on light, food is grown in these beautiful gardens. But for now, rather than asking about life after death, concentrate on enjoying the life that you have, and work on achieving the right balance for you and your children.'

Diana realizes that millions of children have wonderful parents who teach them right from wrong and give discipline when it is needed. Her awareness of child abuse was acute when she was here, and she knows that there is a desperate need to keep a balance between discipline and violence. But she feels that too many children are being brought into the world by parents who are still children themselves, who have never been taught respect or how to behave in a kind way. Her statement reminded me of my meeting with Francis Rossi of the rock band Status Quo. He told me that at school he was taught to swear and how to spit, but he was never taught how to be kind. Today, as a devoted father of eight children, Francis tries to instil a sense of camaraderie and good manners into his children in the hope that they may in turn teach the same principles to their own children. There is no doubt that we all learn from example.

Diana had said that we return to Earth to remember who we really are, to learn and grow from our experiences, and that it is imperative we begin teaching all children the basics of discipline, love and caring for their fellow men and women by example.

If we don't learn from experience, and fulfil our purpose in this lifetime, we keep 'going round in circles' until we do. The bad news, according to Diana, is that our lessons are going to become harder and faster to force us to take notice ... and soon.

It's like life itself – the changing weather patterns, the increasing sickness, the escalating violence all says to us, how many more knocks do you need before you will change? How much more can you take? We are here to 'experience' free will and then to choose. But not enough people are learning from their experiences, and so the cycles keep repeating themselves.

According to Diana, a 2,000-year-old cycle is now ending and another is beginning. It's time to wake up. It's time to remember who we are, what we came to do, and above all to know that it's never too late to change. This reminded me of an 82-year-old lady who wrote to me saying that she had cured her tinnitus, a ringing in the ears which she had suffered for over 40 years, after having acupuncture, changing her diet and taking the right vitamin and mineral supplements. She had helped herself and it gave her a whole new lease of life. I have received thousands of letters from people of all ages who have cured themselves of cancer, eczema, arthritis, heart problems and numerous other conditions. The majority of us can help ourselves if we choose to. Our bodies are perfectly capable of healing themselves when given the right tools for the job. We must stop taking our bodies for granted.

We only get one physical body in each lifetime, and we should worship it as a temple. Above all,

Diana reminded me over and over again to love myself a bit more. How can we expect others to love and respect us, if we don't love and respect ourselves? She said that I should not to be so hard on myself, and to let go of judgement and ego. And if we trust that what we need is for our higher good it will come.

Also she said that, as far as possible, we should do what we love to do, as when we are happy we radiate more light and can receive more light to inspire others. Always realize that you have choices. If you don't like who you are and what you do, work out ways to change for the better. Diana encourages everyone that whatever job you do in life – no matter how menial – give it your best shot. We are all important and we can all make a difference, even those in prisons and institutions, the homeless, alcoholics, drug addicts. No matter how low or abandoned you may feel today, tomorrow you can make a brand new start. You can change your attitude and decide that somehow you are going to help yourself and make a difference. And believe me, once you have offered to work for the light, help will come when you least expect it often from unusual sources. Love yourself, and share that love with others. And if you want to find your purpose, one of the best books I have seen on this subject is by Nick Williams (see page 271).

### *31st August – Oxfordshire*

The first anniversary of Diana's death came and passed. I managed to watch a one-hour special on her life and surprisingly all I felt was compassionate detachment. Back in June when a programme on the car crash in Paris was broadcast, Stuart had immediately noticed how badly it affected me and through my protests had switched off the TV, as he was terrified it might all begin again. But as I watched the documentary, I recalled Lindsey's most recent dream in which Diana had asked us all to think positive thoughts, to remember all the happy times she'd had and to recall just how much she achieved in her short lifetime.

She had predicted that the unusual weather patterns would be gradual but persistent. You would have to be very out of touch indeed not to have noticed the weather changes and the millions of words being written on global warming. Since the terrible storms over Easter that were centred near our home in the Midlands I had begun to take an even keener interest in the weather. July in the UK was a wash out, but globally it was the hottest month on record in the history of the world.

Apparently if we don't act, the weather and Earth changes will become a lot more persistent and records will go on being broken, until we are forced to listen …

As August slipped into September I noticed a tiny report in a newspaper relating how thousands had died in the worst floods in Asia in living memory. Typhoon Rex hit Japan. Hurricane Bonnie hit Carolina at Cape Fear and half a million people fled their homes. We all contribute to the weather and together we can change it – if we make the right choices …

# 19

# The Journey

**ON WEDNESDAY 9TH SEPTEMBER** we left for Australia. Friends had warned us that we were crazy not to break our journey in Bangkok or Singapore, but I had not seen my daughter Victoria for almost two years, and I was determined to think positively and arrive feeling wonderful. After all, the journey is only 23 hours. In the great scheme of things 23 hours is nothing, and yet we can live and die in a second. I was going to live for the moment and not give a thought as to how I might feel when we landed in Sydney.

As our 747 headed southeast out of Heathrow and broke through the clouds into the afternoon sunshine I was in no mood for sleep, I felt like a child going on a great adventure.

Airline journeys always make an ideal time for reflection. Sitting in my comfortable first-class seat I thought about my childhood back in Coventry. In those days I had wild dreams, I wanted the whole fairy tale and now I was living it. My thoughts turned to the millions of people in the world who would give almost anything to have my life. But no single person can make enough money to feed, clothe and help everybody, we can only do our best.

Day turned to dusk as we headed over Turkey, close to Iraq and Iran, then night came over Afghanistan, Pakistan and across northern India. On the tiny TV screen attached to my seat I watched our flight path and thought about what the people below me might be doing. I thought about the hardship being suffered by millions in Iraq and the repressive religious regime in Iran. I also recalled the war and earthquake victims in Afghanistan. It evoked memories of my meeting with Queen Noor the previous October when she had said, 'I have seen much greed, ignorance, religious intolerance and hatred generated by people who like to manipulate others for their own ends. If everyone could think outside of themselves, they would understand how their actions have a knock-on effect that can cause so much destruction. Peace would unleash a positive energy that could have an impact not only on our political process, but on the quality of life for every child and every community.'

She is a special lady whose dear husband, King Hussein, died on 7th February 1999. As I watched all the world leaders attending his funeral in Jordan – the Israelis, Palestinians, Syrians, Americans, Egyptians, Russians and Iraqis, to name but a few – I mused that if they could all make peace for one day in honour of one man, why couldn't they make peace for all time?

Queen Noor and I had also discussed the growing death rate in Jordan from cancers, especially breast and prostate cancers. I thought of the millions of tons of pesticides and herbicides used globally that are known to trigger various cancers. And King Hussein died of cancer – we are creating our own reality. Rich and poor, everyone is being affected. I thought of the floods in Bangladesh. In my newspaper it said that twothirds of the country was under water, 1,000 people had died and 25 million were homeless. I also thought about the work of Muhammad Yunus, and his magical book Banker To The Poor. He has become a wealthy man by loaning sums as little as 50p to the world's poorest people. Trade not aid. He is helping to restore their pride and dignity and Prince Charles has supported his initiative by writing the foreword to his book. There are thousands of ways to make money and to help people and the planet at the same time. I recalled Diana requesting me to encourage people to practise 'socially responsible investing'. In other words not just to invest their money in anything that makes money, but to make sure that their investment in some way helps the planet and its people.

She had said there is nothing wrong with having money, which is simply another form of energy, it's what we do with it that counts …

A warm sultry dawn broke as we landed in Bangkok just two hours later. I longed to leave the confines of the airport to see the city or better still to find a clean bed and fall into it, but it had been my choice to fly straight on, so after an hour we found ourselves back in our seats ready for the next leg of our journey. Dr Serena Roney-Dougal had reminded me back in June about time being relative, and that when you are doing something you love, time flies. I was flying all right, but time was beginning to drag and the thought of another ten hours until we reached Sydney suddenly seemed rather daunting. The fresh faces that had boarded at Heathrow looked gaunt in the sunlight that now flooded the cabin.

Another meal came and went and I continued to follow our route on the little TV screen in front of me, willing the time to pass more quickly. I noticed us passing the Andeman Islands which I had never heard of before. I picked up a magazine from the rack and as I idly flicked through the pages a feature showing a picture of a rain forest caught my eye. As I read on yet another amazing synchronicity occurred – the article was about the 100 surviving Onge tribespeople from the same Andeman Islands we had just passed, and how their ancient plant remedies are now at the centre of an international confrontation.

Weeks later I found another article about this ancient tribe in Time magazine, written by Tim McGirk. An Indian microbiologist has discovered that although they are surrounded by malaria-carrying mosquitos not one of them has caught the deadly disease. The scientist was shown their unique concoction, which the scientist found both contained not only anti-fever properties but also reduced the number of malarial parasites in infected human blood. Realizing that a cure for malaria would be of huge value to a pharmaceutical company, he hoped to be able to make a lot of money himself – but he also wanted the tribe to benefit and be able to continue their culture. When he discovered a senior colleague was trying to file a patent application in his own name, the biologist refused to hand over his findings. To add insult to injury this ancient tribe is now dying from flu strains, bacteria and viruses that are being 'imported' by western visitors.

During the past ten years I have written regularly about native remedies that are so often described as 'snake oil and rubbish' by the orthodox establishment. But today the large drug companies are sending gene specialists to many remote regions of the globe to meet local shamans and medicine men and buy the secrets of their ago-old remedies. For instance, the bark of the African Pygeum tree has long been known to help treatment of enlarged prostates and the market is worth about $220 million a year. Drug companies, though, rarely pass on a share of their profits to the communities that provide the raw materials and knowledge. The Pygeum tree now faces extinction. Balance – we keep forgetting about balance.

As the hours passed I walked the length and breadth of the aircraft to stretch my legs. Some 200 passengers were in cramped seats but many were fast asleep, and yet I hadn't slept a wink. Suddenly I felt very envious of those who can sleep anywhere, anytime. What a wonderful blessing …

# 20

## The Vision

**WHEN WE FINALLY ARRIVED IN** Sydney after our 23-hour journey, I felt absolutely exhausted. Tears flowed as I hugged my daughter and for a brief moment all else was forgotten.

By the time we finally reached our hotel overlooking Sydney harbour and the world famous opera house, I was ready to drop. And yet when I went to flush the loo, I was not too tired to notice that there was a double plunger on the top, if you pressed one side you got a full flush while the other gave you a half flush. Imagine how many millions of gallons of water we could save if we had these toilets in the UK and Europe. I knew in that moment I would love Australia. Meanwhile, I desperately needed a good night's sleep. I took some melatonin – a hormone-like substance secreted by the pineal gland that helps us to sleep – enjoyed a wonderful lavender bath, drank a cup of camomile tea and passed out cold for almost 12 hours. Total bliss.

The next morning we awoke to lashing horizontal rain and cold winds, which made me feel quite at home. Victoria became our enthusiastic tour guide and we enjoyed catching up with friends we had not seen for years. On 14th September we celebrated Vicki's 30th birthday. Stuart made a brief speech and I cried. It was a truly wonderful evening which helped me to finally let go of the guilt I had carried for so many years for sending Vicki to boarding school aged only five when my poor mum became ill and for almost always being away working when it had been her birthday or school play.

On 16th September Stuart and I said goodbye to Vicki for two days and travelled west for two hours by car to stay in the Blue Mountains. Back in May, Diana had predicted that something special would happen in the Blue Mountains and I felt incredibly apprehensive and yet excited ... The sun shone brilliantly as we left Sydney and the spring morning was forecast to be warm with a temperature of around 70 degrees Fahrenheit. But as we drove higher, the temperature dropped and by the time we arrived at the Hotel Lilianfels it was a crisp spring afternoon.

Our room had panoramic views overlooking the mountains and as we walked into our bedroom, the scenery took my breath away. The sheer scale and majesty of these ancient mountains, which have stood for over 250 million years, is breathtaking. We quickly changed into warmer clothes and walked the few hundred yards down the road to stand on one of the viewing platforms which overlooks the rock formation known as the Three Sisters. As I stood there drinking in the view, I was overcome by a sense of just how insignificant I felt compared to the glorious mountains before me that had stood for eons.

We are all here but for the blink of an eye and in the great scheme of things does it really all matter? Humans have done so much damage and we are on the verge of destroying our home, and yet in that moment I knew that some invisible force, call it God, call it nature, whatever feels right to you, would not allow this to happen. We will go on being 'woken up' until we listen. Our awakening can be as easy or as difficult as we make it.

As we walked arm-in-arm back to the hotel, the sun began setting and the clear skies and crisp cold air foretold that a frost was inevitable. I looked back over the mountains and said a silent 'thank you' for my life, for the good and the bad times which had all taught me their own unique lessons, for my wonderful daughter and my dear husband, who has been my rock.

It seemed like a good time for reflection, so back in warmth of our cosy room I sat and watched the dusk fall over the mountains. The millions of eucalyptus trees give off an aroma which at dawn and dusk turns the air a misty, ethereal blue, it is an awesome sight.

Stuart went into the sitting room to catch up on some work and I sat down to meditate in our bedroom, overlooking the incredible view. Silence, the silence was wonderful, I drank it in like a nectar from the gods. I closed my eyes and thought about Diana and wondered if she had ever been to this wonderful place. In that very second I felt the energy in the room change and the air became much cooler.

Slowly, I opened my eyes and to my astonishment Diana appeared before me. She looked like a hologram. All I could see was her head, shoulders, upper body and arms and she radiated a beautiful bluish white light. I was incredibly shocked, but not afraid, and the atmosphere within the room became unbelievably calm and still. Her eyes were mesmerizing and I could feel her words inside my head: 'Remember above all things that each and every one of you comes to Earth to remember who you are, to learn from experience and to serve. This is your sole purpose.'

It was incredible, time stood still, it reminded me of Easter Saturday afternoon when I had felt completely free – when nothing else had mattered. My head was reeling, and I tried to think of something fitting to say, a question to ask. All I could think to say was, 'How can others hear you, and receive the unbelievable and wonderful insights that I have been shown?'

And as I had that thought she touched her heart and a beam of pure white light shot from her heart to mine.

'People can find me and others if they truly open their hearts. You are never alone, we are with you now and always, we are in your hearts.'

My heart and mind ached with a feeling of pure love, and tears streamed down my cheeks. The light within the room intensified and I struggled to control my emotions as Dodi appeared. Beside him stood a young child.

'This is a child of hope. Children are your future, so teach them well. Tell my earthly sons I will love them for all time and will be waiting for them when their moment comes. But we are all children, and it's never too late. Remember these words. Cry for me no more, be happy, for I am home now.'

I was beyond words. Darkness fell over the mountains and the vision, the apparition, faded and disappeared. For a few moments I could not move. The entire incident had lasted no more than two minutes and yet I would hold the memory of what I had seen for all time. I knew it was time to dry my eyes, but I could not bring myself to tell Stuart what had happened, it was too profound and he would think everything was starting again. That night after dinner we walked back down to the floodlit platform overlooking the Three Sisters and sat in silence looking at the heavens. The stars and planets looked so clear, like sparkling baubles on a Christmas tree that I could simply reach out and touch. And as we sat we saw a shooting star speed across the sky. My heart flooded with emotion and in my mind I whispered to Diana, 'Farewell and God's speed.'

As we walked back towards the hotel I heard a faint voice singing. And the song – *Imagine*.

# Epilogue

*or should I say the never-ending story*

**ON OUR FLIGHT BACK TO THE UK** I heard that the Duchess of York's mother, Susan Barrantes, had been tragically killed in a car accident. The long flight gave me plenty of time to tune in and see if Diana might contact me again. Instead I felt Sarah's mother Susan. She apologized for causing the accident by driving too fast. She said that Sarah should try and find a good home for the ponies and then 'let go' because her daughter had more than enough to do without taking on anything else. So sad ... If I saw Sarah again I would give her these messages. Meanwhile, when I asked Diana to make contact all I heard was 'Call Susan, call Susan'. Susan who?

For months I had been desperate for verification that I really had heard the spirit of Diana, that I had not simply been talking to myself, that it had not been my imagination. Suddenly it clicked. Of course, I had to call my old friend Sue Brotherton, a highly experienced medium who has been involved in the spiritual movement for almost 30 years. Sue knows me well enough to realize that something important had happened and agreed to come and spend a night and a day with me in London on 12th October 1998.

Meanwhile, on 26th September Hurricane George hit Florida and the Caribbean, leaving 300 dead, hundreds homeless and a trail of devastation.

A few days later on 1st October I finally received a letter via my friend Lord Feldman from Stephen Lamport, Prince Charles' private secretary. Charles would not grant me a private audience – I was disappointed but I had done my best.

When Sue arrived I told her a little of what had happened to me over Easter and that I truly believed I had been in direct contact with Diana Princess of Wales. Sue was shocked, but the look on my face told her I was deadly serious.

Sue told me not to tell her a single fact that Diana had shared with me, because she would tune in herself, but Sue reminded me that although she can request to tune into a specific spirit, she could offer no guarantees.

At first I wrote down almost everything that Sue picked up, but soon realized there was virtually no point, as I had heard it all before. Not only did Sue corroborate 95 per cent of what I had already written in Diana's name in the manuscript, but when 'hearing' Diana she also used similar phrases and words that I had heard during the previous months.

Remember, no one had seen my notes. No one.

As the hours passed I realized that Diana had said everything she needed to say and listening to Sue gave me enormous comfort. Until that moment, the responsibility of all that I had heard during the previous months had seemed a heavy burden. Hearing Sue lightened my load, and I knew that there must be quite a few others who were hearing Diana too. As the dawn broke Sue said that she was meant to be my 'back-up', to prove to me that what I had heard was indeed from Diana. Many cynics would say it's easy to make up what Diana may or may not want to say, but I had written down what I heard. It was my truth.

Sue continued, 'Diana is aware that there are numerous books about spiritual awakening, but those working with her in the higher realms have endeavoured to make yours so dramatic and profound that people who are ready to listen will take notice. And the cynics, well, you may never convince them'.

I sighed, if only I could hear Diana as clearly as I had back in April, May and June. Sue told me that to be a good medium you need a perfectly relaxed mind. If you are under pressure, you cannot achieve the mind-tomind contact to pick up the details you need. And even then you can only sense a small percentage of all the spirit wishes to convey, as you tune into and blend with their unique frequency. She suggested that if I wanted once again to become a clear channel for Diana or anyone else I should relax my mind more and not try so hard. And anyway, she felt that I already had all the details I needed and should simply carry on writing. And so I did.

In late October Stuart and I travelled to Barbados. For ten days there had been lashing storms and floods in the Caribbean islands. One day as we drove down the west coast we were caught by a torrential downpour which caused millions of gallons of water to run from the hills down the roads and gullies and into the sea. The water rushed passed us down to the ocean and as the water level rose above our wheels hubs, panic rose in my throat. Somehow our car kept going, but others were not so fortunate. This was the beginning of Hurricane Mitch which was to travel onwards with increasing fury and kill over 11,000 people in Honduras, Nicaragua, Panama and Belize.

Being in that flood made me realize that thousands of unusual weather incidents are happening every day somewhere in the world. To hear about it on the news is one thing, but to be in it is quite another. During our ten-day stay we read about the heavy floods in Wales, Manchester and the Midlands which had been the worst in over 30 years. The insurance claims in the UK alone were predicted to top £100 million. Gradual, but persistent. To me it seemed just persistent, nothing gradual about it any more.

On 11th November 1998 at 11 am, along with 43 million people across the UK, I stood quietly to remember the dead from the two great wars. I recalled Diana's words that if we could do this more often and think and believe 100 per cent 'everything is perfect' during those few minutes, our world could be transformed.

I finally saw Sarah, Duchess of York, again for lunch in late November 1998. It seemed as though 100 years had passed since our last meeting. I had written numerous notes for Sarah from Diana, and as I read them to her, she nodded and smiled. Yes, she felt that they sounded so like the Diana she knew. I also gave her the private messages I had received from her mother and Sarah confirmed that my information was correct.

Like every single one of us, Sarah has made mistakes, but she has also done a great deal of good. Through her charity Children in Crisis, Sarah has helped to raise millions of pounds for needy children. She is doing what she can, where she can. No one should ask for more. And as I sat with Sarah I finally recognized that I could not ask her to help me publicly, as the press would have another field day at her expense. She has never read this manuscript and has no idea what it contains, but I told Sarah that I would be writing about our meeting at the Capitol Hotel back in June 1998.

When I had seen Sue Brotherton I had asked her if she could hear something specific for Sarah. Diana had told us that it was time for Fergie to move on. Diana did not want to cause Sarah any problems but had said I should ask Sarah one final question, which I did.

'Back in June when you saw me at the Capitol Hotel and you saw me being overshadowed, did you believe me and all that I told you?' Sarah looked deeply into my eyes as if weighing up my motives and finally sighed, 'Yes, I believed you, I know what I saw and what I heard. Yes I believed you …'

I could have kissed her feet …

Sarah risked much saying this and allowing me to quote her, and I was about to find out just how much she was risking …

In April Diana had told me about men 'above governments' who had begun plotting her downfall. She also told me that these same people had arranged for one of her police body guards, Barry Mannakee, to have an 'accident' resulting in his death in 1988 when they became 'too close'. When I heard these statements I ignored them, as it all sounded too cloak and dagger and such claims would be virtually impossible for me to prove.

But in January 1999 I met a young man at a dinner party who had just left the SAS after 11 years' service. Over coffee I asked him as casually as I could about the possibility of there being a 'body' or group who might be 'above governments' At first he was very guarded, but after much persuasion, and after sharing some of what had happened to me he said, 'You think that Tony Blair is running the UK and to a great extent he is, but there are people above him who have a great deal more power. In the service we referred to them as "The Council".'

I was taken aback, I had read numerous articles and books saying that such a group existed but had never heard such information from such an authoritative source. The ex-SAS man eventually agreed to a private interview as long as he could remain anonymous. We signed confidentiality agreements and met at a London hotel. What he told me sent a cold chill down my spine.

On many occasions he had visited the Royal Close Protection Unit at Buckingham Palace where they would carry out joint exercises with the SAS. I quote: 'During one of these visits the subject of the deceased officer Barry Mannakee, who had guarded Diana, was brought up. At first it was brushed over, but later in the evening after having a few drinks I was told by a member of the Royal Unit that in fact this man's death had been no accident, he had been murdered. Because he and Diana had an affair.'

I was horrified and asked if Charles or any member of the Royal Family could have known that this particular 'accident' was in fact murder.

He honestly did not know …

'And who,' I asked, 'are this Council?'

'The Council are senior figures in the UK – ex-military, senior industrialists, ex-politicians, senior judges, former high-ranking members of the intelligence services and others in high office. But we were never told their names. They gather most of their information from the communications centre, Menwith Hill, in Yorkshire and have hundreds of ways of gathering information by using highly sophisticated technology. In this way they listened to every word Diana and many other people say and said on the phone. The Council would then decide what action to take.'

'So how do you know they really exist?' I asked.

'After 11 years in the SAS and intelligence services, believe me I know. At the highest levels The Council is common knowledge.'

'The Council have the power to destroy people, anybody, either through disinformation within the press or by murder … They plan with incredible precision and they never fail. They can even record from people's mobile phones, then edit the tape to turn it to their advantage. They control people in power, and every first world country has its own council.'

I had to ask him about Diana's death. 'Do you believe there was a plot to kill Diana?'

'In truth I don't know what happened in that tunnel but I do know that if Diana had agreed to marry Dodi or have his child The Council could have organized another accident.'

So there it was, as near as I was going to get. And as I walked away from our meeting, for several days I found myself looking over my shoulder. Some people labelled Diana as being paranoid, she had looked over her shoulder for 17 years. Enough to break a lesser person. Sarah is still doing it. All I could do was pray that my phone wasn't being bugged too.

But I have no proof that what the ex-SAS man told me is true, but he had no reason to lie to me, and I believe what I was told.

When Sue and I sat together once more we jointly asked Diana about the tunnel in Paris again and again. And over and over we both received the same reply, 'It was an accident – it truly was.' All I know is that my story is the truth. Many people reading this book might think that what I went through over Easter was a terrifying ordeal and when it happened it was, but it was also an awesome experience. And I would give anything to recreate the way I felt over Easter and throughout May and June 1998 – anything.

Some of you may ask why did I not approach Diana's brother Earl Spencer or other colleagues. I never wrote to Earl Spencer as I realized that, like Prince Charles, he would be inundated with mail – and I had no direct way to reach him. Neither did I try to contact the only survivor from Diana and Dodi's car crash, Dodi's bodyguard Trevor Rees-Jones. This was because he had been very seriously injured and was still having treatment.

In January 1999, after reading about Princess Diana's ex-butler Paul Burrell's departure from the charitable trust formed after Diana's death, I eventually traced his home address and wrote to him. In February I received a kind reply thanking me 'for offering my professional services' when in fact I had private messages to pass on to him.

Then I began negotiating via an intermediary with Commander Patrick Jephson, who was Princess Diana's personal equerry for almost eight years. But he was a busy man and he did not have time to see me. Again I had personal messages which I hoped would prove irrevocably that I was truly communicating with Diana.

Eventually time became my greatest enemy. Diana agreed that I had done my best and it was time to simply get the book out. And I did.

On 7th April 1999 my husband took me to Paris for my 50th birthday. After everything I had been through I just had to see the scene of the accident. It was such a straight piece of road and not a tunnel at all, only a small underpass. And as we drove over those few fateful yards all I could hear was, Diana saying, 'Let it go now, it really was an accident. Remember me with love in your heart, but let me go.'

As our taxi emerged from the underpass into the bright sunshine I took a deep breath and finally let her go. She had told me there really is no point in going back, and that we should all work together towards a brighter future and finding our own truth. I have found my truth through my experience, and leave you now to find yours.

With Love and Light to you all
Hazel Courteney
July 1999.

# 21 THE JOURNEY CONTINUES

*November 2004*

**HAD I REALLY HEARD** from the spirit of Diana, Princess of Wales? Did I truly become some kind of enlightened spiritual being who could effect miracles? The answer is yes – and no. I became everything and nothing, and today, more than ever, I understand that virtually everything is a paradox, and there are thousands of realities and explanations.

My search for more answers has taken me back to America, Germany and on to India and Bali. I have interviewed spiritual masters whom, in this lifetime, I never believed I might even begin to understand – let alone meet face to face. I have witnessed miracles that have lifted my soul briefly back to the blissful, heightened state that I experienced during the spring and summer of 1998, but I have also plummeted to the depths of despair – and beyond.

It's as if I have lived another lifetime during the past four years. So much has happened – and yet it's only a brief chapter that has been added to my never-ending journey. For our spirit is eternal.

No one ever said that the spiritual path is an easy one, but I now know that it is possible, preferable and far safer to become enlightened in a calm, controlled and loving way, without the need to experience the trauma of a spiritual emergency – when spiritual transformation becomes a crisis, and mine sure became a crisis.

To say what I went through was exceptional is an understatement, but I have heard from hundreds of others around the world who have had, or who are undergoing similar experiences to varying degrees, and I am truly thankful to report that this book has even saved lives.

Many people saw visions of Diana during the night on which she died, not knowing of her death until they awoke the next morning. Numerous mediums around the globe have also seen or heard Diana since her death.

More about this later.

Looking back, I also realize that if my spiritual emergency had not been so dramatic, life-threatening and profound, this book would never have been written. We are all links in a chain – we all come with a purpose – and before I chose to be born into this lifetime, I agreed to go through the experience.

I almost lost my life and my sanity. I lost my wonderful job and with it a good income. When this book was first published in December 1999, a few people were quick to judge me before knowing the whole story. But once they realized that I had far more to lose than to gain by writing this book, and that my experience went way beyond only hearing Diana, attitudes changed.

What I experienced cannot be bought or sold, and no amount of wealth could ever replace how I felt and the gifts I discovered within myself.

But I now know quite a bit more than I did in 1999 and, although I have lots more to learn, I understand what happened more clearly.

When my literary agent suggested I should re-read *Divine Intervention* before writing this afterword, I baulked at the thought of re-living it all again. It was made easier once I put myself in the place of a stranger who had never heard of Hazel Courteney – and read it as a sceptic.

There were times when I thought 'this woman has got to be joking'.

Not because the story might be a total concoction, (I and many witnesses know it to be true); but due to the style of narrative. A lot of the words attributed to Diana, plus the wisdom threaded throughout the book, now seem riddled with clichés and at times extremely naïve.

Yet the underlying message – that we are all special, capable of affecting miracles, and that we can all make a difference through our every thought and deed – comes through loud and clear. There are a million ways to write universal truths, but try to understand that I was in an extremely heightened state of awareness, and that the facts I gave I believed to be absolutely true when I wrote them.

Throughout my life I have had an inner feeling of not being good enough. But as I finished reading the book, I wondered, 'how on earth did I live through it, keep my sanity, and manage to turn such a profound and huge experience – with which human words are pitifully lacking to describe – into a small, readable book?'

I marvel that it was written at all and, for once, I silently gave myself a pat on the back.

So what happened?

On that fateful day in Harrods back in April 1998, I now believe that my base chakra, known as the kundalini (or coiled serpent energy, that resides at the base of our spines) suddenly blew like a volcano. Once activated, the kundalini rises up, awakening all the other chakras, or energy centres, which forms a bridge to super-consciousness. There are spiritual teachers who say that the kundalini cannot be activated unless all the chakras are perfectly balanced. I beg to differ.

How did it feel? Try to imagine that you are an old-fashioned computer that has been ticking along for 20 years or so. Then one day, someone or something connects you to the ultimate computer – the one that contains all knowledge, all languages, all possibilities and all realities – otherwise known as the God Consciousness or the Ultimate Source of All That Is.

The editing abilities and software that kept you running normally are totally overpowered. All your circuits blow, and you have instant access to infinite amounts of unrestricted, unedited information and knowledge. Your mainframe begins to collapse. In a nutshell, that's basically what happened to me.

As my kundalini blew, the veils or filters between this and other worlds were lifted, and the spirit frequency of Diana was then free to enter and communicate without restriction.

My friend, Dr Richard Lawrence, had been right on that Easter Friday when he suggested to my neighbour, Norma, that I might have experienced a 'walk-in'. But I now understand that what happened to me was in no way evil; in fact, once I got used to the energy of Diana inside me, she was full of love, compassion and humour. For almost three months it felt as if there were two of us in one body.

I realized how speaking in tongues can be possible. When you enter these heightened states, the veil may be lifted for a second, a minute or several minutes; you have access to 'All That Is', but in receiving so much information, your brain cannot decipher it all, and out comes a garbled mess.

But I was online to Head Office – and it didn't switch off. As the days passed, the energy inside me and around me became more and more powerful. My whole body felt as though it were spinning – especially my solar plexus. There were days when I felt that at any moment this area could burst into flames. The spinning feeling was all my chakras being awakened (specialist scanners are now able to show these energy centres). Every time I asked a question, I received dozens of answers virtually simultaneously. Not only did I have to cope with the huge amounts of knowledge to which I had instant access, plus the physical phenomena happening around me, but I also had to cope with Diana's emotions – which were awesome – and try to keep an accurate record of everything she said. My body and mind were totally unprepared.

Imagine: on one day I'm a normal working wife going about my business; the next, I am levitating, my eyes are changing colour, and I begin affecting electrical equipment as my energy field becomes more and more powerful. Then there is this voice inside my head, a new personality, and different voices coming out of my mouth. How would you cope?

Initially I was frightened quite literally to death, and on the Easter Saturday when I left my body during the near-death experience, I believe this was caused not only by overload to my brain and nervous system, but also the terrible, almost unimaginable shock. Some of the shock was mine and some was Diana's as her emotions rippled through my body – an almost fatal combination.

For the first few weeks I alternated from occasional feelings of complete bliss and awe – to total terror. But as days turned to weeks and I slowly became more used to everything that was happening, there were several days on which I knew no fear at all. Times when, no matter what was happening around me, I was in a state of totally accepting bliss. If someone had put a gun to my head and said 'I'm going to shoot you' in such a moment, I would have said 'fine', and really meant it. This was because I knew that at our core we are eternal beings of light who cannot die, and in those moments everything felt perfect. I was incapable of telling a lie, and it would have been impossible to hurt any living thing, even a spider – which I would previously have killed without a thought. My physical strength was at times incredible. At one point I arm-wrestled Al, my 17-stone trainer, and he was incredulous at the strength I could summon at will.

Yet I also felt totally humble and, in a non-patronizing way, that I had become everyone's mother and father. Above all, by May 1998 I felt truly as though I had come home, as if this state was something that I had been searching for since the beginning of time. I knew that I (the ultimate 'I' being God) had emanated from the beginning of time, and that when you are in this blissful state, you are always home.

When people asked questions, I already knew the answers. When I looked deeply into a person's eyes, I felt I was seeing into their souls. No one could lie to me, as I could see only the truth. Possible futures and the past became freely available to me. I knew I had the capability to move between dimensions, between worlds and travel through time, but remained wary of doing so – in case I could not return. I also knew that one day linear time as we know it would cease to exist and that we would be able to choose our age.

And yet there were moments when I longed to merge with the ultimate source of bliss and perfection, the consciousness that is God, the cosmic mind. All that I believed I needed to do, was to lie down, relax, merge into and become light. The thought of walking on water at such moments seemed easy.

Like millions of others, I now know there are thousands of other life forms in the universe. The majority of us cannot see them, as they exist on other frequencies – other speed bands. But for those few precious months I could see and communicate with them, and to hear only the spirit world became like child's play.

Once I got used to seeing thoughts as coloured energy, moving around the house, it was great. I did not need a Feng Shui expert to tell me where energies were trapped – I could see them! If someone was sick I could 'see' their illness, tumour, injury or whatever as an energy blockage. Somehow I automatically knew when healing was possible and in such cases I offered healing. But when someone had chosen their illness for whatever reason, I would simply pulse into their energy field the energy of pure, unconditional love that was flowing through me. I could also feel what animals were thinking – you don't need language or words when feeling emotions, and there are numerous psychics who work with, and can easily understand, animals. I could smell negative thoughts and feel the energies emitted by newsprint. When I had a sudden influx of insights, if they felt right, they became my truth – but not necessarily anyone else's truth. A belief is only a thought that you hold to be true – and we are all creating our own reality, but note the word 'own'. One man's beliefs and practices can be offensive and even deadly to others. This is a crucial point for anyone undergoing a heightened spiritual experience.

In the summer of 2000 I was contacted by a man in his thirties who was going through through a huge spiritual emergency. Prior to the experience, he had been practising regular meditation and praying for spiritual growth. He got what he wished for! He and his family ran a busy newsagent's business – just ordinary people going about their lives. His family were desperate for help, as he was claiming to be the ultimate (and only) God, and vehemently suggested that spiritual masters like Sai Baba would want to kneel at his feet and so on. He invited his family to attempt to kill him, as he felt invincible and also demanded that his brothers get on their knees and worship him. Unfortunately, in discovering the ultimate truth, that we are all part of an eternal consciousness – God, he had forgotten that he is part of God in a physical body.

In vain I tried to calm him down, but he was loath to listen. When I spoke with his wife, she said that he had always been rather macho and opinionated. And as the scientist, Dr Serena Roney-Dougal, had told me in Chapter 11, the underlying personality of the person does not change when they have the experience. If they are not helped to integrate the experience, it can go to their head and things can go very awry indeed. I encouraged him to consult specialists who I knew would be able to help him. But no, he was way above all that. His ego had taken over and I am sorry to report that he was been arrested and imprisoned after becoming violent. I pray that the psychiatric treatment and drugs will not exacerbate the situation. Unfortunately, during this time of awakening and transition, such stories are becoming more and more commonplace.

We are beginning to access ancient knowledge within our being. New chakras are opening, and we need to look after our physical bodies and nervous systems so that we can integrate this new knowledge without suffering. We also need to radically reconsider our perceptions of what is normal.

By the time I interviewed Dr Serena Roney-Dougal in Glastonbury in

June 1998, my ego had also begun to get the better of me.

After all, I was making ash, I had almost materialized a ring, I was telepathic, I could appear younger or older at will, and give intense healing by pulsing the

energy through my eyes, and much more. After relating my story to Serena, I looked deep into her eyes and asked, 'Am I becoming a master?' and she looked deeply back into my eyes and said very authoritatively: 'You – are only Hazel'.

Here was a renowned and highly experienced scientist telling me that I was only Hazel and, as I was creating my own reality instantly, who did I become?

Of course – only Hazel.

As I stood before Serena, I suddenly felt the tornado of energy inside and around me being sucked back deep inside from whence it had come – like in the movies when you see a huge genie being sucked back into the tiniest bottle. I remained psychic, I could still hear the voice of Diana and others, but virtually all the other phenomena ceased from that instant. Serena saved my life that day. If I had gone on and on with the energy expanding, without help, my physical body would have died. During May 1998, Meg, the spiritual guru in Australia, told me that I had probably become one of only 13 living masters. She meant well, and it sure boosted my self-esteem, but of course she was wrong. I now know there are thousands, if not hundreds of thousands, of people whose kundalini energy is active. But there are still only a handful of men and women who are truly enlightened – fully integrated, God-realized masters of the self.

For a brief time I was enlightened to a degree, but my body was not ready to handle such an intense amount of divine energy. I had not been prepared.

As Serena said so wisely, it can take up to 20 years to fully integrate all the knowledge and faculties that are available to you once in this heightened state of awareness.

Awakening the kundalini energy is one of the doorways to higher states of being, of realizing your true potential, both physically and mentally. Being truly enlightened is another ball game altogether – and there is great variation in degrees of enlightenment, just as there are people who can tinkle a tune on a piano and those great pianists who are true masters of their art.

In India in November 2000, I sat with the spiritual master Sai Baba, and watched him materialize jewellery and ash from his hand. It was incredible to witness, but such 'miracles' no longer made me feel that I should worship another person as I know that mind-boggling feats are possible once you become whole or Holy – a true master of the self.

Today I believe that there may be a couple of hundred or so Masters of Self like Sai Baba, plus a few thousand who are well on the road to total, integrated enlightenment, and millions more at various stages in between. But during the past few years, when interviewing followers of various spiritual gurus, it really is amazing how many state 'My master/guru is stronger, more powerful and more enlightened than so and so.' They believe that their guru is the most powerful being on the planet and should be worshipped as the one true God. No wonder we ended up with so many gods and religions. In fact, we are all part of God and all parts make the whole. Let this sink in; then begin worshipping yourself instead of others.

However, upon re-reading the book, I am embarrassed at how many times I used the word 'special', and talked of feeling like a spiritual master. But while these experiences are going on, it's really hard to put into words just how truly special you feel.

These days I realize I was only half-way up the mountain, with a long, long way to go. Fully God-realized Masters of Self are able to materialize and de-materialize at will, and they can appear physically in several places at once. They can affect numerous, and virtually limitless, miracles. The minute fraction of these I achieved I used to call my 'tricks'.

I now believe that it is vital to call these gurus – which means someone who removes darkness – Masters of Self, or self-realized people, and not masters of others. The word 'master' infers slaves. At Sai Baba's ashram in November 2000, I watched as 15,000 people from all countries and religious faiths came twice daily to worship this frail old man. Jesus once said, 'know ye not ye are Gods', and Jesus, Buddha, Mohammed, The Dalai Lama, Sai Baba and all the masters in between have told us over and over again that everything they could and can do, we can do also, and I now know this to be true.

Also, in late June 1999 when I visited Swami (which means Master of Self) Satchidananda, the yogi, fully-realized master who lived in Charlottesville, Virginia, I met other people who were also making ash and giving darshan – pulsing divine energy through their eyes. Swami has now passed away but as I sat with him, he reminded me that the cosmic mind is totally neutral. All knowledge is neutral, it's how you use it that counts. You can use a knife to cut an apple or to cut someone's throat. The cosmic mind is neither good nor bad, it simply is – hence when people used to say to me, 'what or who is God?', I used to reply 'God simply is'.

This is why the mantras I AM, SO HUM or OM, are very powerful. Used daily in meditation, they help to accelerate spiritual growth. The brain is simply an instrument through which this cosmic mind can work. The knowledge and powers that are awakened in an enlightened person can be used for good or evil, as we have free will. But once a person becomes totally and fully integrated and reaches the top of the mountain, then they would have no desire to harm anything or anyone, for they are in a state of perfection. But they can still choose, in the knowledge that in harming others they ultimately harm themselves.

Many millions of people around the world continue to revere Jesus today and yet, when he lived, he was the subject of constant derision and was eventually crucified. The press and gossip do the same for many of the true masters who are alive today. As I write, Sai Baba has been accused of assaulting young men. I have no idea if these accusations are true, and wonder if it's Sai Baba's way of saying to the world before he passes, 'Worship yourself, find the God within and don't worship other people who happen to be more awake than you are. Let us teach you, but don't worship us'.

Since this book first appeared I have received numerous letters from people who are experiencing a variety of our potential capabilities. Some are levitating at will, others are able to affect the weather, a few have become telepathic, and so on. Two people I met awoke one day to find stigmata-type injuries that were not self-inflicted. These people are not affiliated to a specific religion. They noted that the injuries healed quickly and that varying degrees of spiritual awakening followed. One, a man in his 40s, is now fully enlightened and works as a teacher and healer in London. The other, a lady in her fifties, is working her way towards total enlightenment and works as a psychic in Oxford, England.

Another woman in her thirties wrote from Australia, relating how her spiritual emergency had been very similar to mine except that her 'walk-in' had been the rock star Michael Hutchence, who had died in a Sydney hotel room in November 1997. Luckily, she was able to verify most of Michael's messages in several conversations with his partner Paula Yates before Paula's tragic death in September 2000. She is a bestselling author and TV personality in Australia and, when we eventually met, she struck me as a sensible, down-to-earth individual who is telling the truth.

The power of the mind is also receiving far more attention. A senior medically trained nurse, sixty-year-old Bernardine Coady, from Peterborough in the UK, has hypnotized herself twice to enable surgeons to cut through bones in her feet. There are thousands of documented cases in which hypnotherapy has been used to heal people, but until now the orthodox medical establishment has remained sceptical. However, in February 2002, Dr David Spiegal, Chair of Psychiatry and Behavioural Studies at Stanford University in the US, announced that brain scans on hypnotized volunteers showed consistent changes – as if the patient was actually seeing what they had been hypnotized to see. The power of the human mind is awesome – we are capable of virtually anything we can imagine and truly believe, but the slightest doubt will prevent things from happening.

In the future, enlightened souls will be able to re-grow limbs and nerves that have been severed through the power of their minds; salamanders are already capable of doing this. We will learn to move physical objects with our thoughts; monks have been doing this for centuries in countries such as Japan and Tibet.

On a physical level, in the UK permission has been granted to experiment on stem cells from human cloned embryos. On one hand, this research offers hope to people such as Christopher Reeve, plus the millions suffering from Parkinson's and Alzheimer's disease, yet it has understandably sparked a great ethical debate. And yet if you can truly begin to comprehend that we are all gods in a physical body and that aeons ago humanity was born from a star-seeded experiment, then as long as we have humility and more reverence for nature, why should we not take more control of our own destiny? Unfortunately, many people have forgotten that to take back this control and use it responsibly we need to let go of our ego and arrogance and consider the long-term implications of our actions. Nuclear power, for example, was once hailed as the answer to all our energy problems but equally it has become a source for destruction.

I now think of God as the ultimate microchip or computer which holds limitless information, that resides in every cell of our body. All we need to do is access it, switch it on... and watch out!

## A NEW BEGINNING

Some say that enlightenment itself is instant, and in some cases it is – but it's how the physical body copes and integrates the knowledge that determines how you come through the experience. There are people who can raise and lower the kundalini at will, but if it blows unexpectedly as mine did, you can go mad or die of shock. This is why it's better to take the spiritual journey in a structured and safe way, through meditation and practices like spinning, yogic breathing and exercise, Qigong, chanting, using crystals, and so on. Such practices, plus eating a healthy, balanced diet, will help you to cope when your own unique awakening begins.

Today I have begun my spiritual journey from scratch again. I have been taught dozens of meditation techniques, tried numerous spiritually uplifting therapies known in the West – and then some. I have chanted for England and listened intently in the hope of hearing the spirit world more clearly once again.

During 2001 I met a wonderful teacher called Michael Jenkins who lectures and teaches on all spiritual subjects in London. During our first lesson he gently chastized me for wistfully repeating 'When I was in that state...', saying, 'How can you lose something that is already inside of you? Stop all this searching outside yourself and go within.' As I sat and meditated with Michael, I slowly became aware of his tremendous energy field and when I opened my eyes, all I could see was a huge amount of pure white light all around Michael's head and body. He laughed, saying 'You think your abilities have gone, and yet now you see they are still there.'

For four years I have known that I need to begin meditating daily, but have resisted incessantly, as I find it difficult to still my ever-active mind. And of course, what you resist is usually what you most need in your life.

Then I attended a course with Dr Deepak Chopra on how to activate our light body. There were around 2000 of us in the lecture theatre and, as we chanted the ancient Sanskrit word Om to music before Deepak spoke, the energies inside the hall gradually increased. By the time I got home, I was back 'on line' – my solar plexus was spinning almost out of control – but this time I lay on our lawn and later ate some porridge to quickly ground myself. This experience reminded me that the more people who can congregate with a positive intention, the sooner we will see positive results on a personal and planetary level. What we send out to the cosmic mind –

God – is what we get back.

As the scientist Roger Coghill told me, the entire universe is filled with tiny charged particles called electrons, and when one single electron moves, it affects every single electron in the universe. Therefore, even if just one per cent of us could begin thinking, acting and behaving in a positive, loving, productive way, then a larger part of the cosmic collective mind that works through our brains would automatically raise the consciousness of everyone else on the planet, and the changes we will witness will be awesome. Meditation or silent prayer will accelerate these positive changes.

As I write, several parts of the world appear to be sinking into an abyss of chaos. On September 11th 2001, I was in New York when the two hijacked airliners smashed at full speed into the World Trade Center. For days I was numb with shock at the enormity and horror of what I had witnessed. In those terrifying moments our history was irrevocably changed. Like millions of others, I wept as I heard how many passengers on the doomed flights and in the World Trade Center had called home to say 'I love you', to their relatives – knowing that they were never coming home. When the ex-Beatle George Harrison passed over in November 2001, his last words were that 'we should all love each other'. Sage advice. The frequency of pure, unconditional love is what will save this planet, and we need to give and receive a lot more of it. Love opens the heart chakra which helps us towards enlightenment.

After Diana's death there was a huge outpouring of grief and love, and for a time consciousness was raised. Unfortunately, many people have returned to old ways of thinking and behaving, and every time we regress, the universal messages and events will be accelerated and amplified until we all change. Hence why those who are physically and mentally prepared and, above all, adaptable – will find the transition easier. In the meantime, how many more innocent people need to die before we begin to listen and act?

We are on the edge of an abyss. We are creating our world and many of our possible futures lie in every person's hands. It is utterly imperative for everyone to try as much as possible to rise above what has happened; to pray for those who have gone on, and to invite and anchor the light – the love frequency – on earth. Let tragedy become a catalyst for peace, not war. Our planet is in enough trouble – we don't need to create more. As H.M. Queen Noor of Jordan once reminded me, we are all links in a chain. How clearly we have seen this since September 11. But if we could all think and act positively from this moment on, believe me we can all help turn this situation around. We are birthing a new consciousness, and birth can be painful or easy. We can choose.

Meanwhile, fanatics continue to plant bombs and kill innocent people and sometimes, themselves, saying it is the will of their God. It is tragic that that so many dreadful deeds are done in the name of what these people consider to be an invisible, external, intangible being. Fanaticism and those who seek power over others and have closed minds need to understand that 'an eye for an eye' has never, and will never, work.

During Deepak Chopra's lecture, he made me smile when he said 'Most people in the West envisage God as a dead white male'. I then asked a Moslem friend who God is and he said he was not sure except that He must be a man!

This evoked memories of the intensely profound moment on that Easter Friday in 1998 when I had said 'I am the weather', not knowing who the 'I' was. For those who find this part hard to take the ultimate 'I' – is God. You can dress this up by saying that we are all part of God and that his/her light/energy/frequency is within us all. But the ultimate truth is that we are all God. Every cell in our body contains all parts of the whole. If you had a hologram of, say, a cake and you cut the hologram in half, you would end up with two whole cakes. We are basically six billion holographic images of the whole. Therefore instead of saying 'Why has God done this?' – start to understand that every one of us is part of God, and at every level we are creating our own reality.

And these days, do I still walk my walk as a health writer and light worker? To be honest, there have been many dark days during the last few years when I have thought about simply giving up my work, going shopping and forgetting what happened to me. But I can't. And what happened in America on September 11 2001 has only strengthened my resolve. Again I reiterate that we must all begin with the self.

My diet goes off the rails now and again, but when I eat a chunk of chocolate or a fabulous piece of apple pie topped with cream, I eat consciously, knowing that a small amount of what you fancy really boosts your immune system and makes you feel good. But if you live on treats, then the arteries can clog and health problems arise. I also exercise and eat organically-grown foods as much as possible.

I really do try and keep a balance in all things and still do what I can, when I can to help my fellow man and the planet. Millions are doing the same.

My big adventure was a gift from the universe and I now truly understand that if I want to experience anything like it again, I am going to have to work for it just like everyone else...

To this end, I had regular lessons with Christopher Hansard, a physician of Tibetan medicine. He taught me various chants to help still my mind before I meditate and says that if I practice regularly, then maybe, just maybe, in a year or so I should see some results. I am already more psychic, and trust that one day more abilities may return. If you would like to contact Christopher, call 020 7881 5800 or log onto www.edenmedicalcentre.com.

The difference today is that I now come from a space of experience. You can write about these happenings, but living them is a different ballgame.

Back in December 1999 when this book was first published, there were many days when I felt like a total fake once the enormity of what I was claiming regarding Princess Diana really hit me. However, when I began receiving dozens of letters of support from people who had also seen and heard Diana, it gave me renewed strength.

The media have continued to give us more information about Diana.

Not all of it has been kind. It's so much easier to say negative things when the person has gone and cannot answer for themselves. We now know that Diana had loved and lost the heart surgeon Hasnat Khan. That she was not all sweetness and light. Are you? Is anyone?

I still believe she was one of the greatest assets our royal family has ever seen. Her sons, William and Harry carry her seed and I pray that one day in their own way they will continue the wonderful work that their mother started. And to my mind there is absolutely no doubt that Diana was a great healer with a huge heart.

During a TV series shown in 2001 to celebrate Diana's life, Christina Lamb, the highly experienced foreign correspondent of The Sunday Times, travelled with Diana to Angola in 1997 during her visit with The Halo Trust to highlight the need to ban land mines. Christina related how she travelled in a cynical frame of mind, believing that Diana only wanted to be seen doing good. But after travelling with Diana for several days Christina changed her opinion, saying that Diana visibly transmitted huge amounts of compassion and love to the injured children, and had an aura about her that the journalist had only previously seen in Nelson Mandela.

There is also one huge point that I must now clarify. On Easter Friday 1998, around midnight, when my eyes were so tightly closed and I 'watched and felt' events unfold, like watching a movie inside my head, I vividly recall the flashing cameras as pictures were taken of Diana and Dodi after the crash. But I also saw and knew other things that I can no longer omit. During the time that I heard Diana, she told me over and over again, that her death was an accident. And I acted like a secretary, I wrote what I was asked to write and remained respectful of her wishes. But in my heart I have always believed that she was murdered.

I believe the absolute truth may never be known. I also believe that the men who truly are 'above governments' can and do dispose of people who have too great a radical and positive impact on global consciousness.

## ALTHORP, ENGLAND, AUGUST 2001

During August last year, my dear friend and Reiki healer, Debbie Flavell, suggested out of the blue that as I had agreed to write this final chapter, it might be a good idea to visit Althorp, Princess Diana's family home and final resting place. It had never crossed my mind to make such a trip, but it felt right. And so on a warm summer day we drove to Northamptonshire.

As we walked up the avenue of English oak trees that Diana's brother Earl Spencer had planted in her memory, I felt quite strange. Then a familiar voice began singing in my head, 'All things bright and beautiful, all creatures great and small, all things wise and wonderful, the good Lord made them all.' I was elated beyond words.

Hundreds of people from all over the world were thronging around Earl Spencer's home and garden. We walked under the Italian-inspired porticoes into the exhibition that Diana's brother has so lovingly built in his magnificent stables. Her wedding dress, which is breathtaking, stands in a glass case with her handmade silk slippers. And as I looked up at the tiara, I heard the word 'Hope'. To me, this signified what she felt on that day. The dress is a complete fairy tale, much prettier than it looked on TV. In various rooms, huge screens were showing edited film clips from her life and funeral, and in front of the final screen are hundreds of dried flowers saved from that dreadful day. When I saw her passport and driver's licence lovingly displayed along with the hundreds of books of remembrance from 125 countries, I somehow felt like an intruder. Yet it also made me realize just how much she meant, and still means, to so many. Before walking to the Oval (an oval pathway that surrounds the island which has become Diana's final resting place) Debbie and I visited the gift shop. I bought a beautiful bound copy of the riveting speech that Earl Spencer had given at Diana's funeral in Westminster Abbey. All profits from sales of the speech are donated to Diana's charities. As I queued to pay, the young assistant suggested that I should ask Earl Spencer to sign it. I looked at her vacantly as if to say, 'How on earth would I do that?'. 'He's standing over there' she laughed. For once,

I was almost lost for words. Debbie edged me towards the Earl, saying 'Go on – tell him about your book'. Suddenly the crowd around him dispersed and there I stood, rooted to the spot. Debbie urged me forward.

He was utterly charming. We chatted easily about some mutual friends and he asked if we had enjoyed the exhibition. And as he signed a copy of his speech, I told him I believed that Diana would have totally approved of what he has done. He smiled, that wonderful warm Spencer smile, we shook hands and I left. No more needed to be said.

Once outside, I could clearly hear Diana roaring with laughter saying 'You didn't expect that, did you?' She really was a caution...

And as Debbie and I walked around the Oval, I was moved beyond words. Diana's mortal remains supposedly lay on a tiny island in the centre of a small, peaceful lake. Swans and ducks serenely swim back and forth in a timeless scene.

The trees whisper to you.

In the centre of the walk is a small temple dedicated to Diana. Inscribed on a plaque are Diana's words from a speech she gave in June 1997:

'Nothing brings me more happiness than trying to help the most vulnerable people in society. 'It is a goal and an essential part of my life – a kind of destiny. Whoever is in distress can call on me. I will come running wherever they are.'

Beautiful letters from around the globe tell me that Diana is appearing to people at times of crisis and is giving healing from the higher realms.

As we drove away I truly felt that Diana and many others in the higher realms are assisting us. By asking for their help we bring more light into ourselves and onto the planet. Through her tragic death, Diana opened the heart chakra of the world. We now need to continue this work by anchoring the light with which she now works. In this way, her earthly life will not have been in vain.

I pray that you have taken what you need from this story and, as always, I wish you love, light, health, and above all, peace in your hearts.

Hazel Courteney
November 2004.

If you would like to read the sequel to this book, Hazel continues her journey in *The Evidence for the Sixth Sense* (Cico Books).

## Useful Books and Addresses

BiCom machine
Contact Applied BioPhysics in the UK, tel: 01938 556800. In Germany, call Regumed in Grafelfing, tel: (89) 8546101. Peter Smith is based at the Hale Clinic in London tel: 0870 1676667.

David Ash
His books including *The New Science of Spirit* (published by Light Publishing) are available from the College of Psychic Studies, 16 Queensbury Place, London SW7, tel: 020 7589 3292. www.collegeofpsychicstudies.co.uk.

Dr Gauld's research papers
Photocopies are available for a small fee from The Society of Psychical Research at 49 Marloes Road, London W8 6LA, tel/fax: 0207 937 8984. www.spr.ac.uk.

Dr Jacob Liberman
He has written several books including *Light, Medicine of the Future* (Bear & Co) and *Take Off Your Glasses and See* (Thorsons); or have a look at his web site on www.ulight.com.

Dr Serena Roney-Dougal
Serena's book *Where Science and Magic Meet* (Vega) is available to order from good book shops. For more information on her research into healing and paranormal subjects log onto her website at www.psi-researchcentre.co.uk.

Horace Dobbs
For more information on Dr Horace Dobbs' work on healing with dolphins, check his web site www.idw.org or call International Dolphin Watch in the UK, tel: 01482 645789.

Jasmuheen
Her book *Living on Light* (Koha Publishing) is available worldwide. In the UK, order from Watkins Bookshop in London, tel: 020 7836 2182; or log onto www.jasmuheen.com.

Joao Teixeira de Faria
You can find out more about Joao by reading *The Book Of Miracles* by Alberto Villoldo, available via www.amazon.com; or try *The Miracle Man of Brazil* by Robert Pellegrino-Estrich, available via www.johnofgod.com.

Karma and Life After Death
There are huge numbers of books available on these subjects, but a few of my favourites are: *The Afterlife Experiments*, by Professor Gary Schwartz (Atria Books); *They Walk Among Us* by Emma Heathcote-James (Metro Publishing); and *A Free Spirit* by Patrick Francis, which beautifully describes life after death and the laws of Karma and is available by calling Dublin in Ireland, tel: 353 (0) 1 452 3793.

Kelvin Heard
Kelvin is a wonderful healer and you can reach him via tel: 07710 794627.

Lives Between Lives
Dr Michael Newton is a clinical hypnotherapist who has documented hundreds of patient cases of lives in-between physical lives. They make fascinating reading. *Lives Between Lives* and *Destiny of Souls* are both published in the USA, Llewellyn Publications.

Meditation
There are hundreds of books regarding meditation – but one of the most interesting I have found is the Merkaba Meditation, which is very powerful. It is taught by qualified practitioners via a scientist called Drunvalo Melchizedek. His books on the secrets of ancient geometry and the Flower of Life workshops, plus details of his work, are available on www.floweroflife.org; or call Phoenix, Arizona, USA, tel: (001) 602 996 0900.

Mental Health
Patrick Holford's book *Mental Health and Illness* (Piatkus) – co written with Dr Carl Pfieffer – is well worth a read. His web site also carries a large amount of valuable advice and information regarding mental health: www.patrickholford.com.

Nick Williams
His magical book about finding your purpose in this lifetime is called *The Work We Were Born To Do* (Element).

Osteoporosis
For lots of information on Hormones, the menopause and all related subjects read *New Natural Alternatives to HRT* by Dr Marilyn Glenville (Kyle Cathie); or log onto www.marilynglenville.com.

Professor Bill McGuirn
His books *Apocalypse* (Cassell) and *A Guide To the End Of The World: Everything you Never Wanted to Know* (Oxford University Press) make sobering reading!

Roger Coghill
Roger has written several books on healing energies, and for more details log onto www.cogreslab.co.uk; tel: 01495 763389.

Seka Nikolic
The healer Seka specialises in treating ME (chronic fatigue syndrome) at the Kailash Centre in North London, tel: 020 7722 3939 or log onto www.orientalhealing.co.uk and www.sekanikolic.com.

Spiritual Emergency
If you believe that you or a friend is going through a spiritual emergency one of the best things you can do is to read the sequel to this book- which is entitled *The Evidence For the Sixth Sense* (Cico Books).

Alternatively, log onto Clinical Psychologist Isabel Clarke's site. She is one of the few people in the UK working within the NHS who specialises in Spiritual Awakenings which become a crisis; www.scispirit/psychosis_spirituality/

Professor Stan Grof is the world's leading authority on Spiritual Emergency. His book *The Stormy Search for Self* (Thorsons) is a godsend; or log onto www.holotropic.com.

Stephen Turoff
For more details on Stephen's life and his work, read *Stephen Turoff Psychic Surgeon*, by Grant Solomon (Thorsons).

Swami Satchidananda Ashram
This magical centre, dedicated to peace, is set in 1000 acres of trees and lakes in Buckingham, Virginia, USA – it teaches internationally accredited yoga, healing and meditation to people from all denominations. I loved it there, tel: (001) 804 969 3121 or 969 3122; log onto www.yogaville.org.

Lynne McTaggart
Her amazing book *The Field* (Harper Collins) offers fascinating research into how many 'miracles' are possible.